THE INTENDANT SYSTEM IN SPANISH AMERICA

BY

LILLIAN ESTELLE FISHER, Ph.D.

GORDIAN PRESS
NEW YORK
1969

Originally Published 1929

Reprinted 1969

Library of Congress Catalog Card Number - 77-91350

Published by GORDIAN PRESS

THE INTENDANT SYSTEM IN
SPANISH AMERICA

PREFACE

The purpose of this work is to supply further information concerning the intendant system in Spanish America. Its establishment in the Spanish colonies and its operation of the four departments of government which it formally recognized, are described, the contemporary arguments for and against it are summarized, and an attempt has been made to evaluate the results of the innovation.

The Ordinance of Intendants for New Spain has been translated from the Spanish to reinforce the above study so that the English reader may learn at first hand what were the provisions of the system, and the functions and powers of the intendants. This Mexican legal code, being more voluminous than the other Ordinances for Spanish America (which it did in fact ultimately supersede in actual use), presents the new institution in greater detail, and has therefore been chosen for translation and study. In the Appendix an illuminating comparison is made between the Ordinance for New Spain and the earlier one for Buenos Aires.

The translator has taken the liberty of arranging the material of the various articles into paragraphs according to the subject matter, in order to make it more readable. Brackets are used to inclose words not found in the Spanish document, but which have been inserted to make the meaning clear. The marginal glosses in manuscript indicate the changes which the ordinance underwent in practical operation, as recorded by some unknown jurist who presumably used the book between 1786 and 1816. His notes are lettered, and inclosed at the end of the corresponding article. The notes originally printed as marginal glosses have been referred to numerals and presented at the foot of the proper pages, together with certain explanatory materials. The *"índice"* or table of contents of the Spanish edition is not reproduced here because of its great length, but a briefer one is substituted. The Appendix is omitted entirely. The ordinance translated is a printed copy of the original manuscript; it was evidently printed for official use, and is rubricked with the legal half-signature, "Sonora," of José de Gálvez, minister of the Indies. It was printed for the Spanish government under the following title: *Real ordenanza para el establecimiento é instrucción de intendentes de exército y provincia en el reino de la Nueva-España.* Madrid, de órden de su magestad, 1786.

In the notes and bibliography the abbreviation AGI is frequently used for Archivo General de Indias. The material which has been utilized is found in original or in transcript in the Bancroft Library and the University of California Library.

Miss Irene A. Wright of Seville, Spain, helped me obtain information on several difficult matters.

I am deeply indebted to Professor Herbert Ingram Priestley for his valuable suggestions and criticism, and for reading the introductory chapters and the entire translation.

CONTENTS

IV

V

THE INTENDANT SYSTEM IN SPANISH AMERICA

————

I

ESTABLISHMENT OF THE INTENDANCIES

The initiation of the intendancies was a progressive movement in Spanish colonial administration, coming after many years of effort. A gubernatorial system that had become corrupt and inefficient was thus regulated in the interest of efficiency and higher financial return. Many of the errors in the Laws of the Indies, which had been collected in a haphazard manner, were rectified. The introduction of the intendant system was moreover an attempt at reform to meet the new conditions that arose after the Seven Years' War. It was first tried as a kind of experiment in Havana, thereafter being gradually applied in Buenos Aires, Peru, New Spain, and the whole of Spanish America.

Reforms were very badly needed throughout all the vast domains of Spanish America by the middle of the eighteenth century. The old administrative system, inaugurated shortly after the conquest, was still used with but few variations. After two centuries and a half, it was natural that new problems and relationships should arise and the old inflexible system become inadequate.

A new republic had sprung up in the north and insisted upon trading with its Spanish neighbors. A newborn spirit of democracy, with its more progressive ideas, began to stir Europe and was soon to infiltrate into the distant Spanish colonies, the inhabitants of which, belonging to a new generation, had lost the fervor of devotion to the mother country characteristic of the *conquistadores*. The long years of separation and the hardships of frontier life had gradually centered their interests upon America, their native land. The slow means of communication with Spain accentuated their estrangement, and caused their obedience to relax, in spite of the watchful eye of the king. The age-long ban against certain colonial manufactures, industries, and free trade had created actual suffering in some parts of the dependencies, therefore even officials had long been willing to wink at the laws. The old commercial system of monopoly and exclusion had long outgrown its usefulness, but was still retained with all its antiquated theories. Smuggling became so universal that the royal revenues decreased, the persistence of piracy compelling the use of armed convoys. Moreover, the population of the viceroyalties had greatly increased since the early days and this caused new problems of government to arise.

The energetic administration of the early viceregal period languished as the kings became more careless in the choice of their highest representatives in the New World. This was especially noticeable in the caliber and efficiency of the early eighteenth-century viceroys as compared with those of the sixteenth century. None were outstanding and of the aggressive type like Antonio de Mendoza, the second Velasco, or Francisco de Toledo. Most of them were men of medium capacities and some were weak. After the seventeenth century it had become the custom to appoint military men to this high office, and only too often they were lacking in administrative ability. Positions as high as the viceroyalties had sometimes been sold to obtain funds for continental wars, a practice which probably accounts for a few of the least capable viceroys.

For over two centuries the complications of the administrative functions had grown greater, thus increasing the work of a viceroy without adding to the efficiency of the government. The minute instructions of the mother country, which had a perfect mania for regulation, grew more detailed. The endless red tape employed in colonial administration inevitably detracted from its vigor and progressiveness, the viceroy being dependent to a high degree upon his secretaries because of the great cumbersomeness of administration, involving masses of papers, reports, and opinions which concerned the most minute details.

Consequently there was lax obedience to royal and viceregal orders. The well-known saying which characterized Spanish colonial administration, "I obey but do not execute" (*obedezco pero no cumplo*), shows the spirit with which they were carried out. Procrastination and delay became the rule. Many viceroys were so accustomed to this inertia that their orders were often worded so as to leave a loophole. The less aggressive viceroys could enforce only those measures not in direct opposition to the wishes of the local magistrates, who were apt to take their own time in carrying out the viceroy's commands. Some measures were not made effective for years, and by that time they had lost all their force. A common time-saving form of decree on the part of a busy viceroy was, "Let it be as the fiscal requests" (*como pide el Señor fiscal*).

The viceroys were overworked because almost everything was expected of them; their duties ranging from the highest administrative, financial, religious, military, and judicial functions of the supreme representative of the king in America to those of mentor and adviser of the people. The routine of their offices, alone, sometimes requiring from four to six hours daily. The great Mendoza declared that Indian affairs alone were enough to drive a viceroy mad, while many people were ready to offer advice and suggestions, but few to really aid him.[1] It took the

[1] *Instrucciones que los vireyes de Nueva España dejaron a sus sucesores* (Mexico, 1867), 238.

home government a long time to realize this situation: the impression actually prevailed in Spain that a viceroy's work was easy. It was thought that the Indians were submissive and not difficult to control, and that the chief executive had plenty of leisure, whereas, while in Spain a viceroy had many assistants to aid him in the performance of his duties, in America everything had to pass through the viceroy's own hands.[2]

Moreover, such assistants as the American viceroys had were far from distinguished. The *alcaldes mayores*, who were supposed to aid them in minor matters, were more often the cause of added trouble and work. The judges of the *audiencia*, who exercised the highest judicial authority in the colonies, were the viceroy's chief assistants, but they frequently quarreled among themselves, with the minor officials, and with the viceroy himself. Sometimes they embarrassed him by disputing his powers. As a last resort, the viceroy had to depend almost entirely upon his secretaries and assessor. Yet without capable subordinate officials, a viceroy, were he the greatest man in the world, could not govern well his extensive domains.[3]

Many of these minor officials had become corrupt; even governors, especially in the frontier provinces, worked for their own advantage and tried to amass fortunes. The *corregidores* engaged in trade, oppressed the Indians, and constantly had dissensions with ecclesiastics. Complaints came from Peru that they appropriated the best pieces of land for themselves, took away water rights from the natives, and enslaved the poor by making them work their estates.[4] In New Spain the *corregidores* refrained from reporting the true state of affairs in their towns to the viceroy because they desired to make a good impression

---

[2] (*Instrucciones que los vireyes de Nueva España dejaron a sus sucesores* (Mexico, 1867), art. 2, p. 243. For further information concerning the functions of American viceroys see Fisher, Lillian E., *Viceregal Administration in the Spanish-American Colonies* (Berkeley, 1926).

[3] *Informe y plan de intendencias, que conviene establecer en las provincias de este reyno de Nueva España*, MS, AGI.

[4] *Documentos inéditos . . . . de Indias* (Madrid, 1864–1884), XI, 197.

upon him and to win his favor.[5] Inevitably the administration often had to move in serious matters without adequate assistance from subordinate officials whose conception of their duties was wholly self-centered.

The *alcaldes mayores*, who governed divisions of each province called *alcaldías mayores* were even more dishonest, chiefly because they were poor and did not receive salaries. As a result they were forced to engage in trade, in which they tyrannized over the Indians, compelling them to work and to buy what they did not need[6] from the provisions which the *alcaldes* were allowed to vend. Frequently they were lax in the performance of their judicial duties, consenting, for a remuneration, to make the sentences of criminals lighter. Many *alcaldes* enriched themselves considerably within the five years of their term of office, taking away from the treasury each year, by illicit operations and frauds in tribute collection, five or six hundred thousand *pesos*. They were usually men of inferior intelligence, who appointed greedy lieutenants of still lower station in life with no sense of honor to work for them in the smaller towns. Such *alcaldes mayores* as were of good birth, education, and honesty were often so burdened with debts, contracted before obtaining possession of their offices, that they persuaded themselves that it was justifiable to enrich themselves with the royal tributes and revenues. Thus they indemnified themselves for their labor, their expenses, the salary which they did not receive, and for the half-annate that was collected from them.[7]

The *Recopilación de leyes de los reinos de las Indias*, a monument to the colonial genius of Spain, dating from the sixteenth century on, provided the legal system in force in the Spanish

---

[5] Villaroel, Hipólito, *Enfermedades políticas que padece la capital de esta Nueva España* . . . . MS, I, pt. II, pp. 99–100.

[6] *Documentos inéditos o muy raros para la historia de México* (Mexico, 1905–1911), VII, 71–72. There were about 200 *alcaldías* in New Spain.

[7] *Informe y plan de intendencias* . . . . *de Nueva España*, MS, AGI.

colonies. These Laws of the Indies differed from those of modern codes in that they were not brief and severe formulas, but rather paternal advice, in which were recapitulated the causes for their enactment. They were full of benevolent theories difficult to put into practice, especially when these had to be executed by men like the *conquistadores*,[8] ungovernable and warlike in spirit. At first the laws made by the Council of the Indies and sent to America to be enforced by viceroys and *audiencias* worked well. As time passed and new conditions arose many of the laws of the *Recopilación* became a dead letter, and had to be supplemented by numerous royal *cédulas* or decrees to meet particular circumstances. Massive volumes of these *cédulas* were accumulated, and administrators had to consult them just as they did the *Recopilación* to see what the laws really were,[9] as many of the *cédulas* contradicted the codified laws. This added to the delay and confusion of law enforcement. Jurists in Spain and America began to realize the need for a recodification of the Laws of the Indies, but like everything else this important act was postponed.

During the early eighteenth century little assistance in the way of reform came from the mother country. Spain was in a deplorable condition at the end of the Hapsburg rule. Its treasury was empty, its army was a mere shadow, commerce and industry were ruined, crime and public disorders were frequent, and ignorance and misery generally prevailed. The accession of the Bourbon dynasty brought disastrous wars which only added to the distress. After almost fourteen years of fighting, the Bourbon right to the Spanish throne was guaranteed when the Archduke Charles became emperor and renounced his claims to

---

[8] For the manner in which the Laws of the Indies were collected see Fabié, Antonio María, *Ensayo histórico de la legislación española en sus estados de ultramar* (Madrid, 1896).

[9] In New Spain alone 156 huge volumes of *cédulas* were collected by 1797. *Instrucciones que los vireyes* . . . . art. 10, p. 130.

Spain. However, peace did not last long, for Philip V revived his claim to the French throne at the death of Louis XIV, bringing Spain into a series of conflicts with the English, French, Dutch, and Austrians. Few advantages came from these costly wars, save the securing of the Italian duchies of Parma and Tuscany and Sicily for the Spanish princes, Charles and Philip.

The work of administrative reconstruction along all lines began in Spain, in spite of these sad conditions. Energetic measures were taken toward centralization of administration after the French fashion. The active Alberoni and other ministers applied most of their reforms to the mother country, which had to be revived immediately, rather than to the colonies. These men realized that other countries like England far surpassed Spain in economic development, although they did not have huge quantities of gold and silver coming from the Indies. Therefore, manufactures, industry, and commerce were promoted. The financial and military systems were reinvigorated. Some attempt was also made to centralize administration in the colonies. The Council of the Indies was reorganized in 1720 with a view to centralization, its legislative function being thenceforth absorbed by the king, who legislated through his ministers only, or *por la vía reservada*. The functions of the *Casa de Contratación*, or Board of Trade, were restricted and in 1717 it was moved from Seville to Cádiz. The next year the intendant system, which had been used in France since the time of Richelieu, was introduced into Spain.[10] At first the new régime was not very successful in Spain, and it was suppressed until in 1749, after which time continuous effort was made to extend it to America.

---

[10] Danvila y Collado, Manuel, *Significación que tuvieron en el gobierno de América la Casa de la Contratación de Sevilla y el Consejo Supremo de Indias* (Madrid, 1792), 37 *et seq*. For an account of French influence in Spain consult Sister Mary Austin, *The reforms of Charles the Third in New Spain in the light of the Pacte de Famille*, MS (Ph.D., thesis, Dept. of History, University of California), Berkeley, 1927.

It should be borne in mind that this Ordinance is of one piece with all the reforms undertaken by the able ministers of Charles III, who began their struggle for efficient government immediately upon his accession, and continued to fight obscurantism, provincialism, sloth, and decrepit tradition until after his death. The general visitation or judicial inspection of all the American colonies was enthusiastically urged by the indefatigable José Campillo y Cosío before his death in 1743, and with that general housecleaning the intendancies were to be extended to all Spanish America. The identical program was urged in the late 1750's by Bernard Ward, clever and studious Irish-born economist who gave his energies to the study of the Spanish economic problem. The adoption of the program moved slowly, for causes too numerous to mention here. But the general visitation of the various parts of America did take place over a span of years, under the active cooperation of energetic men like José de Areche in Peru and José de Gálvez in New Spain.

The most notable features of the reforms introduced into the New World were: (1) the widespread enlistment of colonial troops in bodies of militia, for the defense of the wide realm; this set the empire in America upon an entirely new basis of defense; (2) the adoption of practically free trade for Spanish ships, under the Grand Pragmatic of Free Commerce of 1778; this measure reversed the colonial commercial policy of nearly three centuries, and developed a tremendous wave of prosperity; (3) the expulsion of the Company of Jesus from all the Spanish colonies, as also from Spain, in the interest of a regalistic control that resented the erection of an *imperium in imperio* which threatened the integrity of the empire; (4) the systematization of the colonies by erecting them into uniformly governed intendancies in place of the old "kingdoms," provinces, "governments," and the like; this reorganization was especially directed toward reform of the fiscal system and increase of the revenues so as to provide money for all the other reforms.

The influence of the great Choiseul of France in working out the conceptions of the Pacte de Famille, the long studies of commerce by the Abbé Béliardi in Spain itself, the visitations of America by Areche, Gálvez, and their contemporaries in the other provinces, the long and devious stories of Spanish diplomatic relations with France and England during the reign of Charles III, the preparation and conduct of his wars, the rise and fall of his ministers, all constitute essential phases of the problem of resuscitation of the empire to which that competent and resourceful monarch directed his will and unceasing attention.

The intendant system as used in Spain finally became so successful that it was considered wise to extend it to the colonies, where it was hoped that administration might be improved by a greater centralization as had been the case in the mother country. The new system was first employed in Havana in 1764, no doubt as a kind of experiment, the Spanish Ordinance of 1749 being taken as a model. The first American Ordinance of October 31, 1764, was short compared with later ones. It consisted of sixty-eight articles proper, but eighteen more articles in regard to general administrators, eighteen relative to the general accountant, and twenty which concerned the treasury-general were added to these, making a total of one hundred and twenty-four articles.[11]

This system thus inaugurated of course closely resembled its prototype. The intendant of Havana had cognizance of the two departments of treasury and war in the same manner as intendants of Castile. At first there was some doubt about his functions, which were not well defined, but royal decrees of 1765 and 1767 made them more explicit.[12] The first thirty-one of the principal

---

[11] Zamora y Coronado, José María, *Biblioteca de legislación ultramarina* (Madrid, 1844–1846), III, 606.

[12] Danvila y Collado, *op. cit.*, 42.

sixty-eight articles instruct the intendant concerning his duties toward the treasury and the improvement of finances; the remainder treat of his obligations in the department of war. The substance of this Ordinance in regard to the two departments of finance and war is similar to the Ordinance of 1786 for New Spain, but the articles are briefer and more condensed, and less definite. The two departments of *policía* and justice are omitted entirely, since the intendant of Cuba had no jurisdiction in those matters.[13]

The Spanish document of 1749, the model for the first American Ordinance, consisted of one hundred and forty-six articles, which were, as compared with the Ordinance of 1786, a mere outline of instructions. The chief difference between the Ordinances of 1749 and of 1764 was that the intendants in Spain had control of all four departments of the government—treasury, war, justice, and police. From time to time it was necessary to supplement the Spanish Ordinance with royal decrees. In this way defects were eliminated and the system was made workable.[14]

The intendant of Cuba was to reside in Havana and have authority in matters of war and treasury over the whole island. This connoted the management of civil, ecclesiastical, and military revenues, which had previously belonged to the captain-general. The intendant was also given charge of matters concerning contraband trade, fortifications, and royal lands, and he was made equal in rank with the captain-general.[15] The latter official was expected (though vainly) to get along peacefully with the intendant and communicate with him in regard to anything of importance which might arise. The intendant received his instructions from the king, and was permitted to correspond directly with

[13] Zamora y Coronado, III, 598 *et seq.*

[14] *Colección de reales cédulas* (Madrid, 1749–1799), I, *et seq.*

[15] Zamora y Coronado, III, 598 *et seq.* For a list of the intendants serving in Havana from 1764 to 1813 see Valdés, Antonio José, *Historia de la isla de Cuba* (Havana, 1876–1877), III, 413.

him, and usually reported to him all important matters and the measures which he had taken. Some of these reports are full of interesting information and correctly depict conditions in the West Indies.[16] The intendant presided over the tribunal of accounts at Havana, and in 1775 helped to supervise the finances of the Windward Islands and Louisiana, as well as Cuba.

The great reformer, Charles III, after he had rejuvenated Spain, decided to apply sweeping reforms to the colonies. The first experiments, which concerned free trade and the centralization of the government under the intendancy in Cuba, did not seem to cause any bad results, therefore the sovereign decided to extend the new model gradually to all the viceroyalties. Undoubtedly these reforms would greatly improve conditions in the colonies, but there was also an element of selfishness to be found—they would increase the prosperity and greatness of the mother country. However, Spanish statesmen could not help being aroused to the need of colonial reform. The Indian population was debauched and seemed to be growing more discontented, so much so that it was feared that the natives might become so inflamed by foreign influences that they would revolt. No one could be blind to the corruption that existed in administration.

The appointment of José de Gálvez, visitor-general of New Spain, was a vital part of the reform program. The title of intendant of army was conferred upon him, in order that he might instruct the people of Mexico concerning the new system, since they were so ignorant that they even called subaltern administrators super-intendents.[17] Gálvez and Viceroy Croix discussed the Plan for the intendancies of New Spain and signed it on

---

[16] *Consejo de estado*, February 3, 1813, papeleta 106, AGI, 88–19 (Audiencia de Mexico); Havana, Sept. 28, 1783, num. 168, AGI, 80–1–24 (Audiencia de Santo Domingo).

[17] *Informe y plan de intendencias* . . . . *de Nueva España.* MS, AGI; Gálvez to the king, Nov. 24, 1781, AGI, 90–2–13. Gálvez seems to have retained his title of intendant during the whole period of the visitation.

January 15, 1768. It is an interesting document full of wise suggestions.] Gálvez thought that the intendant system had brought great benefit to Spain, and therefore should be applied extensively to the Spanish colonies because of their decadent condition. On the other hand, many Americans opposed the idea of assimilating the administration to that of the mother country. They preferred the old conditions under the ancient system, which they venerated. Others did not even take the trouble to examine the inveterate abuses, thinking them incurable. But the visitor declared that the only real remedy for corruption among officials and *alcaldes mayores* would be to establish the intendant system. The first important result expected was the relief of the viceroy from his intolerable burden of office detail. It was not possible for one mortal to attend to everything alone, or with the aid of inferiors who only embarrassed him. It was absurd to think of the chief executive maintaining in peace and justice three million people with the aid of officials who sought only to enrich themselves. Even the extraordinary measure of the general visitation, since it recurred only at intervals of several years, was not sufficient to keep the government at maximum efficiency.

The suggested innovation would greatly simplify matters, as officials coming to America to serve would not have to learn new rules different from those in use in Spain. Originally it was thought that eleven intendancies would be sufficient for Mexico, one general intendancy of army in Mexico City and the rest in the chief cities of the provinces, though this idea was subsequently modified. All the intendants should be exclusively subject to the viceroy as the highest official in the country and superintendent of the revenues. This latter suggestion of the visitor-general was also subsequently amended.

The salary for the intendants of Puebla, Oaxaca, Yucatan, Valladolid, Guanajuato, and San Luis Potosí was to be 6,000 *pesos*. The intendants of Guadalajara, Durango, Sonora, and the Californias were to receive 8,000 *pesos,* and the intendant of army in the capital 12,000 *pesos,* to enable him to maintain suitable comparative luster in the presence of the viceroy. As these new salaries were to be higher than those received by former officials, it was argued that at first sight they appeared too large; but it seemed, and was indeed proved in the sequel, that the amount could easily be made up to the royal treasury by the usefulness of the new system. The tributes alone would produce half a million more *pesos* when the corruption of the *alcaldes mayores* should be eliminated, and the energy and zeal of the new officials would cause the other diminishing revenues to be considerably augmented. The general benefit to the kingdom when disorders were checked would bring about the same result.

Suggestions are offered in this Plan whereby to raise the additional amounts for salaries without its costing the treasury anything over current expenses. If the *corregimientos* were united to the intendancies the salaries of the *corregidores,* each amounting to 4,800 *pesos,* would be saved. The 6,000 *pesos* which the *corregidor* of Mexico City received could be allowed on the intendant's salary. In Guadalajara the intendant might serve as president of the *audiencia,* so that his salary would have to be increased only 3,000 *pesos* over that of the president. In Durango the intendant's salary would only have to be raised 2,000 *pesos* more than the governor received, and this extra expense could be made up from the enlarged revenues of the city. The same thing might be done in other cities. Only in Oaxaca and Campeche were the municipal funds not sufficient to be assigned for part of the intendant's salary. For many years in the former region most of the revenues had been used for the purposes of religion, which had suffered because of bad economic conditions under the *encomienda* system and the extortions of the general accountant. Oaxaca was one of the richest provinces of all New Spain on account of the cochineal industry and the commerce in woolen blankets, therefore if the notorious corruption of the *alcaldes mayores* could once be stopped, the region would have plenty of public funds.   A large part of the increase would come from stopping the habitual exactions of the *alcaldes mayores,* who obtained for themselves from ten to fifteen thousand *pesos* in compensation for no real public service.   Indeed, their heavy exactions had caused the Indians to destroy the cochineal insect on many of the plantations of Oaxaca.   In the intendancies of the Californias and Sonora salaries of intendants could be provided for by decreasing expenditures for missions and military purposes.   This presaged the later governmental appropriation of the Pious Fund.   These two intendancies were to be immediately subject to a *comandancia general* of the frontier created for the purposes of better military administration.

The offices of *corregidores* and *alcaldes mayores* were to be abolished, and the intendants might appoint subdelegates in the larger towns of their district to collect the revenues in place of the older officers; but they were to leave the administration of royal justice in first instance to newly created Spanish *alcaldes ordinarios,* who also could assist in the collection of tributes.   The subdelegates were to be paid reasonable salaries for their services, as was done in Spain.   It was no doubt correctly feared that if they did not receive a moderate remuneration, the same corrupt conditions would result as under the *alcaldes mayores.*

There was the problem of what to do with the retired *alcaldes mayores.*   Gálvez showed that this difficulty could be overcome if they were allowed to become subdelegates, at least until the intendants were able to appoint their own assistants; and their diligence might be solicited by paying them four to five per cent of the amount of the tributes which they should increase in their district.   Thus the *alcaldes* might complete their terms of office, and be left also with the exercise of ordinary jurisdiction.   Spaniards alone were to be chosen as subdelegates, even for revenue collection in Indian towns.   If there were a scarcity of Spaniards for these offices, it was suggested that administrators of the monopolies of tobacco, powder, and playing cards might be intrusted with the duties of subdelegates.

Another problem connected with the Plan was how to replace the *repartimientos*, or practically forced sales which had provided the Indians with food and tools, at great profit to the *alcaldes mayores*. This was met by the suggestion that the Indians might obtain their supplies from the same merchants who furnished them to the *alcaldes mayores*, and hence obviously at lower prices. The proposed intendants were to be guided by the Spanish Ordinance of 1749, except in regard to the encouragement of manufacture, which was prohibited in the colonies. They were to have jurisdiction in the four departments of finance, war, justice, and police.[18]

The Plan received royal approval with the reservation that sufficient time should be taken to choose suitable men for the new positions. Therefore Gálvez and Viceroy Croix took some preliminary measures to put the Plan of intendancies into effect provisionally. In 1768, after the royal sanction was obtained, they granted Pedro Corbalán ad interim powers of intendancy for Sonora and Sinaloa, which in 1773 still existed. The governor of Vera Cruz was also allowed to exercise certain functions of an intendant in financial matters.[19] In 1775 the governor of Louisiana exercised the powers of intendant over the treasury, with the royal approval.[20] There was some doubt as to whether the powers which the intendant exercised in Cuba held good in Louisiana. The king decided that they should be so exercised, though only over the royal treasury.[21]

---

[18] *Informe y plan de intendencias . . . . de Nueva España.* MS, AGI.

[19] Priestley, H. I., *José de Gálvez* (Berkeley, 1916), 20. King to the viceroy, June 3, 1773. *Reales cédulas,* N. 150 *libro* 102 (Archivo General); *ibid.,* Dec. 21, 1773, N. 161, *libro* 103 (Archivo General).

[20] Bernardo de Otero to Arriaga, June 15, 1775, AGI, 86–5–21.

[21] The king to the *contador* and *tesorero* of Louisiana, July 21, 1776, AGI, 86–5–24 (Audiencia de Santo Domingo).

Among the matters considered by Gálvez was the project to erect a new viceroyalty in the frontier provinces of the north of New Spain. The organization of the *Provincias Internas* by a royal order of August 22, 1776, was intended to be the preliminary step. The new government comprised the older units of Nueva Vizcaya, Coahuila, Texas, New Mexico, Sinaloa, Sonora, and the Californias.[22] After the introduction of the intendancies the question of the new viceroyalty was dropped, however, and the northern territories still constituted the *Provincias Internas*, and were under the control of a commandant-general. So they remained, with recurrent regroupings into eastern and western provinces, until the independence of Mexico.

Under the galvanic influence of the great visitor the plan to introduce the system of intendancies into all of the viceroyalty continued. On March 1, 1777, the king ordered the viceroy of Mexico to summon a *junta* to examine the lists of employees in the *corregimientos* and *alcaldías mayores* and decide upon the best way to unite small *alcaldías* with others. The new divisions were to be classified as first, second, or third in rank, and a map of them was to be sent to the king. Circular letters were written to the *alcaldes* to gain information concerning the old boundaries, conditions in general, and the number of civil and ecclesiastical officials who served in the districts. A map of each division was also requested. Since many of the *alcaldes mayores* were ignorant of the extent of their own jurisdictions, and because the task was disagreeable to them, the reports were very slow in coming in. When these were finally submitted to the *junta* they were found to be indefinite, and few maps had been made.

The *junta* convened some months later and, when it had examined the reports of the *alcaldes,* it redivided the *alcaldías.*

---

[22] For a further account of the *Provincias Internas* consult Beleña, E. B., *Recopilación sumaria de todos de los autos acordados de la real audiencia y sala del crimen de esta Nueva España* (Mexico, 1787), I, pt. III, 290–291.

It was considered advisable not to disturb some of the *alcaldías,* such as the eleven belonging to the Marqués del Valle and the Duke of Atlisco. It was further found impossible to make the general map which the king desired. By October, when the *junta* met to consider the establishment of the intendancies, the boundaries of all the *alcaldías* but twenty-nine had been determined. The next step was to decide which *alcaldías* should be included in each intendancy. Finally the boundaries for the intendancies of New Spain were all mapped out and a report was sent to the king.[23]

In the same year on September 8 the king appointed an intendant of army and treasury for Venezuela, to reside in the chief city, Caracas.[24] This large intendancy included Cumaná, Guayana, Maracaibo, and the islands of Margarita and Trinidad, besides the province of Venezuela proper. The next attempt made to introduce the intendant system into America was in Buenos Aires. Early in 1778 the sovereign created the office of general superintendent of the army and treasury for that city. The new official was to have complete direction and management of all the departments of the treasury, and in 1779 Juan de la Piedra was commissioned intendant. He set out from Spain with a large number of Spanish families who were to settle on the coasts of Patagonia. They reached their destination but the colonizing scheme proved to be unfortunate, like so many others, because of epidemics and deaths. The new intendant seemed to take his work seriously and made an extensive visitation of all his provinces in order to obtain information concerning them.[25]

---

[23] Secretary Soria to the king, Oct. 9, 1777, AGI, 146–6–14, *num.* 2. This MS, and AGI, 146–6–14, *num.* 1, give the boundaries of the intendancies and a list of the *alcaldías.* The divisions are also indicated in the Appendix of the Ordenanza from which the accompanying translation was made.

[24] Robertson, Wm. S., *History of the Latin-American Nations* (New York, 1922), 120.

[25] Zinny, Antonio, *Historia de los gobernadores de las provincias Argentinas* (Buenos Aires, 1879–1882), I, Introduction, xxxvii–xxxviii.

About the same time Rafael de Sobremonte, an ex-secretary of the viceroyalty, became intendant of the provinces of Córdova and Tucuman. He served successfully in this office for many years, and seems to have been one of the outstanding intendants. It is said that he raised Córdova to a point of efficiency and prosperity hitherto unknown, giving the province a new lease of life. Sobremonte's activities included putting down disorder caused by thieves near Córdova; he also built an aqueduct, he established *alcaldes de barrio* in the four wards of the city, regulated the supply of meat, lighted the streets, improved the gildhalls, founded gilds of artisans, formed bodies of militia, established elementary rural schools, and introduced a chair of jurisprudence into the university of the city. His stupendous energy and permeating influence were felt in the neighboring regions. He secured the frontiers near Mendoza, promoted mining, built roads and bridges, and improved the mail delivery.[26] His career is of special interest because the earlier intendancies have usually been neglected in accounts of the subject.

There is evidence that José de Gálvez, as minister of the Indies, had an active part in forming the Ordinances of Intendants both for Buenos Aires and Mexico. In 1778 he seems to have made many suggestions concerning the new laws that were about to be enacted. His recommendations were that only one province should be included in each intendancy, and that certain provisions of the law should be stated more clearly and be slightly modified. He always had proposals to offer for exceptional cases which might arise. The collection of tribute was placed by the measure under *alcaldes ordinarios* and subdelegates who were in the chief Indian towns and districts, but if both of these officials were lacking Gálvez thought that the Ordinance should mention who should do this. He also noted that

---

[26] Zinny, *Historia de los gobernadores de las provincias Argentinas*, I, 163–165. Sobremonte later became viceroy of Buenos Aires.

if subdelegates were established in all the chief Indian towns, as was to be inferred from the article, there would be too many of them in each intendancy, and inconveniences would result. Again, it was not declared who should elect *alcaldes ordinarios* in Spanish towns which did not have them or an *ayuntamiento*. Gálvez thought that the article which referred to this matter should state exactly who could elect them. Changes were suggested for the election of Indian governors, and Gálvez also proposed that one of the government notaries should always attend the *juntas* to attest their resolutions. The first draft of the article relative to this matter only said that a notary was always to be present, but he did not have to be a notary of the superior government. If both were allowed they might substitute for each other when necessary.

The Ordinance prescribed that the accounts of municipal finance should be presented at the beginning of January; but the great minister advised that the wording should be changed "to all the month," since it would be difficult to submit the accounts on the first of January. Gálvez provided the part which required that *alcaldes ordinarios* and subdelegates who collected the tributes should be responsible for them. The former were to be deprived of their goods if they delayed in the collection, and the latter had to give bonds to the satisfaction of the treasury officials. Many similar changes were due to the influence and superior intellect of Gálvez, but they cannot be mentioned here because of lack of space.[27]

In 1782 Charles III finally issued the Ordinance of Intendants for Buenos Aires, which provided for the establishment of intendancies throughout the entire viceroyalty of La Plata. The printed Ordinance covers three hundred and twenty-five pages with an index of fifty-seven more pages, and consists of two hundred and seventy-six articles. Although very similar to the

---

[27] Gálvez, José de, *Proposals concerning the intendancies*, Oct. 4, 1778, AGI, 146–6–14.

later document of 1786 for New Spain, it is much shorter. Two hundred and nineteen of the articles are the same as those of the Mexican Ordinance.[28] The document begins with a preamble stating the general purpose for which it is issued; the first eleven articles treat of the intendant system as a whole; articles twelve to fifty-three of the department of justice; articles fifty-three to seventy-one of the department of general administration or *policía;* articles seventy-one to two hundred and twenty of the department of finance; and the remainder, from two hundred and twenty to two hundred and seventy-five, of the department of war. The last article, two hundred and seventy-six, enjoins all colonial officials to obey the Ordinance, which was given the force of law, and was intended to be the political code for the colony, all other laws contrary to it being annulled.

The document was modified in 1783, and from this date until Buenos Aires won her independence this important piece of colonial legislation was the legal code for the viceroyalty. Not at all surprisingly it also served as a kind of constitutional basis for the free government that was established later. The viceroyalty was divided into eight intendancies which took their names from the capital cities. For the most part, the territory of each intendancy was made to coincide with the bishopric within which its capital city was situated. The eight intendancies were: Buenos Aires, Asunción, Tucuman, Santa Cruz de la Sierra, La Paz, Mendoza, La Plata, and Potosí. The intendant-general of army and royal treasury resided in Buenos Aires.[29] Later another intendancy was added which included the Patagonian coast and the Falkland Islands.[30] All the old political governments of the viceroyalty, except those of Montevideo and the thirty towns of the Jesuit missions, were to be abolished

---

28 For a comparison of the two Ordinances see the Appendix.

29 *Real ordenanza para el establecimiento é introducción de intendentes de exército y provincia en .el virreinato de Buenos-Aires* (Madrid, 1782), art. 1.

30 Pinkerton, John, *Modern Geography* (London, 1807), III, 541–542.

The Intendancies of Peru.

within five years. In the excepted regions the departments of
justice and general administration remained united to the department of war, the military governor controlling those districts and serving as an intendant.[31] Mojos and Chiquitos also
continued as military governments immediately subordinate to
the viceroy.

To tell the truth there was not a great deal of difference
between the new intendant-governors and the military governors.
The former had charge of the four departments of government
and exercised the vice-patronage (of the church) in the district,
whereas by law the latter had jurisdiction in matters of war,
policía, and justice only. In finance the governor of Montevideo was subject to the intendant of Buenos Aires, and the
governor of the *Misiones* to both the intendant of Buenos Aires
and the intendant of Paraguay. The governors of Mojos and
Chiquitos were subordinate, in matters relative to the treasury,
to the *audiencia* of La Plata. The intendants had power to subdelegate control of financial matters to the military governors
and frequently did so. The king chose the military governors
just as he did the intendants, but the viceroy could make ad
interim appointments.[32]

The salary of the intendant-general of Buenos Aires, who
presided over the tribunal of accounts and audited all those of
the viceroyalty, was ten thousand *pesos*. The intendant of Potosí
was likewise granted ten thousand *pesos,* since he was also the
director of the mint.[33] The remuneration of intendants in the
viceroyalty of La Plata was lower than in New Spain.[34]

In 1784, two and one-half months after his arrival in Peru,
Viceroy Teodoro de Croix made plans to introduce the new

---

[31] *Ordenanza* . . . . *de intendentes* . . . . *de Buenos Aires*, art. 7.

[32] *Revista del Archivo General de Buenos Aires* (Buenos Aires, 1869–
1872), IV, 104–105, 243.

[33] *Ordenanza* . . . . *de intendentes* . . . . *de Buenos Aires*, art. 273;
Pinkerton, *op. cit.*, III, 539, 541.

[34] See art. 303 of the *Ordinance of Intendants of New Spain.*

system into his viceroyalty. The visitor-general submitted to him a list of the intendancies that were to be formed, with the dioceses to be included in them, their capitals, and the number of officials serving in them. The viceroy ordered that the proper appointments should be given to the intendants who had been named, he being the only official in the colonies who could confirm the appointments after they were received from Spain, as he represented the supreme authority and person of the king. Croix published a proclamation in Lima enjoining obedience to the new system; copies of the Ordinance of Buenos Aires were sent to all the tribunals of the capital and to the provinces; account was given to the king concerning the measures taken, the royal approval was obtained on January 24, 1785, and the new régime was definitely established in the viceroyalty of Peru.[35] The eight intendancies of Lima, Trujillo, Tarma, Huancavelica, Guamanga, Cuzco, Puno, and Arequipa were created. They were also divided into fifty-seven districts or *partidos,* over which subdelegates were placed.[36]

The application of the Ordinance of Intendants to Chile was delayed until the relation which this southern region was to have to Peru under the new system could be determined. This matter was finally decided in 1784. Chile was to remain dependent upon the viceroyalty of Peru in military administration and financial affairs. The next year Viceroy Croix consulted with the president and regent of the *audiencia* of Chile about the number of intendancies to be established in that province, the *partidos* to be included in each one, the officials, subtreasuries; *junta superior,* and many other matters which the Ordinance

---

[35] *Memorias de los vireyes que han gobernado el Peru* (Lima, 1859), V, 70–71. When there was a dispute over religious jurisdiction in the intendancy of Tarma, Croix sent to the proper authorities Article 8 of the Ordinance of Mexico and Article 6 of the Ordinance of Buenos Aires. *Ibid.,* V, 56. Quesada, N. G., *Historia colonial Argentina* (Buenos Aires, 1915), 257.

[36] Moses, Bernard, *Spain's Declining Power in South America 1730–1806* (Berkeley, 1919), 246.

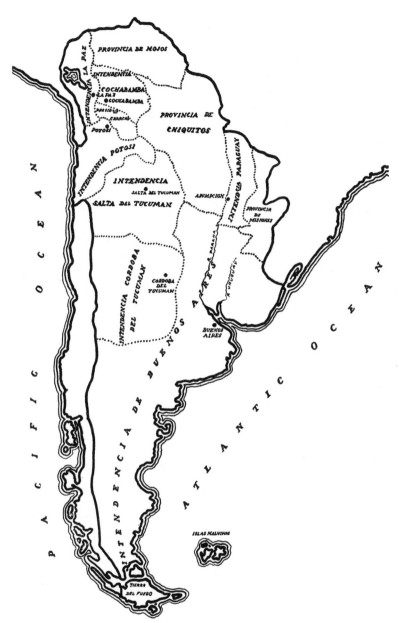

Map showing the boundaries of the intendancies in the viceroyalty
of La Plata. *In* Biedma and Beyer, *Atlas histórico de la república Argentina.*

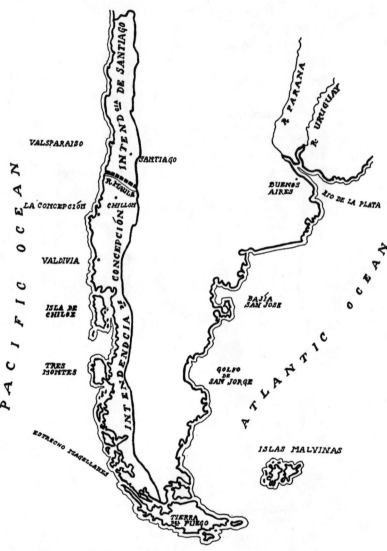

The intendancies of Chile. *In* Biedma and Beyer, *Atlas histórico de la república Argentina.*

mentioned.[37]   It was decided that two intendancies would be
sufficient—the intendancy of army at Santiago de Chile and the
intendancy of province at Concepción; the two were to correspond to the two bishoprics of the same names, and were
actually much smaller than any of the intendancies in Peru, on
account of their narrowness and extreme length.   The northern
part of the country from the southern boundary of Peru to the
Maule River constituted the intendancy of Santiago, and the
region between the Maule and the Araucanian frontier that of
Concepción.   Viceroy Croix was commissioned to inaugurate
the two intendancies, which he did as soon as possible.

The president of the *audiencia* of Chile, Ambrosio Benavides,
was chosen intendant of army in Santiago, and Brigadier Ambrosio O'Higgins, who had been governor of the frontier for
some years, intendant of province in Concepción.   The *corregidores* in the two new intendancies remained as subdelegates, but
they did not have the right of *repartimiento* as before.   The
governors of Valparaiso, Valdivia, and Juan Fernández also
became subdelegates.   Thus there was little real change in the
new government of Chile inasmuch as old officials remained in
office.   They merely had different titles and more powers for
the better regulation of financial matters. Viceroy Croix thought
it would be better for Chile to be less dependent upon Peru, as
thus the delays incident to great distance and poor communications might be avoided.   Croix sent copies of the Ordinance of
Intendants to the president and regent of the *audiencia* of Chile
so that they could form the *junta superior de hacienda* or Board
of Finance, and the president assume his duties as intendant of
army.   These officials were ordered to inform O'Higgins of his
title as intendant of province, and the two intendants were to
choose their lieutenant-assessors.   Account of what they did was
to be given to both the viceroy of Peru and the king.   The ques-

---

[37] *Memorias de los vireyes que han gobernado el Peru,* V, 72.

tion as to whether Chiloé and Coquimbo should belong to Chile or Peru was to be settled later. The new system of intendancies was duly established in Chile by the beginning of 1786 and the king approved it on February 6, 1787. A later project to make La Serena the capital of a third intendancy was considered and rejected.[38]

In 1786 the Ordinance of Intendants for New Spain was promulgated. It was an attempt to supplement the Laws of the Indies, simplify them, and make them workable. The king expected the work to be a reform that would last for all time, and indeed, though it proved to have defects, it was a remarkable piece of legislation. The Ordinance was to apply to other parts of Spanish America as far as conditions would allow. It was sent to Havana and ordered to be put into effect, thereby replacing the Ordinance of 1764.[39] It was hoped that many financial improvements would result and abuses in administration be corrected.

The printed Ordinance for New Spain consists of four hundred and ten pages containing a preamble and three hundred and six articles; there is also a sixty-page index, and an appendix showing supporting legislation. The arrangement of the articles is the same as in the Ordinance of Buenos Aires. The first fourteen treat of the intendant system as a whole; articles fifteen to fifty-six of the department of justice; articles fifty-

---

[38] Quesada, *Historia colonial Argentina*, 285–296. It was decided later that the province of Chiloé should be dependent upon the viceroy of Peru. Chile still retains the name intendant for the officials over its eighty-two departments, but now the president appoints the intendants for a term of three years. The departments are divided into 901 subdelegations and these into 3,228 districts. Sweet, Wm. W., *A History of Latin America* (ed. 3, New York, 1929), 300.

[39] Zamora y Coronado, III, 606. At first Viceroy Croix seems to have used both the Ordinances of Buenos Aires and Mexico in Peru. *Memorias de los vireyes que han gobernado el Peru*, V, 56–57; *ibid.*, VI, 12. Miss Irene Wright was unable to find for the writer in the Archives of Seville a special Ordinance of Intendants for Peru. The Ordinance of Buenos Aires was first employed there and later it seems to have been replaced by the Ordinance of Mexico.

seven to seventy-four of the department of *policía;* articles seventy-five to two hundred and forty-nine of the department of finance; articles two hundred and fifty to three hundred and five of the department of war; and article three hundred and six declares that the document has the force of law and is to be obeyed.

The primary purpose of the new system was to relieve the overworked viceroy of the eighteenth century, who, because of the shortness of his term, could not become familiar with all the conditions of the viceroyalty. The intendants would have a chance to be better informed locally and could specialize in their line of work.[40] They could aid the viceroy in the collection of revenues, the administration of justice, and in all economic matters. They could be real assistants to him, and thus supply a need which had always been felt in the colonies. For this reason the intendants were to be carefully chosen from among Spanish-born subjects, since they were considered more efficient than creoles or *mestizos.*

The far-reaching aim of the entire reform was to make the revenues more ample through more efficient collections, for it was desperately necessary to secure greater wealth and strength wherewith to check England in the great rivalry for colonial possessions. At the same time, the creation of this office limited the power of the viceroy, as it took away his supreme control over financial matters. In regard to the treasury the general intendant of army and treasury was to act with absolute independence of the viceroy, but the latter was to continue to exercise all his other powers according to the Laws of the Indies. The viceroy still gave instructions to the intendants, just as he had done with the former governors, and they were obliged to inform him concerning all the appointments which were made. They were subordinate to him in matters of general administration,

---

[40] Revillagigedo to Floridablanca, Oct. 30, 1790, AGI, leg. 1, *num.* 55; Villarroel, *Enfermedades políticas* . . . . MS, I, pt. II, p. 16.

worship, public instruction, and the judiciary. In military affairs they had to respect the general of the army and all the rights of the viceroy and the commandant-general of the frontier.[41] They were also subject to the *audiencias* and to the *junta superior de hacienda*. The subdelegates as inferior officials were subordinate to the same authorities indirectly and to the intendants directly.[42]

Twelve intendancies and three provinces were established in New Spain. The capital cities of the intendancies were: Mexico City, Puebla, Vera Cruz, Mérida de Yucatan, Antequera de Oaxaca, Valladolid de Michoacan, Guanajuato, San Luis Potosí, Guadalajara, Zacatecas, Durango, and Arispe. In size the intendancies were not uniform; some were ten, twenty, or thirty times larger than others. The intendancy of San Luis Potosí was more extensive than the whole of Spain, Sonora and Durango were larger than the British Isles, but Guanajuato was no larger than two or three departments of France. Also there was no uniformity in regard to population. The intendancies with the most inhabitants were Mexico, Puebla, Guadalajara, and Oaxaca. The intendancy of Mexico had a population of over a million and a half, and the capital of the viceroyalty was situated within it.[43]

The intendants took full charge of finances and were immediately responsible to the intendant-general, who in turn was directly subject to the Council of the Indies. They were appointed by the king and performed the duties of the former governors in civil administration and cases of justice. The intendants were obliged to submit their commissions to the viceroys for confirmation.[44] In 1787, upon the petition of the people of

[41] *Ordenanza . . . . de intendentes . . . . de Nueva España*, arts. 2, 7, 299–302.

[42] *Account of Valiente concerning the system of government in America*, Sept. 16, 1809, *AGI*, 141–5–11.

[43] Humboldt, Alexander, *Ensayo político sobre Nueva España* (Paris, 1836), I, 292–297.

[44] *Ordenanza . . . . de intendentes . . . . de Nueva España*, arts. 1–4; *Cedulario*, MS, II, 158.

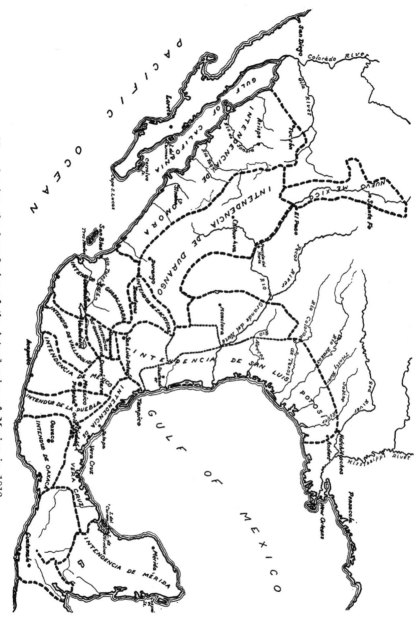

Map showing the boundaries of the intendancies of Mexico in 1812. Taken with the author's permission from Priestley, *José de Gálvez*, 450.

the *audiencia* of Buenos Aires, the king decreed that they were to pass afterward to the *audiencia* for its information. The commissions of subdelegates were also to go first to the viceroy and then to the *audiencia*. Intendants who resided within the district of subordinate *audiencias* had to notify them of the subdelegates they appointed. On March 21, 1793, the king ordered that such intendants should take the oath of office before the *audiencia*.[45] The intendant-general, also called the superintendent-subdelegate, presided over the *junta superior de hacienda* in the capital of the viceroyalty. Next to the viceroy and *audiencia* this board exercised the highest authority in the country. Its meetings were to be held at least once a week on the days determined by the intendant-general, and he could summon extraordinary sessions. The *junta* had the power to correspond directly with the king by the *vía reservada*. Matters of justice might be appealed over the intendants' heads to the *audiencias,* just as had been done with the former governors.[46]

The salaries of intendants in New Spain were high enough for them to maintain the dignity of their offices. The intendant-general of army received 12,000 *pesos;* the intendants of Puebla, Vera Cruz, Guadalajara, and Arispe 7,000 *pesos;* those of Oaxaca, Valladolid, Guanajuato, San Luis Potosí, Zacatecas, and Durango 6,000 *pesos;* and the intendant of Yucatan 5,000 *pesos.*[47] Intendants of province had to give 10,000 *pesos* bond for their offices, but the superintendent-subdelegate was exempt from this obligation because of his high position.[48]

A complete change likewise took place in the local government. The old *alcaldías mayores* and *corregimientos* were suppressed and united to the intendancies. Subdelegates replaced *corregidores* and *alcaldes mayores,* who had long been the cause

---

45 *Ordenes de la Corona,* MS, I, 5–6; *Cedulario,* MS, III, 10–11.
46 *Ordenanza* .... *de intendentes* .... *de Nueva España,* arts. 4, 6.
47 *Ibid.,* art. 303.
48 *Ibid.,* art. 304.

of abuses in misappropriation of royal revenues.[49]   The new subordinate officials were put in charge of *partidos*, as the divisions of the intendancies were then called, and they served without fees.   They were directly subject to the intendant of province, who at first appointed them, but in 1787 the viceroy was granted this power.   In practice the intendants proposed three names (a *terna*) from which the viceroy usually chose one. Subdelegates were appointed to serve for five years.[50]   The effectiveness of the new system depended largely upon these officials, since good local government is always the basis for all successful national administration.[51]

While the old officials were being suppressed the intendants served as chief justices of their provinces, but they were not to interfere with the *alcaldes ordinarios*, who remained as judges of first instance.   The latter officials were rather to be the chief assistants of the intendants in judicial matters in the smaller towns and villages.   Two *alcaldes* were chosen for each town by the *ayuntamiento* or town council, but where there was no council the intendants appointed an *alcalde* every consecutive year.[52]   In Indian towns the ancient custom of choosing governors or *alcaldes* was not to be interfered with.   The chief duty of the Indian magistrates was to collect the tribute.   To prevent disturbances during elections a Spanish judge or a Spaniard whom he might designate was to preside over the native *juntas*. The subdelegates or *alcaldes ordinarios* had to give account to the intendant concerning the outcome of the native elections so that he might approve them.   Preference was always to be given to

---

[49] *Ordenanza . . . . de intendentes . . . . de Nueva España*, arts. 7, 9.

[50] *Ibid.*, art 12; Revillagigedo, *Dictamen . . . . sobre la ordenanza de intendentes . . . .* May 5, 1791, MS, *num.* 402, arts 131–132; Revillagigedo, J. V., *Instrucción reservada . . . .* (Mexico, 1831), arts. 859–861; see the *Revista del Archivo General de Buenos Aires*, IV, 245 *et seq.* for the manner in which the intendants proposed to the viceroy the names of subdelegates.

[51] Revillagigedo, *Instrucción reservada*, arts. 847–848.

[52] *Ordenanza . . . . de intendentes . . . . de Nueva España*, art. 11.

Indians who knew Spanish or who were exceptionally skilled in agriculture or industry.[53]

Certain military administrations, just as in the viceroyalty of La Plata, were allowed to remain. In New Spain most of them were found in the frontier provinces or in strategic points. They were Yucatan, Tabasco, Vera Cruz, Acapulco, Nuevo León, Nuevo Santander, Coahuila, Texas, and New Mexico. In these more remote regions the departments of justice and general administration were united to the military department. The department of finance was under the intendants and subject to the *junta superior de hacienda*. Gradually all of these places except Yucatan, Vera Cruz, and Campeche were to be brought under the control of subdelegates after the success of the new system of intendants should become a reality.[54]

In Mexico the right of the ecclesiastical vice-patronage was to be exercised by all the intendants except those of Mexico City, Guadalajara, Arispe, Mérida, and Vera Cruz. In the capital the viceroy was to perform these functions, in Guadalajara the regent of the *audiencia,* in Arispe the commandant-general of the frontier, and in Yucatan the governor and captain-general. Likewise in the viceroyalty of La Plata all the intendants except those of Buenos Aires and La Plata exercised the vice-patronage in their provinces. In Buenos Aires the viceroy who resided there held it and in La Plata the president of the *audiencia.*[55]

In 1787 the intendancy of Nicaragua was established. As soon as Juan de Ayssa became intendant-governor of the province, he dispatched official letters to the *corregidores* inserting in them articles 6, 7, and 272 of the Ordinance of Intendants, since they pertained to those officials. The Ordinance was published by means of proclamations in the towns of his jurisdiction. At

---

[53] *Ibid.*, arts. 13–15.

[54] *Ibid.*, art. 10.

[55] *Ibid.*, art. 8; *Ordenanza . . . . de intendentes . . . . de Buenos Aires,* art. 6.

first the *corregidor* of Sutiava refused to recognize or obey the intendant because a special command from the superior government had not preceded his orders. The needed document soon arrived and with it came the intendant's title, which greatly simplified the problem. The intendant was enjoined to put the Ordinance into effect, suppressing the *corregimientos* of Sutiava, Matagalpa, and Nicoya, which were to be included in the new intendancy. The intendant was ordered to appoint subdelegates for the *partidos,* but not to overlook the three *corregidores,* who were to serve in the minor offices. Costa Rica was to remain a military government, like that of Montevideo, as it was so far distant from the residence of the intendant. Its governor had jurisdiction in all the departments of government except finance. The intendant appointed judges in whom he had confidence to collect the revenues of Costa Rica and to take care of all affairs relating to the treasury. The military government might not interfere with them in any way.[56]

By 1790 the intendant system had been extended to all Spanish America. From New Spain it had been introduced even into the distant Philippines in 1784. The judge of the Manila *audiencia,* González Carbajal, became the first intendant, with an additional salary of three thousand *pesos.* In 1786 four intendancies were there established, but they lasted scarely a year. The intendant-general, González Carbajal, became a member of the *audiencia* of Mexico in 1787, whereupon the superintendency of the treasury of the Philippines was restored to the governor, who received the title of superintendent-subdelegate of the royal treasury. There had been a number of disputes between the governor and the intendant, but after 1787 everything remained peaceful until 1819, when the captaincy-general was again separated from the financial control. Again in 1824 the superintendency of the treasury was united to the government. One single intendancy

---

[56] Fernández, León, *Colección de documentos para la historia de Costa Rica* (Barcelona, 1881–1907), X, 212–213.

of provinces was allowed to remain, and this was subordinate to the governor. There was another separation in 1829 and a union in 1842.[57]

About 1790 three other intendancies were established in Central America. They coincided with the captaincies-general of Chiapas or Guatemala, Honduras, and Salvador.[58] In 1803 the intendancy of Porto Rico was planned, but was not created until 1811. Alejandro Ramírez, secretary to the president of Guatemala, was appointed intendant with a salary of four thousand *pesos* and six hundred *pesos* for secretarial expenses. He was to observe the regulations of the Ordinance of Intendants of New Spain, aid the industry of the island, encourage its commerce and agriculture, and improve its administration.[59] The other West Indian intendancies besides Havana and Porto Rico were Puerto Príncipe and Santiago de Cuba. The intendancy of Puerto Príncipe was established in 1813, José de Vildósola serving as the first intendant.[60]

To sum up: in the foregoing account it has been emphasized that administrative and financial reform was badly needed to meet new conditions and to overcome the defects of a colonial organization which had lost much of its early efficiency. As the viceroys were overworked not much assistance in the way of reform could be expected from them without modification of their functions. It needs perhaps to be said again that the Bourbon reforms of the eighteenth century, this new system being one of them, were directed toward preparing Spain to challenge, with France, the supremacy of England in the colonial field. Finally Charles III, one of the most enlightened sovereigns

---

[57] Zamora y Coronado, III, 620–621.

[58] Robertson, *op. cit.*, 122. For the provinces included in the four Central American intendancies of Nicaragua, Chiapas, Honduras, and Salvador see Juarros, Domingo, *Statistical and Commercial History of the Kingdom of Guatemala* (London, 1823), 12 *et seq.*, 207.

[59] Zamora .y Coronado, III, 619–620.

[60] *Diccionario universal de historia y de geografía* (Mexico, 1853–1856), IV, 293; Valdes, III, 557.

of Spain, rose to the situation and applied sweeping reforms to the American dependencies after he had revivified the mother country. Among his reforms was the intendant system, which, had its first experiment in Havana. It proved to be successful there, and later the visitor-general, José de Gálvez, was sent to introduce the system into New Spain.

In the meantime intendancies were established in Venezuela and the viceroyalty of La Plata. After much discussion, the drawing up of many plans, and the insistence of Gálvez, who became the Minister of the Indies, the Ordinance of Intendants of Buenos Aires was issued in 1782. The intendant system was then applied to Peru and Chile. In 1786 the Ordinance of Intendants of New Spain was promulgated. This remarkable piece of legislation was to apply to all of Spanish America in so far as conditions would permit. By the latter part of the century the new system had spread to all of Spanish America and to the Philippines.

II

The Four Departments of Government Under
the Intendant System

There were four departments (perhaps phases would be the better word) of government in the Spanish colonial system—the departments of justice, general administration (*policía*), finance, and war. Before the establishment of the intendancies the viceroy was at the head of all four of them, but with the introduction of the new system he was relieved of the functions connected with the division of finance, and the intendants were to assist him in the three other *causas*.

It would be interesting to show which of the Laws of the Indies were incorporated in the Ordinance of Intendants, but lack of space will not permit.[1] The most noticeable difference between the *Recopilación* and the Ordinance is the latter's omission of ecclesiastical matters. The Ordinance of Intendants has only one article which treats strictly of the vice-patronage, while the whole first book of the *Recopilación* deals with the church. The importance of ecclesiastic affairs of the early days had clearly given place to regalism as represented by the centralized government of Charles III. It must be understood that the *Recopilación* was not actually superseded, although the frame of government was effectively revamped and its operation systematized.

The intendants were not always lawyers, and in order to perform the duties connected with the department of justice they had to be aided by a lieutenant-lawyer or assessor, who

---

[1] Refer to the footnotes of the translation for the corresponding laws of the *Recopilación*.

exercised for them contentious civil and criminal jurisdiction in the capitals of the intendancies. At the same time he could substitute for the intendant in case of absence or illness. If the intendent and his lieutenant-assessor both died or were incapacitated then the senior judge of the treasury temporarily performed the functions of the office. When this happened to both the intendant-general and his assessor, the senior judge of the tribunal of accounts served for the first official, and he whom the viceroy chose with the advice of his council for the second. Lieutenant-assessors had to be examined and approved by the *audiencias* and were appointed by the king.[2] The Council of the Indies submitted to the king three names for each lieutenancy and he chose for a term of five years the person whom he thought most fit for the position. The salary of the intendant-general's assessor was to be two thousand *pesos* besides perquisites, and of the others fifteen hundred *pesos* besides perquisites. The intendants could not remove their assessors except for just causes approved by the king and the Council of the Indies, but these assistants might be suspended by the *junta superior*.[3] Appeals from the decisions or sentences of lieutenant-assessors went to the *audiencia*, but they were never to be deprived of their cognizance in judicial matters, since they received their titles from the king.[4]

On August 22, 1793, the king made a very important decision concerning intendants when he declared that intendants and other judges for whom he had appointed assessors would not be held responsible for the decisions or sentences which they gave through or with their advice. They could not make use of assessors whom the king did not appoint for them. When intendants did not agree with their assessors they could suspend the decision or sentence and consult the superior authority,

---

[2] *Ordenanza . . . . de indendentes . . . . de Nueva España*, arts. 15–17.
[3] *Ibid.*, art. 18.
[4] *Ibid.*, art. 19.

stating the reasons why they did this in an official document or *expediente*. When subordinate judges or *alcaldes ordinarios* determined cases with the opinion of assessors whom they themselves appointed they were not to be held responsible, but only the assessor, provided there had been no fraud in the decision.[5]

As heads of the departments of justice the intendants had many functions to perform in their districts.[6] First, they or their lieutenants presided over all municipal councils and public functions of their capitals. Account of what was done or discussed in the town councils had to be given them, so that they might arrange for putting the resolutions into effect.[7] They were to study the Laws of the Indies carefully, so that they might wisely administer justice for the good of the people and enforce the laws.[8] It was especially charged upon them to protect the Indians and prevent local officials from tyrannizing over them as the *alcaldes mayores* had done, to reprimand such officials for misdeeds, and if they did not heed the correction to refer their cases to a higher tribunal.[9] They were to see that the local justices did not delay judicial cases or exact excessive revenues.[10] In addition, judges of *residencia* were sent out by the Council of the Indies, and judges of commission by the *audiencias*, to see that local officials were doing their duty, but they were not to be sent out to investigate the intendants.[11] These latter were to make frequent visitations of their provinces to gain information whereby they might promote agriculture, industry, commerce, and mining. In case it proved impossible to do this at least

[5] *Cedulario*, MS, I, 167.

[6] Donald E. Smith has given a concise summary of the duties of intendants under the four *causas* in his book, *The Viceroy of New Spain* (Berkeley, 1913), 260 *et seq.*

[7] *Ordenanza* . . . . *de intendentes* . . . . *de Nueva España*, art. 20.

[8] *Ibid.*, art. 21.

[9] *Ibid.*, art. 22.

[10] *Ibid.*, art. 23.

[11] *Ibid.*, art. 24.

every year they might send a trustworthy subdelegate as a substitute.[12]

The Ordinance then diverges from strictly judicial affairs and treats of financial matters. The *junta superior de hacienda* was required to inspect the finances of Spanish cities and the communal funds of Indian towns, the king reserving the right to appoint the general accountant for all these funds.[13] The *junta* might ask the intendants for information concerning them, and communicate its measures to them through the general accountant of municipal finance, who was also the permanent secretary of the *junta*.[14] In order that they might not be ignorant of municipal finances, as soon as they began to serve in their offices the intendants were to ask each one of the cities, towns, or villages within their jurisdictions for an exact account of these funds, and of the municipal taxes which the towns collected.[15] From the information obtained in this manner the intendants were required to draw up a provisional ordinance for municipal finance and submit it to the *junta superior* and that body was expected to report it to the king.[16]

A municipal *junta* was to be established in each Spanish city, town, or village for the control of financial matters, serving as a body quite distinct from the town council. The senior *alcalde ordinario* was to preside over it, and the town council was not to interfere with it in any way. The business of the *junta* was to sell offices connected with the branches of municipal finance to the highest bidders,[17] and lease the revenues of the town to collectors. The intendants were to supervise the proceedings of the municipal *juntas* in order to prevent abuses. In their capitals they could do this directly or through their

---

[12] *Ordenanza . . . . de intendentes . . . . de Nueva España*, arts. 26–28.
[13] *Ibid.*, art. 28.
[14] *Ibid.*, art. 29.
[15] *Ibid.*, arts. 31–33.
[16] *Ibid.*, art. 33.
[17] *Ibid.*, art. 36.

lieutenant-assessors and in the smaller towns by means of the justices.[18]   When he thought best the intendant of province might grant revenue-leases for longer than a year and report them to the *junta superior*, but they were not to exceed five years.[19]

Each municipal *junta* annually appointed a steward to take charge of all funds on hand. He received as a remuneration for his work one and one-half per cent of what he collected. At the end of the year he made a report of the revenue collection to the municipal *junta*. If a favorable balance was shown the steward deposited the funds in the coffer of the three keys in the presence of the members of the *junta*. The account was certified by a notary and signed by all the members of the retiring *junta*. The certified account was then presented to the town council and if approved was returned to the *junta* which sent the original with the certified records to the intendant.[20]

All the funds of the local treasuries except those needed for current expenditures were sent to the treasury of the province, which also had three keys, one in the possession of the intendant, and the others in the hands of the accountant and the treasurer.[21] The Spanish subdelegates in the smaller divisions of the provinces had practically the same supervision over municipal finance as the intendants had in the capitals.[22]

When all the local accounts were closed for the year the intendants sent the *junta superior* an "extract" of each one properly certified by the principal accountant of his province. At any time the *junta* might require the general accounting-office of municipal finance in the capital to review these accounts and the intendants had to provide the records.[23] The municipal *juntas*

18 *Ibid.*, arts. 37–39.
19 *Ibid.*, art. 39.
20 *Ibid.*, arts. 40–43.
21 *Ibid.*, art. 43.
22 *Ibid.*, art. 44.
23 *Ibid.*, art. 46.

and inferior justices were always to obey without delay the intendant's orders for drawing up documents which related to municipal finance.[24] Whenever municipal *juntas* or inferior justices considered themselves aggrieved by the intendant's measures they might appeal directly to the *junta superior*.[25] The treasury officials of their provinces were always to cooperate with intendants, and four per cent of the income from the municipal funds in Spanish communities, and two per cent in Indian towns, were to be set aside for their traveling expenses and salaries, which intendants might determine with the approval of the *junta superior*.[26]

The intendants were to watch over clerks and notaries so that they would not be careless in drawing up documents or try to falsify them.[27] They had to see that the pecuniary penalties and fines imposed by *alcaldes ordinarios* and subdelegates were not concealed or misapplied, and they corresponded directly with the regents of the *audiencias* about this matter.[28] The last article under the department of justice declares that intendants should make reports at all times to the viceroy and higher tribunals concerning any important matters. In addition they were permitted to communicate directly with the king when serious events occurred.[29]

Intendants no doubt frequently availed themselves of this latter privilege. Several instances illustrate the character of their correspondence. In 1785 the intendant of Louisiana wrote to the king about the confiscation in New Orleans of a brigantine from Jamaica suspected of illicit trading. The sovereign approved of the confiscation, perhaps because the treasury received 66,484 *pesos* after the intendant had obtained his share.[30] In 1788 the intendant of Durango communicated with the king

---

[24] *Ordenanza . . . . de intendentes . . . . de Nueva España*, art. 49.

[25] *Ibid.*, art. 50.   [26] *Ibid.*, art. 51.   [27] *Ibid.*, art. 54.

[28] *Ibid.*, art. 55.   [29] *Ibid.*, art. 56.

[30] *Consejo de Indias*, April 7, 1790, AGI, 86–5–22 (Audiencia de Santo Domingo.

relative to the unfortunate condition of that province because of repeated Indian raids. The monarch urged the viceroy to take proper measures to remedy the situation.[31] Again in the same year the intendant of Louisiana, enclosing a letter from the commandant at Natchitoches, entreated the king to fix the boundary of the *comandancia* at the Sabine River. The viceroy was urged to do this, since it would create a definite demarcation and make smuggling more difficult.[32]

The intendant of Louisiana wrote to the king in 1801 asking what to do in the case of an American trader, Evan Jones, who carried on commerce through his position of United States consul. The fiscal and the intendant's assessor had differed in their opinions as to the course to pursue. The sovereign answered that Jones could trade only if he should take the oath of allegiance to him and as a subject come under the laws of Spain.[33] In February of 1802, Venturo Morales, the intendant ad interim of Louisiana, reported to the king the measures he had taken to prevent injuries which resulted from the right of Americans to deposit their goods in New Orleans before they shipped them to foreign ports. It seems that some Americans smuggled their merchandise into the city by landing it several leagues above the municipality to avoid the payment of duty.[34] Again in June of the same year the intendant of Louisiana sought the royal approval for spending 230 *pesos* on the guard he had placed at the mouth of the Arkansas River.[35]

---

[31] Porlier to the viceroy of Mexico, Feb. 21, 1788, MS. *Reales cédulas* 1752–1789, *num.* 108, *lib.* 134, p. 172 (Archivo General).

[32] Valdez to the viceroy of Mexico, Nov. 1, 1789, MS. *Reales cédulas* 1755–1790, P. Y. 78, *lib.* 142, p. 241 (Archivo General).

[33] Lopez Angulo to the king, July 13, 1801, AGI, 86–5–23 (Audiencia de Santo Domingo).

[34] Intendant of Louisiana to the King, Feb. 28, 1802, AGI, 87–1–29, *num.* 66 (Audiencia de Santo Domingo).

[35] Intendant of Louisiana to the king, June 12, 1802, AGI, 87–1–29, *num.* 109 (Audiencia de Santo Domingo).

During the trouble between Great Britain and France before the peace of Amiens the intendant of Louisiana had suspended the trade of neutrals, and sought the royal approval therefor.[36] He also reported the illicit commerce of neutrals and advised that prompt measures should be taken either to make the trade legal or to suppress it. He also asked the king to tell him definitely the terms of the treaty of peace of 1802 with England so that he might know what measures to take.[37] In 1813 the intendant of Santo Domingo corresponded with the king concerning the deplorable condition of that island, and asked that something be done to prevent its total ruin.[38] Viceroys sometimes showed their jealousy of the independence of the intendants in their communications to the king.

Probably with greater frequency the intendants wrote first to the viceroy or some superior official asking his intervention with the monarch. In 1782 the intendant of Louisiana addressed the viceroy of Mexico asking royal approval for the expenditure of 4,303 *pesos* on the garrison of Mobile.[39] In 1784 the governor of Louisiana wrote to the king that the intendant had confiscated some Negroes of the English on the way to Jamaica, and sought the royal approval on behalf of the official.[40] In 1797 the intendant ad interim of New Orleans reported to the captain-general of Cuba the arrival in that city of the first vessel from the United States, and sought the royal sanction for having permitted its captain to sell the cargo after he had paid the dues of foreigners.[41] He likewise asked that the Englishman, William

[36] Intendant of Louisiana to the king, Oct. 21, 1802, AGI, 87–1–28 (Audiencia de Santo Domingo).

[37] Intendant of Louisiana to the king, 1802, AGI, 87–1–29, *num.* 75 (Audiencia de Santo Domingo).

[38] *Consejo de estado*, Feb. 3, 1813, *papeleta* 106, AGI, 88–19.

[39] Intendant of Louisiana to the viceroy, April 30, 1782, AGI, 87–3–10, *num.* 112 (Audiencia de Santo Domingo).

[40] Governor of Louisiana to the king, Jan. 15, 1784, AGI, 87–3–10, *num.* 51 (Audiencia de Santo Domingo).

[41] Diego Gardoqui to the captain-general of Cuba, Jan. 21, 1797, AGI, 87–1–24, *num.* 85 (Audiencia de Santo Domingo).

Panton, be permitted to continue his trade with the Indian tribes near Pensacola.[42] Two years later the intendant of the same city wrote to the captain-general of Cuba asking for a royal decision in a quarrel which he had with the governor.[43]

In the second department, that of general administration or *policía*, the intendant's duties were just as numerous as those of the former governors. A new and heavy requirement of them was that maps of all the intendancies, showing boundaries and such topographical features as mountains, forests, rivers, and lakes, were to be made by capable engineers,[44] who were to furnish the intendants information about the climate, quality of the lands, minerals, products, industry, commerce, navigable rivers or those which could be deepened, places where irrigation canals and mills might be erected, bridges, roads, lands containing timber for construction of vessels, and about ports large enough for commerce.[45]

Under *policía* fell the quaint injunction to pay careful attention to the morals of the people, prevent laziness and vice, but not intermeddle with the private affairs of useful persons. Vagabonds were to be put to work and professional beggars sent to workhouses. Turbulent and vicious people were to be sentenced to work in the mines and at the *presidios*.[46]

The department of *policía* was concerned chiefly with the encouragement of various forms of industry. There was need for this, since industry had been greatly hampered before the period of free trade. The cultivation of native crops which would not compete with Spanish products was to be increased as much as possible. The cochineal industry, a profitable enterprise

[42] Diego Gardoqui to the captain-general of Cuba, March 3, 1797, AGI, 87–1–24, *num*. 94 (Audiencia de Santo Domingo).

[43] Soler to the captain-general of Cuba, March 31, 1799, AGI, 87–1–25, *num*. 286 (Audiencia de Santo Domingo).

[44] *Ordenanza* . . . . *de intendentes* . . . . *de Nueva España*, art. 57.

[45] *Ibid.*, art. 58.

[46] *Ibid.*, arts. 59–61.

which had declined in Mexico, was to be extended and new lands were to be set aside for it. Similar action was prescribed to promote the raising of hemp, flax, cotton, wild silk, and wheat. Measures were to be taken to work uncultivated lands. Waste and royal lands were to be sold at reasonable prices to those who desired them, even to Indians or the castes, who were to cultivate them for their own profit.[47]

In 1796 the land question was exclusively intrusted to viceroys and presidents of *audiencias,* who could appoint subdelegates to sell unoccupied lands, reporting the appointments to the Secretary of State of the Indies. All persons who had held uncultivated lands since the year 1700 were to show their titles to the subdelegates, but if they could not do this or if their titles had not been confirmed they were to be allowed to keep their lands, and obtain new titles for them. All new titles issued had to be confirmed by the proper authorities, and appeal was allowed from the decisions of subdelegates to the *audiencias.* Persons who had claimed in their holdings more lands than they had purchased, whether confirmed or not, were to appear before the subdelegate for a composition as to the excess. If they did not do this the surplus was to be considered crown land and might be sold to whoever desired it. All grants issued under the Ordinance of Intendants required the approval of the *junta superior.* Within their provinces the intendants were to be special judges of incidental questions relative to sales, compositions, and distributions of crown lands. In the distant provinces of Caracas, Havana, Cartagena, Panama, Buenos Aires, Yucatan, Cumaná, Margarita, and Porto Rico the confirmation of landgrants was to be made by the governors with the aid of treasury officials who also could determine appeals from the decisions of subdelegates.[48]

---

[47] *Ordenanza . . . . de intendentes . . . . de Nueva España,* arts. 61–63.

[48] Cedulario, MS, I, 28–29; Hall, Frederic, *The Laws of Mexico* (San Francisco, 1885), 28–29, 40, 74.

Irrigation was to be developed, and cattle-raising, especially for wool-production, was to be encouraged. The intendants had to protect the forests and the mines, repair bridges and roads, encourage the use of wheeled vehicles to facilitate communication and transportation of crops, build inns, lodging houses, and taverns for the convenience of travelers, and keep the country safe by the employment of mounted police of the *Santa Hermandad.*[49]

In the towns, also, they had many functions to perform in connection with this department. What the viceroy did for the capital, the intendants were expected to do for their own cities and towns. These obligations included supervision of cleaning, paving, and widening the streets, and of erecting and repairing both public and private buildings. They had to see that the dwellings in Indian towns were built in good style, and that their own capitals were inclosed by walls for protection. They suggested to the *junta superior* the means of raising funds for public buildings when the surplus amounts from municipal finance were not sufficient for such projects.[50] They exercised the same supervision over churches as over other public edifices. None were to be constructed without the plans being submitted to the *junta superior* for approval, and repairs were to be promptly made when needed.[51]   All other municipal services such as the water supply and protection against fire were under their general direction. Every four months they were to make crop reports to the viceroy or to the commandant-general of the frontier, and to the intendant-general in Mexico. Intendants had to see that trade in the products of the country was always free, administer the public granaries of the capitals and other towns of their provinces, and draw up regulations for them. The latter were

---

[49] *Ordenanza . . . . de intendentes . . . . de Nueva España*, arts. 63–68.
[50] *Ibid.*, arts. 68–70.
[51] *Ibid.*, art. 70.

to be submitted to the viceroy or some higher authority for approval, and finally to the Council of the Indies. An important duty was to prevent corners in foodstuffs by hucksters and retailers of grain, for which purpose the intendants might establish public storehouses if they thought best.[52] In 1786 Intendant Francisco de Sanz prohibited wheat export from Buenos Aires, since this would too greatly decrease the supplies of the city.[53]

The coinage also demanded the attention of those busy officers. They and their subdelegates had to watch constantly that the current gold and silver coins were not defaced or counterfeited. They could make as many investigations as were needed, inspecting silversmith's shops, stores, and public workshops for this purpose.[54]

The third department, that of finance, was by far the most important division of government under the new system. It was regarded as the especial feature of the state's activities, for it was by means of more efficient tax collection that most of the reforms in other lines were expected to come. Through it colonial administration was to be reinvigorated, great benefit was to result to all the people, and above all the sinews were to be provided for a coming war with England. For these reasons the part of the Ordinance which treats of finance is much longer and more detailed than the other divisions. Here the intendants were weighted with heavy responsibility, as they were given exclusive cognizance of all legal cases relating to the treasury and its branches, other officials or tribunals being rigidly denied interference with them.[55] In the smaller divisions of the intendancies the subdelegates were judges of first instance in matters which pertained to the treasury, and appeal from their decisions

---

[52] *Ordenanza . . . . de intendentes . . . . de Nueva España,* arts. 71–74.

[53] Acuerdo de cabildo, May 1786. *Documentos para la historia del virreinato del Rio de la Plata* (Buenos Aires, 1912–1913), I, 203.

[54] *Ordenanza . . . . de intendentes . . . . de Nueva España,* art. 74.

[55] *Ibid.,* arts. 75–77.

was always allowed to the intendants, who determined the cases by means of their assessors.[56] The *junta superior* was the highest court of appeals in financial matters in America and litigants had recourse to it over the intendants' decisions. For this reason neither intendants nor their assessors were permitted to be present when lawsuits appealed from their verdicts were being discussed in the *junta*. Final appeals, if they were important enough, went to the king through the Minister of the Indies.[57]

Cases connected with the monopolies of tobacco, *alcabalas*, *pulque*, powder, and playing cards, although those revenues were not administered by intendants, were decided in first instance either by them or their subdelegates. These officials had to see that the rules provided for each branch were kept and all violations punished.[58] They took charge of cases concerning estates confiscated on account of a judicial sentence, but they might not interfere with such lawsuits which were under the cognizance of the viceroy. Likewise cases which pertained to prizes taken at sea, shipwrecks, vessels seeking refuge, and unclaimed property belonged to their jurisdiction.[59]

All royal decrees relative to finances were enforced by the intendants and their subordinates, and if necessary they were empowered to call upon captains-general or commandants of troops to aid them. When conflicts over financial matters occurred between intendants and other tribunals the former were to report them to the *junta superior,* which took corrective measures pending appeal to the king. So also when doubt arose about the powers of the *junta* the viceroy determined the matter and notified the king.[60] Because of the dignity attached to their offices intendants, their families, and servants were permitted to

---

56 *Ibid.*, art. 77.
57 *Ibid.*, art. 78.
58 *Ibid.*, arts. 79–81.
59 *Ibid.*, arts. 81–84.
60 *Ibid.*, arts. 84–86.

enjoy military privileges and the benefit of the military pension system (*montepío militar*). No inferior tribunal or official could try the cases of persons who possessed the military *fuero*. They were honored by having the *junta superior* take cognizance of them directly in first instance, and appeals from its decisions went to the king. The highest treasury officials enjoyed similar privileges and the intendants took cognizance of all their lawsuits in first instance, permitting recourse to the *junta superior* and from it to the king. When doubt arose over the cases of persons enjoying military privileges, because of the great distance from the Council of War in Spain, the viceroy was enjoined to summon and preside over a special *junta,* which was to consist of the intendant-general and the regent of the *audiencia,* in which such matters might be determined.[61]

Subordinate administrators of royal revenues enjoyed merely the privilege of treasury officials in civil and criminal suits arising from their positions. In such cases the intendants were their sole judges, but in non-official matters they were subject in first instance to the ordinary justices. Subordinate revenue officials were to furnish information whenever the ordinary royal jurisdiction should need this for the trial of cases, and to do the same thing for the intendants.[62] They were not to hold other municipal offices as these would interfere with their financial obligations. They could not be arrested for any crime until their immediate superiors had been informed, so that other individuals might be put in their places. Neither might any person who had charge of treasury funds be imprisond before being conducted to the subtreasury where his papers and funds were deposited in order that the money should be counted in his presence and the papers, books, accounts, and securities be examined.[63]

---

[61] *Ordenanza . . . . de intendentes . . . . de Nueva España,* arts. 86–88, 94.

[62] *Ibid.,* arts. 89–90.

[63] *Ibid.,* arts. 90–94.

In their supervision of the subtreasuries the intendants were to decide where it would be best to locate other minor treasuries, presenting the matter to the *junta superior* for executive action pending royal approval. The salary of officials for any new subtreasuries was to be determined by the intendants with the advice of the *junta superior*.[64] Usually these salaries were smaller than those of the general accountant and treasurer of Mexico City, who received four thousand *pesos*, and the chief accountants and treasurers of province, three thousand *pesos*, except those of Mérida and Arispe who got only twenty-five hundred *pesos*. Treasury officials were forbidden to engage in trade or receive any other emoluments.[65]

The intendants were to see that funds were not paid from subtreasuries by warrants drawn by the officers who administered them,[66] nor might the superintendent-subdelegate in Mexico, nor intendants of province, nor any other persons draw upon the treasury without special royal permission. Any official who issued a warrant without a royal order would be held responsible.[67] Before salaries, pensions, or other expenditures could be paid the intendant-general had to put his countersign upon the orders, a memorandum had to be made in the auditor's office, and another by the judges of the treasury. Then the payments had to be authorized by the *junta superior*. In extraordinary expenditures the process was more complicated. First, a provincial *junta* of the treasury had to be held in the intendancy to discuss and vote upon them. Next the intendant of province gave account of the decision to the *junta superior* in the capital through the superintendent-subdelegate as its president. Finally

---

[64] *Ibid.*, arts. 96, 98. There were fifteen proprietary subtreasuries in Mexico and twelve in the viceroyalty of La Plata.

[65] *Ibid.*, art. 99. In the viceroyalty of La Plata the salary of treasury officials was lower than in Mexico.

[66] *Ibid.*, art. 101.

[67] *Ibid.*, art. 102.

the royal approval had to be obtained,[68] for the king had long been aware that leakage from the treasury was one of the main defects of colonial administration.

When treasury officials had any doubts which concerned the making of payments they were to submit the matter to the intendant who should decide it in consultation with the *junta* in the more serious cases, when the treasury officials were not held accountable but only the intendant or *junta* if either had given the order for payment.[69] Intendants had power to suspend payments and to transfer funds from one treasury to another within their territory, but only the intendant-general could convey them from one province to another.[70] For the sake of uniformity in financial administration each intendant was to keep a general account book of finances relative to his province. It was to show the funds that entered into the treasury from the various divisions of finance, expenditures, the real estate of the royal patrimony, and the salaries of all financial employees. Every intendant was to send a copy of this book to the intendant-general so that he might cause a general book of finances to be made for the whole viceroyalty.[71]

One of the important duties of intendants was to provide for the punctual collection of revenues, and for their increase if it could be done honestly. They had to see that lessees of revenues did not oppress the people by collecting too much from them, and that they paid punctually into the treasury the full amount. Aid to the farmers was provided by granting them delay in the payment of taxes during the months when their crops were being raised, and justices and subordinate officials were under secret surveillance as to how they conducted themselves in the assessment and exaction of revenues. The intendants heard the com-

---

68 *Ordenanza* .... *de intendentes* .... *de Nueva España*, arts. 103–106.
69 *Ibid.*, art. 106.
70 *Ibid.*, arts. 107–109
71 *Ibid.*, arts. 109–114.

plaints of those who felt aggrieved by assessments, and punished tax-collectors who proved to be defaulters. If the town were incapable of paying taxes by reason of some calamity the intendants investigated the cause and gave account to the *junta superior* so that it might extend the time for making payment.[72]

The tribute was one of the principal sources of royal revenue, therefore the intendants and their subdelegates were ordered to pay special attention to this branch, which had its central accounting office in the capital. Formerly the *corregidores* and *alcaldes mayores* had collected this revenue, with much incident peculation; but after the establishment of the intendancies the duty was intrusted to the *alcaldes ordinarios*, and subdelegates, who were held rigidly responsible for the collection. They entered the tribute money into the treasury three times a year in Mexico and twice a year in the viceroyalty of La Plata.[73] In order that the intendants might be sufficiently advised about this revenue, the tribunal of accounts and treasury officials were to submit to them any information which they might have relative to it.[74] *Alcaldes ordinarios* and subdelegates received as a remuneration for collecting the tax five per cent of the amount that entered the treasury from this branch, while Indian tax-gathers got only one per cent[75] of what they obtained from their tribesmen.

Intendants had also to see that correct tax lists of all the inhabitants of their provinces were made, and they were to make visitations every five years to learn whether these were correct. Since there had been so many frauds in reporting the number of tribute payers, the intendant-general was ordered to draw up an ordinance which would prevent them. It was to be submitted to the *junta superior* for correction and approval and

---

[72] *Ibid.*, arts. 116–125.
[73] *Ibid.*, arts. 126, 129.
[74] *Ibid.*, art. 131.
[75] *Ibid.*, art. 132. In Buenos Aires they received only three per cent.

finally to the king. It was then to be sent to the intendants of province and their subdelegates who should put it into effect.[76] The Indians had to pay tribute between the ages of eighteen and fifty, and it was very important that the tax lists should be as accurate as possible. The only persons exempted were *caciques,* their eldest sons, Indian *alcaldes,* and women. Intendants were to provide that vagabonds of the tribute-paying class should be put to work under good masters who would see that their tribute was paid.[77]

The sales tax (*alcabala*) formed another very important revenue. It was paid at the rate of six per cent in Mexico when the Ordinance of Intendants was issued. Intendants were to take measures to check fraud in the collection, to prevent the people from evading payment, and were always to give account of their measures to the *junta superior.*[78] A great increase of revenue was expected from this division when the old abuses should be eliminated.[79] In New Spain *pulque* drinking was another profitable source of revenue. Because of the many evils connected with its use, the intendants and subordinate judges were to visit the *pulque* shops frequently and see that harmful mixtures were not made with *pulque.*[80] Villarroel declared that this branch brought into the treasury a revenue of half a million *pesos,* but the beverage was the chief cause of vice and crime and the state lost through it thousands of men.[81] This criticism is even yet valid in Mexico.

Other revenues from powder and playing cards were also supervised by the intendants.[82] The old royal fifth from gold, silver, copper, and other metals still remained and brought con-

---

[76] *Ordenanza . . . . de intendentes . . . . de Nueva España,* art. 134.
[77] *Ibid.,* arts. 136–139.
[78] *Ibid.,* arts. 142, 144.
[79] Cedulario, MS, I, 9–12.
[80] *Ordenanza . . . . de intendentes . . . . de Nueva España,* art. 146.
[81] *Enfermedades políticas· . . . .* MS, IV, pt. VI, p. 25.
[82] *Ordenanza . . . . de intendentes . . . . de Nueva España,* arts. 148–150.

siderable revenue into the treasury. For this reason the intendants were expected to do their best to encourage mining. They were to preside over the tribunals of mining in their provinces, and in the smaller towns their subdelegates were to have cognizance of mining cases.[83] Intendants were to see that all the subtreasuries located in the mining regions had plenty of quicksilver to distribute to miners for the extraction of gold and silver, and that it was never lacking in the various magazines and other places where it was needed.[84]

Intendants had to oversee the division of revenue from the stamped paper required for all legal documents. The superintendent-subdelegate sent the paper to the intendants of province, who distributed it among the subtreasuries and tobacco administrators. The paper came from Spain and each intendant of province was to report to the intendant-general the amount needed for his province so that shipment could be made twice a year.[85] In Mexico City there were special accounting-offices for dues from titles of nobility and half-annates, both of these branches of revenue being under the control of the intendants for their provinces. Revenues from salt mines and from a tax on grocery stores were also administered by them. They designated the number of such stores permitted for every town and gave them their licenses. If the stores refused or delayed to pay the tax, the intendants or their subdelegates could close them. They were to see that proper weights were used and that the food sold was of good quality.[86]

In both Spain and America revenue was collected from salable and transferable offices. When vacancies in positions occurred, the positions were sold at auction, the intendants submitting the bids to a *junta* of auctions which investigated them and sent

[83] *Ibid.*, arts. 150–152.
[84] *Ibid.,* art. 154.
[85] *Ibid.*, arts. 156–158.
[86] *Ibid.*, arts. 158–162.

them to the *junta superior* in the capital, which made the award. The viceroy was informed by the president of the *junta* concerning the persons whose bids were accepted so that he might issue their titles. If the offices sold happened to be in the frontier provinces the commandant-general granted the titles and sent them to the intendants concerned.[87] Bulls of the Holy Crusade (indulgences) still continued to produce revenue, the intendants having cognizance in first instance of cases arising from them, and allowing appeal to the *junta superior*.[88]

Another source of revenue came from ecclesiastical tithes, the income being used for religious purposes. *Juntas* for the administration of tithes were to be established in the most important cities and the intendants presided over them in their places of residence, with a casting vote in cases of disagreement. This *junta* made arrangements for leasing the collection of the tithes, and chose its administrators, who might not be ecclesiastics.[89] At the end of the year they had to present a sworn account of their collections to the *junta de diezmos* for its examination and approval.[90] Intendants were to see that the rules for administration of the tithes were properly observed and the various parts kept separate for the purposes designated. Two fourth parts (i.e., half) were set aside for bishops and chapters, and two-ninths of the remainder for the royal treasury; another ninth and one-half was to be used for building funds of churches and cathedrals; and still another ninth and one-half was to be applied to hospitals.[91] The king considered this division of finance so important that he reserved the right to choose the accountants, but the intendant-general might make ad interim appointments. In the selection of minor officials of the account-

---

[87] *Ordenanza .... de intendentes .... de Nueva España,* arts. 162–164.
[88] *Ibid.,* arts. 165–168.
[89] *Ibid.,* arts. 168–173.
[90] *Ibid.,* arts. 176, 178.
[91] *Ibid.,* arts. 184, 187–190.

ing-office of tithes the church *cabildos* submitted the names of individuals to the intendant from whom he chose one to fill the position. These accountants might only be removed by the recommendation of intendants of province to the intendant-general, but they were subject to the *cabildos* and factor-judges as well as to the intendants and treasury officials.[92] Intendants were to require them to make punctually the special reports concerning the different divisions of the tithes demanded.[93]

Vacancies in ecclesiastical positions brought additional income into the royal treasury. These funds were handled, like those of the direct revenue, by treasury officials, since they belonged to the crown, but they were not used for strictly religious purposes. Forty thousand *pesos* were deducted for the Order of Charles III, and one-third of the net amount was used for widows and orphans of soldiers.[94] Ecclesiastical half-annates and *mesadas* formed another source of revenue. These salary taxes were levied upon members of the clergy as well as upon seculars. Every person who received an ecclesiastical office with and income of at least three hundred ducats had to pay the *mesada* and the *averías* or expenses incurred in his transportation.[95] He also had to give bond to the satisfaction of the treasury officials that the payment would be made, and he was not to be installed in his office until it was known that the security had been given. If the *mesada* was not paid within four months by the newly appointed officials themselves, treasury officials were to compel their guarantors or the treasurer of the chapter to pay it.[96]

Over other minor revenues, such as those from cockfights and monopolies of snow, alum, and leather, the intendants exercised

---

[92] *Ordenanza . . . . de intendentes . . . . de Nueva España*, arts. 194, 196–198.
[93] *Ibid.*, art. 200.
[94] *Ibid.*, arts. 204–209.
[95] *Ibid.*, arts. 209–211, 214, 219.
[96] *Ibid.*, art. 217.

a special supervision.[97] *Espolios* or the tax on property left by prelates at their death was likewise claimed by the king. The intendants had to see that the treasury officials exacted it, or that the right of collection was leased to trustworthy individuals, and that there was no concealment of the wealth of deceased churchmen. They were to decide cases arising from *espolios* and allow the *audiencia* of the territory to examine the proceedings.[98] They were commanded to see that *cabildos* of cathedrals which received a portion of the tithes paid the priests of their dioceses promptly, and that priests did not impose exorbitant parochial dues upon the Indians. They were to require the archbishops to make schedules concerning the dues and these were to be inspected and approved by the *audiencia*.[99]

The intendants had to transmit monthly all the funds from minor treasuries to the principal subtreasury of the province, and finally all the surplus funds of the chief subtreasuries to the capital.[100] Once a week intendants were to hold a *junta* of government at their houses to which treasury officials, administrators, and chief accountants of revenue brought a memorandum properly signed, showing funds on hand and the condition of the collection. Means to improve and increase revenues were discussed During the first week of each month the *junta* considered the monthly revenue statements which were required. If serious matters arose which the local *juntas* could not help to determine, the intendants reported them to the *junta superior* for its decision.[101]

On the first day of each month intendants and subdelegates attended the very formal and watchful ceremony of opening the coffers and checking the contents against the books of the treas-

---

97 *Ordenanza* . . . . *de intendentes* . . . . *de Nueva España*, art. 222.
98 *Ibid.*, arts. 225, 227–230.
99 *Ibid.*, arts. 223–225.
100 *Ibid.*, art. 230.
101 *Ibid.*, arts. 232–234.

ury officials. When the coffers were inspected another statement of receipts and expenditures was given to them. They compared the first one with it and put their signature on the former if correct. When there were differences they had to investigate the causes. The subdelegates submitted five copies of each of their monthly statements to the intendants. Every intendant of province kept one and sent the rest to the superintendent-subdelegate. The latter official retained one, transmitted another to the tribunal of accounts and the other two to the king. From these prolix documents the yearly statement of the whole royal treasury was compiled.[102]

The inspection of the coffers at the end of the year was the big event. The same process took place as at the end of the month, except that it was more detailed. Again statements were made for each treasury and forwarded in the same manner to the intendant-general; however, they were annual statements this time.[103] Intendents kept a very close surveillance over all financial employees to prevent frauds. They had power to take action directly against contraband trade and make confiscations, allowing appeal to the *junta superior*.[104]

A great many of the reports of intendants to their superiors refer to smuggling and interlopers. In 1778 Gálvez, as intendant-general of army, reported to the king concerning the arrival in Havana of a schooner from Carolina loaded with rice, which had a passport for the French colony of Santo Domingo, but arrangements were made to sell the cargo in Havana.[105] Soon the American products were welcomed and were not looked upon as contraband. Therefore in 1780 Gálvez reduced the dues on imports and exports at Havana.[106] In 1783 the intendant of

---

102 *Ibid.*, arts. 234–237.
103 *Ibid.*, art. 273.
104 *Ibid.*, arts. 238–241.
105 José de Gálvez to the king, June 11, 1778, AGI, 81–4–36, *num.* 3.
106 José de Gálvez to the king, Oct. 4, 1780, AGI, 146–2–7, *num.* 690 (Indiferente General).

New Orleans reported the measures he had taken with an English boat, the "Feliz Retorno," which came from Jamaica with thirty-six contraband Negroes on board.[107] In the same year another English boat which contained Negroes was confiscated by Intendant Navarro of New Orleans.[108]

During the French Revolution the intendants were kept busy discovering and watching Frenchmen. In 1795 and 1796 they were ordered to report with reference to foreigners in Mexico. Intendants were empowered to arrest any Frenchmen of suspicious conduct, expel them, and confiscate their goods.[109] They were also to watch for any printing which alluded to the French Revolution.[110]

Next to the *junta superior* the tribunal of accounts was the most important financial authority and court of appeals. If doubts arose in the tribunal of accounts cases might have recourse to the *junta superior*. For the sake of uniformity the tribunal drew up an instruction to which all officials who made financial reports had to conform.[111] Many persons aspired to obtain financial positions, but intendants had to see that they were not accepted without the proper examination. In the capital the intendant-general and in the provinces the other intendants had to decide upon them. If after they had been chosen their conduct proved to be bad the same officials could suspend them from office. Intendants were to require all financial employees to work seven hours a day and fine them if they were absent without proper excuse.[112] The last article under the department of finance declares that the superintendent-subdelegate of

107 Testimonio concerning measures of confiscation . . . . , Dec. 9, 1783, AGI, 86–7–20 (Audiencia de Santo Domingo).

108 *Ibid.*, Dec. 29, 1783, AGI, 86–7–20 (Audiencia de Santo Domingo).

109 Aguilar sobre expulsion de los Franceses de Nueva España, 1795-96, AGI, *Est. Mex. leg.* 5.

110 Branciforte to the king, Nov. 26, 1796, AGI, *num.* 376, *Est. Mex. leg* 6.

111 *Ordenanza . . . . de intendentes . . . . de Nueva España*, arts. 242–245.

112 *Ibid.*, arts. 245–248.

the treasury was to have the same powers in the colonies as did his superintendent in Spain.[113]

The fourth department of which intendants had local charge was that of war as it affected the treasury, leaving strictly military affairs to the captain-general and commanders. The chief duties of the intendants in war affairs were to pay the troops and furnish supplies. Troops were to be paid during the review held at the end of the month. Intendants were expected to examine the adjustments of salaries of the troops formed by the accounting-offices and to calculate the discounts deducted from their pay for the *montepío* and military hospitals. Also on the last day of the month they were to arrange that the supplies of all the following month be furnished on credit by the treasuries, and treasury officials were to maintain a strict account of those advances.[114]

The intendant had to keep check on troops transferred from one province to another so that they might not be paid twice or receive too many supplies. At the same time troops on the march had to be provided for. Salaries were not to be advanced on credit to soldiers and were always to be paid in money. If the funds assigned were not sufficient, intendants were to see that they were first applied to furnishing supplies.[115] Reserves of provisions had to be collected into depositories and they might not be taken out of the storehouses without the orders of the intendants. Army contractors had to distribute the supplies as the intendants desired, and the latter were required to see that there was no connivance or profit between officers and contractors.[116]

The troops were not to live off the country wherein they were stationed or through which they marched. Intendants were to command contractors to pay for foods used on the march at

[113] *Ordenanza . . . . de intendentes . . . . de Nueva España,* art. 249.
[114] *Ibid.,* arts. 250–255.
[115] *Ibid.,* arts. 255–258.
[116] *Ibid.,* arts. 259–261.

current prices. They themselves were empowered to visit storehouses where supplies were kept, so that provisions of good
quality might be furnished. The greatest economy was to be
used in provisioning the troops and the most capable administrators were to be chosen by the intendants for this work.[117]
The intendants also had to see that the people of the provinces,
when they rendered aid to the military forces, did not suffer in
any way from levies made upon them. Payment was to be made
for everything obtained and fair play was to be the rule; care
had to be taken that beasts of burden were not all procured from
one locality since this would interfere with agriculture. Intendants called upon local justices to assist them in the matter of
supplies.[118]

The intendants were required to see that contractors submitted, at least every four months, all bills and original receipts
for supplies furnished to the principal accounting-office of the
province. The receipts were to be examined and summed up
monthly by the paymaster of each regiment, signed by him, and
approved by the commander. Great care was to be taken that
the estimates for supplies were correct, so that there might be
no waste.[119] The intendants took cognizance of any judicial
cases arising from supplying the troops, appeal going to the
junta superior.

Providing quarters for the troops was another duty of the
intendants. When quartering in private houses was resorted
to arrangements were to be made to protect the inhabitants
from inconveniences and unusual expense. Strict discipline and
good conduct toward the townsmen and natives were enjoined.
If soldiers committed misdeeds the intendants reported them
to the viceroy or commandant-general of the frontier. When
troops left the towns in which they were stationed their *sargen-*

---

[117] *Ordenanza .... de intendentes .... de Nueva España,* arts. 261–264.
[118] *Ibid.,* arts. 265–274.
[119] *Ibid.,* arts. 274–277.

tos mayores were required to obtain a certificate from the justices stating that the soldiers had not been guilty of misdemeanors and had not taken any money even as a voluntary gift. All damages were to be paid and if the guilty persons could not be found the corps to which they belonged was held responsible.[120]

Military reviews took place in the provinces every month. The judges of the treasury as commissaries of war witnessed them, and in distant places where there were no such commissaries the intendants appointed trustworthy persons to do this. The summaries of review were the bases of distribution of supplies and payment of salaries. The intendants also had authority to examine these summaries and revise anything in them which did not conform to the regulations. If the allowances to the troops were found to be legitimate the intendants kept one of the summaries and sent three to the intendant-general, who retained one and transmitted the other two to the Council of the Indies. If any of the judges of the treasury as commissaries of war made mistakes or granted more allowances than belonged to the corps, the intendants could fine them and cause the injury to the treasury to be righted; they were also expected to prevent frauds in reviews, such as the passing of soldiers from one regiment to another so as to increase the allowances.[121]

Military hospitals were also under the care of the intendants, and they proposed to the intendant-general the names of persons who should serve in them. They were to cause the proper officials to visit these hospitals twice a day.[122] Likewise the intendants had to provide permanent quarters for troops and inspect magazines of war in the fortified places of their districts. They were to obtain frequent information with reference to the munitions on hand, so that with the consent of the intendant-

---

120 *Ibid.*, arts. 278–282.
121 *Ibid.*, arts. 282–286.
122 *Ibid.*, arts. 288–290.

general they might dispose of useless articles and replace those lacking. Intendants were to inspect such magazines frequently through the treasury officials, see to the repair or manufacture of arms by armorers, furnish supplies for artillery and their transportation, and provide for the repair of fortifications, ruined barracks and magazines. They were to see that the engineers inspected fortifications regularly, and reported their needs and the cost of repairs, so that the viceroy or the commandant-general and superintendent-subdelegate might be notified and decide what should be done.[123]

Most of the extraordinary expenditures were in connection with military matters; in these the intendants took prompt but provisional measures with the advice of a provisional *junta* of the treasury and made them known later to the *junta superior*, which in turn reported to the king. The commandants frequently called upon the intendants for financial assistance. Such a case happened in 1788, when Juan Ugalde, the commandant-general of the eastern frontier provinces of New Spain, requested the intendant of San Luis Potosí to give him thirty thousand *pesos* to fight hostile Indians.[124] In 1819 we find the intendant of Zacatecas sending the extraordinary aid of fifteen thousand pesos to Saltillo to pay the troops.[125]

While the intendants had no part in actual military operations, it was their duty to see that their territories were well defended. In 1797 the intendant of Guadalajara sent many reports to the viceroy saying that he did not have sufficient troops to defend the coasts and lands under his control. Finally he was permitted to establish a battalion of provincial militia for his capital, a regiment of dragoons for the towns of Lagos

---

[123] *Ordenanza .... de intendentes .... de Nueva España*, arts. 291–297.

[124] *Ibid.*, arts. 297–299; *Provincias Internas*, San Luis Potosí, Aug. 12, 1788, *tom.* 111, 743 *num.* 4, *expediente* 4 *fojas* 16 (Archivo General).

[125] Commandant-general to the viceroy, *ibid.*, May 16, 1819, *tom.* 252, *num.* 934 (Archivo General).

and Aguas Calientes, and "flying" companies for other parts of the intendancy.[126] In the same year the intendant of New Orleans believed his province to be in danger on account of foreign wars, and asked for naval supplies to arm one or two frigates to clear the seas of corsairs.[127] It is to be observed that this great Ordinance made no provision for an intendancy of marine, although the king had asked in 1785 that this should be done; hence the intendants of the seacoast provinces were placed in charge of marine affairs.[128]

When money for defense was not required immediately in emergency the intendants often appealed to the viceroy for it. In 1781 the intendant of New Orleans did this declaring that his funds were not sufficient for the expenses for the fortifications of Pensacola and Mobile, other fortresses and hospitals, and for Indian affairs. No financial help had come from Havana, therefore he asked for an additional sum of three hundred thousand *pesos* besides the usual subsidy for extraordinary expenses.[129]

All of the officials of the commissary department were directly under the intendants, who in turn were subordinate to the intendant-general of the army. The latter official and also the intendants of province had to recognize the viceroy and the commandant-general of the frontier as their superiors, and had to communicate everything of importance to them in peace or war.[130] The intendants usually cooperated judiciously, although a few cases of insubordination have been found. In 1787 Mangino, the intendant-general of Mexico, disputed the authority of Viceroy Núñez de Haro in certain matters. Because of his haughtiness Mangino was soon recalled by the king, and the

---

[126] Branciforte to the Prince of Peace, Aug. 30, 1797, AGI, *num.* 498. *Est. Mex. leg.* 7.

[127] Hormazas to the captain-general of Cuba, Dec. 16, 1797, AGI, 146–2–9, *num.* 11 (Indiferente General).

[128] *Real decreto*, May 31, 1785, AGI, 141–5–11.

[129] Intendant of Louisiana to the viceroy, July 24, 1781, AGI, 87–3–10, *num.* 54 (Audiencia de Santo Domingo).

[130] *Ordenanza .... de intendentes .... de Nueva España*, art. 299.

superintendency reverted to the viceroy.[131] There was a notable case in Peru, when Viceroy Croix ordered the intendant, Francisco Hurtado, not to trade with the island of Chiloé. The intendant refused and denounced both the viceroy and his assessor. Needless to say, Hurtado was speedily removed.[132]

The proper cooperation was of course much more common. Before 1782, under the administration of Viceroy Flórez in Nueva Granada, the intendant Pedro Fernández de la Madrid was present at a *junta* with the viceroy, the governor, and the treasury officials to help decide upon measures to be taken in the war against England.[133] In 1820 the intendant of Durango and the commandant-general of the *Provincias Internas* of the east cooperated. On February 28, the intendant sent word concerning the arrival at the port of Mexatlan of the merchant frigate "Cleopatra" and of its sudden departure for San Blas.[124] On July 31, the commandant conferred with the same intendant about decreasing expenses. They agreed to take out of active service several companies of infantry and cavalry.[135]

On the other hand viceroys and superior authorities had to respect and aid all the measures taken by the intendants, and invite them to be present at *juntas* of war. The intendant-general was to have prescribed military honors accorded him by the latter officials when he inspected the troops, and funeral honors when he died.[136]

Like other officials the intendants were subject to the *residencia* at the end of their term, and were permitted to take the *residencias* of their subordinates, but in 1799 the viceroys and

---

131 Rivera Cambas, Manuel, *Los gobernantes de México* (Mexico, 1872–1873), I, 460–461.

132 *Memorias de los vireyes que han gobernado el Peru*, V, 125–129.

133 Groot, José Manuel, *Historia eclesiástica y civil de Nueva Granada* (Bogotá, 1889–1893), II, 231.

134 Conde to the viceroy, Feb. 28, 1820, *Provincias Internas*, tom. 252, num. 519 (Archivo General).

135 *Ibid.*, July 31, 1820, tom. 252, num. 663 (Archivo General).

136 *Ordenanza* .... *de intendentes* .... *de Nueva España*, arts. 300–303; king to the viceroy, March 23,1792. *Reales cédulas* 1790–1795, V, num. 65, *lib.* 145 (Archivo General).

audiencias were allowed to name judges of *residencia* to try sub-delegates and the political and military governors.[137] The *residencia* helped to restrain the intendants as it did all other colonial officials. Subordinate officials also acted as a check, for even they had the right to complain of the conduct of their superiors, and sometimes did so. About 1795 Josef de Orue, accountant of the army, reported concerning the conduct of Estevàn Miró, intendant of New Orleans. He complained that the intendant and his assessor had not treated him well; and that they allowed one Arturo Strother to take two thousand *pesos* out of the city clandestinely.[138] In 1796 it happened that the intendant of New Orleans, Juan Morales, had a grudge against the chief revenue official, José Navarro. It was the duty of Navarro's immediate superior to defend him, which he did very enthusiastically, but at the same time he showed the real character of the intendant and did not make very complimentary remarks about him.[139] In 1799 the Spanish minister in Philadelphia wrote to the viceroy and complained of the lack of funds since the last war with France. Some fifty thousand *pesos* were sent to Havana, but the intendant was so slow to transmit them to Philadelphia that the minister grumbled to the viceroy about the intendant.[140] Viceroys were also expected to notify the king of any misconduct on the part of the intendants. In 1793 Revillagigedo reported that the intendant of San Luis Potosí was subject to drunkenness, and quarreled with the *juntas* and officials. He was too indolent in the performance of his duties to satisfy the energetic viceroy.[141]

---

[137] *Ordenanza . . . . de intendentes . . . . de Nueva España*, art. 305; *Consejo de Indias*, April 2, 1799, arts. 90, 102, AGI, 141-3-17 (Indiferente General).

[138] *Expedientes sobre la aprehensión de 2000 pesos*, 1795-1799, AGI, 86-5-22 (Audiencia de Santo Domingo).

[139] New Orleans, Aug. 10, 1796, AGI, 86-7-9 (Audiencia de Santo Domingo).

[140] *Varias cartas sobre pago del situado del ministro Español en Filadelfia*, 1799, *papeleta* 75, AGI, 89-1-12 (Audiencia de Mexico).

[141] Revillagigedo to Gardoquí, June 30, 1793, MS, *num.* 21.

Finally, in the last article of the Ordinance of Intendants all the high civil and ecclesiastical authorities are commanded to observe the regulations in what pertains to them. The Ordinance is declared to have the force of law and all other laws, customs, and measures contrary to it are annulled.[142]

From this survey it may be seen that the duties of the intendants in the four departments of government were not only numerous, but detailed and exacting. To recapitulate in brief: in the department of justice with the aid of their assessors who had legal training intendants took cognizance of cases which related to the royal treasury and the financial system of the viceroyalties. Appeal from their decisions went to the *junta superior de hacienda,* the highest financial authority in the colonies. In government (*gobierno*) they exercised the administrative functions of the former governors, whom they superseded. They also had to determine where the money was to come from for any public improvements.

The department of finance was their especial field and most urgent care. Under it they supervised the treasury, subtreasuries, the various branches of revenue, the collection of revenues, all the officials of finance in the country, and the monthly and annual financial statements. It was their prime duty to increase the revenues and guard against financial frauds. In the department of war again they had charge of finances. They saw that the troops were paid and were provided with food and military supplies. They controlled depositories where provisions were stored, and also magazines of war. All the officials of the commissary were subordinate to them. Intendants were likewise held responsible for furnishing soldiers with lodgings and providing military hospitals. They had to see that the monthly reviews were held and that the statements of review were correct, since the pay and allowances of the troops were based upon them.

---

[142] *Ordenanza .... de intendentes .... de Nueva España,* art. 306.

III

Results of the Intendant System

The question whether the intendant system was proving successful in Spanish America was much debated among officers who administered it. There were powerful supporters of the reform, yet it aroused a great deal of adverse criticism from the very beginning. There is no doubt that it checked many of the evils against which it was aimed, but it did not score the complete triumph that was expected.

Like all innovations the intendant system at first created many points of friction. Complaints came from all sides. In 1769 Cagigal, governor of Havana, voiced his disapproval of the new system. He asserted that there were disorders in the administration of the treasury and that the intendant did not remedy the scandalous conditions. The orders and threats of the intendant did not cause certain officials to improve their conduct. The royal revenues had increased considerably, but Cagigal attributed this to the honesty of the majority of the financial employees and not to the establishment of the intendancy. He thought that the old management of the treasury was more simple, less costly, and provoked fewer quarrels. He believed that the intendancies were not suitable to America, since they decreased the governor's power and made him less able to protect the people and to prevent disorder. This of course was an interested view. Cagigal declared that the intendant might quite properly control finances, but when it came to having charge of the fortress it was another matter, since the governor was the only person who should take care of it. The intendant ought to be satisfied with furnishing from the treasury the money needed for military purposes. Another useful suggestion made to the king was that the intendant should submit a copy of his instruction to the governor, as this would prevent discord between the two officials. The intendant was ordered to keep on friendly terms with the governor, but this was rather difficult to do because the latter official did not desire to subject himself to the authority of the former. The whole secret of the trouble was that the governor's power had been limited and he could not give up gracefully some of the functions which he had hitherto exercised. Cagigal was displeased because all his judicial power in financial matters, except in regard to illicit commerce, was taken away. He proposed to the king that his authority should be extended to include other cases besides those of contraband. The governor ended his criticism of the new system by saying that the intendancy of Cuba would never be of service, because two independent heads in the same country so far distant from the court could never be conciliated.[1]

Many people in Mexico were likewise doubtful of the new administrative system, and some even thought that the country would be ruined by it. There were even rumors that the intendancies were only temporary and would be abolished after the death of Gálvez. Some men, including Viceroy Rivillagigedo, correctly enough attributed the innovation to the insistent zeal of this strong-willed Minister of the Indies. Many of these hostile reports spread to the region of San Luis Potosí before the first intendant arrived, making his office extremely difficult. The people received him not as an intendant, but simply as an *alcalde mayor*. The new official tried with all his ability to win the confidence of the people, and since he was a very just and upright man, he succeeded in making friends of most of the inhabitants, but there were some wealthy individuals who re-

---

[1] Bucareli to the king, Oct. 16, 1769, AGI, 80–1–7, *num.* 1220 (Audiencia de Santo Domingo).

mained obstinate and would have nothing to do with him. They had dominated over the *alcaldes mayores* for so long that they hated an official who would not show partiality. They bitterly opposed the measures of the intendant and the administration. In spite of these hindrances, conditions were soon greatly improved in the intendancy.[2]

Another and more general cause of antagonism was the interference with the viceroy's powers. Although the intendants supplied the great need of intermediary officials between the viceroys and the *alcaldes mayores*, or subdelegates, the viceroys had exercised supreme power for so long that they were unwilling to have it decreased, even if their administrative burdens should be thereby lightened. On the other hand Viceroy Revillagigedo averred that the intendants provided for the people a more immediate and prompt recourse in their judicial cases. They no longer had to incur the expense of long journeys or neglect their interests and occupations by going to the capital. He adds, however, "but it is very certain that an establishment which at first sight seems to have been so useful, has produced proportionally very few of the advantages which should be hoped from it." It met with disfavor from the beginning and its modification was constantly predicted.[3]

Viceroy Bucareli sharply opposed the introduction of the intendant system into New Spain. He could not see the need of intendants with so many enlarged powers, and he feared that they would not check confusion but only cause greater expense. He was certain that they would never be able to perform their many duties on account of the difficulty of finding enough capable subordinates for the *partidos* of such large intendancies. He did not believe that the treasury would be better administered than before.[4]

---

[2] Salcedo to Revillagigedo, Dec. 4, 1792, *papeleta* 77, AGI, 89–6–19, *num.* 512 (Audiencia de Mexico).

[3] *Instrucción reservada*, art. 830.

[4] Rivera Cambas, I, 427.

One of the serious points of contention was the transfer to the intendants of the functions of the ecclesiastical patronage, which had pertained only to the viceroys. In many cases prelates refused to recognize the rights of the intendants in this field. The archbishop of Lima expressed to Viceroy Croix his doubts about the intendant of Tarma who was to fill vacant parishes, and told the king that this power should remain with the viceroy. Croix consulted his council and it was agreed to observe to the letter the article of the Ordinance which treated of the vice-patronage. The councilors informed the archbishop of their decision and sent him a copy of the last article of the document which enjoined archbishops and bishops to obey the laws.[5]

The bishop of Guamanga likewise protested that the intendant, the Marqués de Lara, a man well known for his honor and peaceful disposition, should not act as vice-patron. This caused Croix to turn the tables and investigate the past conduct of the bishop. It was found that while he had had some disagreements with the *corregidores,* he had usually got along with them on fairly friendly terms because they were his inferiors, but he had observed no conformity whatever to the wishes of the new intendant. The ceremony in honor of the intendant when he went to church was slightingly celebrated, and the proposal of individuals for the position of *alcalde ordinario* was disputed as if this were an ancient ecclesiastical right. There were also some clashes over ecclesiastical and civil jurisdiction. Ecclesiastics treated the *regidores* badly and derided other persons who supported the intendancy. The opponents of the new system even went so far as to stab a clerk of the *ayuntamiento* for sympathizing with it. The intendant had such a hard time that he often appealed to the viceroy to be released from his duties. All the measures taken by Croix to restore harmony between the bishop and the intendant were of no avail.[6] In Arequipa the intendant

---

[5] *Memorias de los vireyes que han gobernado el Perú,* V, 30–31.
[6] *Ibid.,* 34–38.

and the bishop differed so much over matters of vice-patronage that it led to a real dissension. The intendant summoned a council of lawyers to examine the conduct of the bishop. As a result the angered prelate rejected the measures of the intendant and refused to install his appointees in their church offices.[7]

The same embarrassment occurred in Mexico in regard to the question of the patronage. The first intendant of Durango was Felipe Díaz de Ortega, a knight of the Order of Charles III, who took his duties seriously and worked actively to improve the province. He summoned the inhabitants to a conference and invited them to erect a public granary by voluntary contributions, so that there might always be grain on hand during years of crop failure. He appropriated over eighteen hundred *pesos* to begin the work. In spite of his many good achievements, Ortega had serious disagreements with the commandant Ugarte over the royal patronage. These became so lively that they were finally submitted to the viceroy for decision. Ortega served until 1792 when he was succeeded by Francisco Potau de Portugal.[8]

Antagonism arose when it was learned that the intendant was to preside over *juntas de diezmos* instead of the viceroy. In 1792 various colonial ministers protested to the king that the viceroy should be a member of the *juntas* as formerly, and when he could not be present then the intendant might substitute. Where there was no *audiencia* they were perfectly willing that the intendant should attend the *juntas* as vice-patron.[9]

At first many doubts arose concerning certain other points of the new laws. There was the all important question of ceremony, which had never ceased to distress many officials before the time of the intendants. It came up immediately in Lima in regard to

---

[7] *Ibid.*, 66–67.

[8] *Documentos históricos sobre Durango*, MS, 110–111, 255–256.

[9] Circular of Aug. 23, 1786, concerning the distribution of the *diezmos* of the churches of the Indies, AGI, 141–6–6.

the seat which the intendant-general, Jorge Escobedo, was to have at public functions. The viceroy's assessor held several private conferences with the intendant but no agreement could be reached. The intendant pretended to be ignorant of the matter and suggested that the king be consulted, and this was finally done as a last resort.[10] Intendants of province were usually accorded the same fairly elaborate ceremonies and receptions as the old governors. On January 6, 1796, Bernardo Bonavia y Zapata, a knight of the Order of Alcántara, took possession of his office in Durango. He went first to the townhall where his office was conferred upon him with the accustomed ceremony. He then proceeded to the cathedral church and was received by the chapter. Accompanied by the chapter, prelates, religious, and government employees, he returned to the townhall where he was magnificently entertained for two days with dinners, various refreshments, and dances.[11]

Another uncertain matter at first was the relationship which the governors of the frontier provinces of New Spain were to have with the intendant. The matter had to be determined by Viceroy Revillagigedo. In 1790 he declared that the governor of Texas was subject to the intendant of San Luis Potosí in financial and military matters.[12] Two years later he stated that the governors of Nuevo León, Nuevo Santander, Coahuila, and Texas were subdelegates of the intendants in finance and war according to the Ordinance of Intendants. The governor of Texas did not comply readily and tried to interfere with the jurisdiction of the intendant of San Luis Potosí, therefore the latter official had real grounds for complaint.[13]

---

[10] *Memorias de los vireyes que han gobernado el Peru*, V, 83.

[11] *Gazetas de Mexico*, 1796–1797, VIII, 77.

[12] Revillagigedo to the governor of Texas, Feb. 10, 1790. *Provincias Internas*, tom. 99, *num. 6, expediente 2, foja* 344.

[13] Revillagigedo to the king, Nov. 5, 1792, *papeleta* 206, AGI, 103–7–22 (Audiencia de Guadalajara).

Flórez, who became viceroy of Mexico in 1787, did not have much to say either for or against the intendant system. He declared that his term was too short for him to know all the results of the Ordinance; therefore he proceeded cautiously, not daring to enact a great number of measures or give decisive advice. He mentioned, however, that there was room for improvement in many of the articles of the Ordinance.[14]

Others were not so sparing in their criticism. Villarroel, a Mexican attorney who had been an *alcalde mayor*, was quite outspoken in his opinions of the system, and averred that the government of New Spain had not been improved. Not even the viceroys escaped his sarcasm; most of them he declared, returned to Spain with a very superficial knowledge of their viceroyalties, and many were more interested in other affairs than in the duties of their office.[15] He demonstrated that the viceroys had not been sensibly relieved of their official burdens, since many of them still spent from four to six hours daily in the dispatch of contentious *expedientes* which the two secretaries of the government submitted to them for proper reference. Much valuable time was lost in this manner that might have been used for more important matters.[16] It is said that the famous and efficient Revillagigedo spent this amount of time in mere routine, and toiled during part of the night to meet all the obligations of his office.[17]

Villarroel believed that a fixed system of government was necessary, with no variation in the decrees issued, since this would cause confusion and arbitrary interpretations. He admitted that the royal intentions in legislation had always been good, but the desired results in administration were not attained

---

14 *Instrucciones que los vireyes* .... arts. 46–50, pp. 123–124.
15 *Enfermedades políticas* .... MS, I, pt. II, pp. 9–10, 23–24.
16 *Ibid.*, I, pt. II, pp. 2–3.
17 Rivera Cambas, I, 486.

because of the negligence and selfishness of the officials. Many old laws which were wise and of great usefulness had been annulled by the Ordinance. He regarded the new system as unconstitutional and arbitrary since it rendered invalid laws that had proved beneficial. Nevertheless, it had the royal approval and to oppose it would be a serious crime. Thus the colonial government was made uniform with that of Spain, whereas in actuality very different rules should apply to America because conditions were not the same there as in the mother country. He maintained that the beneficial Laws of the Indies were annulled without any formality, for economic purposes, which should have been determined as special cases.[18]

This same observant critic asserted that the Ordinance was directly aimed at reducing the powers of the viceroy, his dignity and character. This was a bad beginning for a new law code and for the administration of a country. The loss of his financial powers reduced the viceroy, according to Villarroel, to a mere governor or captain-general. He said that "A body without a head is no more than a worthless trunk," and such was his opinion of the government in New Spain under the intendant system.[19] He complained that justice was no longer known except in name. Judges punished some and showed compassion to others. Sometimes they diminished the penalty or did not make investigations, while vice increased.[20] Public funds were wastefully spent, and mining, which was one of the chief sources of royal revenue, had decreased. Commerce suffered by the introduction of illicit goods. Foreigners brought their merchandise into the country and took away the silver that was so necessary for the monarchy.[21]

One of the chief reasons why Villarroel considered the new system unsatisfactory was that the Indians were not much better

---

[18] *Enfermedades políticas* .... MS, IV, pt. VI, pp. 7–10, 56–70.
[19] *Ibid.*, pp. 42–56, 71.   [20] *Ibid.*, pp. 10–12.   [21] *Ibid.*, pp. 15, 23–24.

off than before. It is true that many of the abuses practiced by the old *corregidores* and *alcaldes mayores* under the *repartimientos* had been eliminated, but the natives were deprived even of the guidance and restraint which they had profited by under the old régime. They were indeed given more responsibility but did not know how to use it and frequently fell into indolence. Therefore Villarroel thought the natives had received more benefit under the *repartimientos*.[22] The principal purpose of the intendancies being to increase the royal revenues, the result would be real oppression of the people, many of whom were too poor to pay additional taxes.[23]

The most important remedies suggested by Villarroel to make the intendant system work were: to restore to the viceroy his former powers, including the superintendency of the treasury, and make the intendants entirely subordinate to him; to reinstate the *alcaldes mayores* who should be more carefully chosen; to bring back the *repartimientos* since they were very necessary for the workers, the Indians, the *alcaldes*, and the treasury; and to redistribute the lands and divide the larger estates. The *junta superior* should, he thought, be deprived of some of its power and not consist of such high officials as the Ordinance provided. The viceroy ought to preside over it. Two or three members should be lawyers and the other men experienced in economic affairs.[24]

Another objection to the new organization was that there were few outstanding figures among the intendants or their sub-delegates. The first intendants, with a few exceptions, were not familiar with the country over which they were to rule. On the whole they were men of limited capacities and not much of an improvement over the former officials; while under the old régime there had been a number of highly capable governors,

---

22 *Enfermedades políticas* . . . . MS, IV, pt. VI, 36 *et seq.*; 85.
23 *Ibid.*, p. 34.
24 *Ibid.*, 125 *et seq.*

some of whom had become viceroys.[25]   The Spanish-American intendant was never a powerful and influential personage like the French intendant. The subdelegates did not prove to be the unqualified success expected. Their opponents accused them of becoming despotic, and of being blind tools of the intendants, the commandant-general, or the judges of the *audiencia*, from whom they hoped to receive favors. They had no will of their own but only reflected that of their superiors. They were sycophantic before the rich and powerful, who alone could bring their interests before the higher authorities; they were oppressors of the poor and weak; and they devoted their time to their own private business and interests. Many encouraged idleness in others by their own indolence and vice.[26] The subdelegates received poor pay and had very little opportunity for promotion. They received as remuneration five per cent of the tribute collected, but this could scarcely pay their expenses, as in some cases it only amounted to about three hundred *pesos*. A royal decree of March 28, 1787, commanded that subdelegates in Mexico be granted some aid in expenses, but Viceroy Flórez suspended the order and it was never put into effect.[27]

After three years' trial one important change was made in the intendant system of New Spain. In 1789 the superintendency of the treasury was restored to the viceroy. At the same time the control of the income from land tax (*censos*), municipal finances, and the management of the proceeds from Indian communities were again conferred upon him.[28] Experience had proved that two heads almost equal in power caused many difficulties; therefore the intendant-general was made subordinate to the viceroy. In regard to drawing upon the royal treasury

---

[25] Revillagigedo, *Instrucción reservada*, arts. 834–836.

[26] Escudero, J. A., *Noticias estadísticas del estado de Chihuahua* (Mexico, 1834), 21–23.

[27] Revillagigedo, *Instrucción reservada*, arts. 850–853, 855.

[28] Revillagigedo, *Dictamen* .... *sobre la ordenanza de intendentes* .... MS, *num.* 402, arts. 6, 230–231.

for funds, the same rules held for the viceroy as for the intendant. In 1790, however, the king was willing to waive the general rules in cases of urgency, and allow the viceroy to use such funds as he thought best.[29] By a royal decree of December 2, 1794, it was declared that the supervision of all public works, such as roads and bridges, pertained to the viceroy, just as they had before the intendancies were established.[30] The restoration of the financial administration to the viceroy placed on his shoulders again much of the drudgery which the Ordinance had shifted. For this reason several viceroys suggested to the king that the *intendant-corregidor* for the province of Mexico should be restored.[31]

Revillagigedo was very frank in discussing the good and bad features of the system. He asserted that the new administrative régime had been approved by many wise men in order to remedy disorders and had had good results in New Spain in spite of contrary opinions. The revenue from tribute had greatly increased, in 1794 amounting to 19,000,000 *pesos*, or three times as much as when it was first reformed under Gálvez. Administrative expenses had been correspondingly augmented to 4,800,000 *pesos*, but even then there remained a surplus revenue of 14,200,000 *pesos*.[32] Revillagigedo maintained that the simplicity of the system was in its favor, as it required a smaller number of officials than the earlier arrangement. Only through the intendancies was it possible for him to govern moderately and with energy a country where indolence and inaction were so deep-rooted. He believed that though no human plans were perfect at the beginning, the new administration would triumph

---

[29] King to the viceroy, Feb. 27, 1793, AGI, *Est. Mex. leg.* 2.

[30] Becker, J., *La política española en las Indias* (Madrid, 1920), 65.

[31] Revillagigedo to Floridablanca, Jan. 15, 1790, AGI, *leg.* 1, *num.* 55. *Papeles de Estado* (Audiencia de Mexico); *Instrucciones que los vireyes* .... Marquina to Iturrigaray, art. 309.

[32] Revillagigedo, *Instrucción reservada*, arts. 741–743.

in the end.   Therefore he took active measures to regulate it.[33]
He saw to it that the intendancies were well operated and that
many difficulties were overcome, but like all new undertakings it
required time.   The contradictions which arose should be looked
upon as mistakes which were only temporary, and were being
remedied as rapidly as possible.[34]   He feared that the ills of the
kingdom would be irremediable if the intendancies were to be
extinguished, and their chiefs were the persons who must
cure them.[35]

This earnest administrator went on to say that while the
people obeyed the new laws, the innovations caused much difference of opinion.   True lovers of the public welfare applauded
the system, but selfish and vain men were not enthusiastic about
it.   Yet many believed that further reforms were necessary,
since the later royal decrees had caused variation in some of
the articles of the Ordinance.   This viceroy thought that the
new system was wise and of great usefulness, and sapiently
declared that there was no reason to worry about the destruction
of the viceroyalty, because this had been predicted many times
before when innovations had been introduced.   In spite of the
imperfections of the reform, he did not desire it to be abandoned,
since it would be very difficult to restore the old régime, as its
laws and regulations were so greatly different.   He did not
know of any better laws under which he could serve the king
than those of the Ordinance, therefore he supported it.[36]

Nevertheless he wished certain changes to be made.   First, he
recommended   that   the   twelve   intendants   should   be   directly

[33] Revillagigedo to Floridablanca, Jan. 15, 1790, AGI, *leg. 1, num.* 55.
Papeles de Estado (Audiencia de Mexico); *ibid.*, Oct. 30, 1790, MS, *num.* 97
reservada.

[34] *Ibid.*, June 1, 1791, AGI, 1–69, *num.* 35. *Papeles de Estado* (Audiencia de Mexico).

[35] Revillagigedo to Lerena, Aug. 29, 1790, MS. *num.* 55 *reservada.*

[36] *Dictamen .... sobre la ordenanza de intendentes ....* MS, *num.* 402,
arts. 7–26.

subordinate to the viceroy in everything, for if this had been done his power would not have been decreased. This submission of the intendants to the viceroy he would have made political rather than economic, in which respect they were wisely under the *junta superior*.[37] He thought too that the ecclesiastical vice-patronage should reside only in the viceroy who was the supreme representative of the king in America. His powers were diminished when this right was granted even to the president of the *audiencia* of Guadalajara and to the commandant-general of the *Provincias Internas*. The latter should be primarily a military chief and must not have other cares; therefore it would be best to relieve him of the vice-patronage. All the intendants, except of Yucatan because of the distance, should be subdelegates of the viceroy in matters of the patronage and give account to him in regard to the churches in their districts, and they ought not to have any more distinctions in religious matters than the former governors.[38]

Next he argued that the intendants were expected to assist the viceroy, and not to be like the old justices and *alcaldes mayores*, who had been a disorderly and untrustworthy group of men influenced by the will of merchants and traders. They were expected to be persons of respectable character, of distinction, and efficiency. Furthermore, they should be familiar with the country and the inclinations of the people. It was essential that they have good health and be young enough to bear the tiresome burdens of their offices and to visit their provinces with frequency.[39] Revillagigedo believed that the intendants on the whole served well and enjoyed a sufficient salary. The physical strength of a viceroy was insufficient for his many duties, there-

---

[37] *Dictamen* .... *sobre la ordenanza de intendentes* .... MS, *num*. 402, art. 117.

[38] *Ibid., arts*. 125–129.

[39] Revillagigedo to Floridablanca, June 1, 1791, AGI, 1–69, *num*. 35. *Papeles de Estado* (Audiencia de Mexico).

fore the intendants could and should relieve him in matters which he was not able to perform. It would be very well for instance for them to retain such work as inspecting the coffers and other burdensome functions, but leave all serious affairs to the viceroy. He desired the intendants to have capable assessors who had legal training and a knowledge of the country. He thought there should be two of them in Mexcio City, as in Madrid and Cádiz. This would add to the expense of administration, but the greater utility would offset it.[40] He said that some of the assessors were efficient, but only too many were incapable, greedy, and of bad conduct. He saw no reason why well informed *alcaldes mayores* of honor and good character should not be appointed assessors. The viceroy might submit annually to the Minister of the Indies a list of the most worthy lawyers in the country who had been examined by the *audiencia* and approved by the intendants. Then the king could choose whomever he desired for the positions.[41]

In Revillagigedo's opinion, there should be twenty-two intendancies in New Spain, instead of the twelve created. This would mean more officials and a redistribution of the districts or *partidos* with resultant increase in efficiency. He asserted that there would be better results if some of the intendancies were served by military chieftains. They should be divided into three classes. The first should include the intendancies of Yucatan, Vera Cruz, Mexico, Guadalajara, and Sonora. Those of Yucatan and Vera Cruz should be considered of a superior order, and brigadiers or field marshals should control them. In Guadalajara and Mexico, since they were not such strategic places, a colonel might serve; and over those of Puebla and Sonora there could be an honorable second-class military official. He proposed the

---

[40] Revillagigedo to Floridablanca, Jan. 15, 1790, AGI, *leg.* 1, *num.* 55. *Papeles de Estado* (Audiencia de Mexico); Revillagigedo to Lerena, March 27, 1791, MS, *num.* 7 *reservada*.

[41] *Dictamen* .... *sobre la ordenanza de intendentes* .... MS, *num.* 402, arts. 215–222, 242.

formation of four other intendancies—one for the four *Provincias Internas* of the east, another for Chihuahua, another for Querétaro, and another for Tabasco. There should be a military chief only over the last. Salaries were to correspond to the classes of intendancies, the largest were to be twelve thousand *pesos* for Mexico, ten thousand for Yucatan, and eight thousand for Vera Cruz.[42] The three highest military intendants might be the chiefs of the army of Mexico, therefore the sub-inspector general of the troops would no longer be needed, as the intendants could perform his functions without additional pay. Moreover, three classes of intendancies would make opportunity for promotion from one group to another, as incentive for greater efficiency; the three principal military intendancies could be reserved for those having the highest careers in the army of New Spain.[43] The intendancy of Mexico might serve as a model for all óthers because in it was found the most nearly complete machinery for the four departments of government.[44]

An important change suggested by Revillagigedo was in regard to the *junta superior*. He thought that it should be divided into two parts, one of which should take charge of contentious matters only, and the other of economic and administrative affairs. The first he would have made up of the viceroy as president, of the regent of the *audiencia,* of the senior member, of two judges appointed annually by the viceroy, and of the fiscal of the treasury. The second should consist of the viceroy, of the intendant of Mexico, the senior judge of the royal subtreasuries, the superintendent of the customhouse of Mexico City, the directors of *alcabala,* tobacco, powder, and playing cards, and of the general accountant of tributes and assessments. The viceroy was not to attend the former *junta* when a case of

---

[42] *Dictamen* .... *sobre la ordenanza de intendentes* .... MS, *num.* 402, art. 31 *et seq; Instrucción reservada,* arts. 836–843.

[43] *Ibid.,* arts. 83, 87, 99–100, 105.

[44] *Ibid.,* art. 35.

which he had been judge was being determined, but no decision was to be put into effect without his consent and approval. His sanction had also to be obtained for everything done in the latter *junta;* in each body he should have only a casting vote.[45]

The question of the cognizance of cases relative to confiscation on the sea was doubtful, since there was a variation between the instructions to naval commanders and the Ordinance of Intendants. Article 240 of the Ordinance granted this power to intendants, but it was not declared to extend to contraband on the high sea or outside of the boundaries of the respective intendancies. As these cases occurred frequently with coastguard boats, it seemed best to Revillagigedo that they be granted exclusively to the intendants of Vera Cruz and Yucatan, with the obligation that they should report to the viceroy concerning their measures and that they allow appeal to the *junta superior*.[46]

One of the chief problems in the establishment of the intendant system had been the *repartimientos* of supplies to the Indians, and what should replace them. There was still such a difference of opinion in regard to them in 1791 that Revillagigedo decided to ask all the intendants what they thought about them. The answers varied greatly. The intendants of Valladolid, Puebla, and Oaxaca were opposed to the *repartimientos* and wanted to follow the Ordinance to the letter. The intendant of Mexico disapproved of them but was a little more lenient. The intendants of Zacatecas, Vera Cruz, Yucatan, Guanajuato, and Guadalajara favored them. Those of San Luis Potosí and Sonora believed that they might be permitted in special cases, and the intendant of Durango asked that they might not be introduced into his territory. Some intendants maintained that the Indians were better off since the *repartimientos* were suppressed and that no injury had resulted to the treasury. Others thought that

---

[45] *Dictamen* .... *sobre la ordenanza de intendentes* .... MS, *num.* 402, art. 111 *et seq; Instrucción reservada,* arts. 820–822, 827.

[46] Revillagigedo to Gardoqui, March 31, 1792, MS, *num.* 17.

their abolition was harmful to the natives, and that it made them lazy and unable to pay tribute.[47] The viceroy himself thought that the article prohibiting the *repartimientos* was one of the most important parts of the Ordinance of Intendants, and that nothing would be more serious than to break it. Some people still hoped that the *repartimientos* would be restored.[48]

Another matter that had not been settled satisfactorily was the salary of the subdelegates. Abuses were still attributed to those officials because of their low remuneration; they had not, perforce, ceased to carry on trade and commerce with the Indians and others. They differed little from the old *corregidores* and *alcaldes mayores*, except that they did not charge interest, or tyrannize over debtors with cruel punishment, because the intendants carefully watched their transactions and corrected them for misdeeds.[49] Revillagigedo felt certain that the subdelegates would work better as soon as they received higher salaries. Therefore he thought that they should be divided into three classes—thirty in the first group, sixty in the second, and eighty in the third. The pay of those in the first class should be one thousand *pesos*, of those in the second six hundred *pesos*, and of those in the third four hundred *pesos*, not high salaries in fact for the services exacted. He thought that they could be assigned four per cent from the sale of stamped paper and two per cent to four per cent from the municipal funds, besides the five per cent they received from tributes. The subdelegates had suffered greatly on account of financial difficulties and had often been forced to do the will of their guarantors, who were usually inhabitants of their districts; thus they were deprived of freedom to act as they wished. The *residencia* was another burden to them because of the cost and the delay involved. Revillagigedo

---

[47] *Dictamen* .... *sobre la ordenanza de intendentes* .... MS, *num.* 402, art. 141 *et seq.*

[48] Revillagigedo, Nov. 26, 1790, MS, *num.* 162 *reservada.*

[49] Revillagigedo, *Dictamen* .... *sobre la ordenanza de intendentes* .... MS, *num.* 402, art. 134; *Instrucción reservada,* art. 847.

desired that the subdelegates should be of such good character that they would not need bonds, or the *residencia,* or to pay the half-annate. He declared that when they were well paid justice would be so much improved that the tribunal of *La Acordada* would become useless and its expenses could be saved.[50] The treasury officials he also would have divided into three classes and have their salaries graded accordingly. Those of the first class he would have paid four thousand *pesos,* the second three thousand, and the third from twenty-five hundred down to eighteen hundred *pesos.*[51]

Revillagigedo suggested but few changes in the Ordinance in regard to military matters. He thought that the frontier troops should not be paid every month, but at the beginning of the year or every six months; that their supplies need not be furnished each month; and that there were not sufficient hospitals and quarters for troops in Mexico.[52]

In 1795 and 1796 Viceroy Branciforte expressed rather mildly his opinions about the intendancies of Mexico. He had found it very difficult to enforce article 12 of the Ordinance, which prohibited *repartimientos,* and thought that the subdelegates needed them in order to be able to subsist in their offices.[53] He felt that while the viceroy still retained many powers, those of subordinate magistrates were increasing, some of them being able to act with absolute independence. He complained that the intendant of Guadalajara, who was president of the *audiencia* and military commandant of his district, considered himself to have independent powers. Royal orders and *cédulas* which should have been submitted first to the viceroy went to him and he placed his approval directly on them. The same thing hap-

---

[50] *Instrucción reservada,* arts. 856–873; *Dictamen . . . . sobre la ordenanza de intendentes . . . .* MS, *num.* 402, arts. 152–154, 205.

[51] Revillagigedo, *Instrucción reservada,* art. 879.

[52] *Dictamen . . . . sobre la ordenanza de intendentes . . . .* MS, *num.* 402, arts. 518–522.

[53] Branciforte to Varela, March 30, 1795, MS, *num.* 982 *reservada.*

pened with the intendant of Vera Cruz.[54] Branciforte also argued that the superior government should be authorized to appoint judges to take the *residencias* of subdelegates at the end of their terms.[55]

The public-spirited Abad Queipo, Bishop of Michoacán, in 1799, described the wretched condition of the Indians and castes of Mexico under the intendant system. He avowed that they lived in the greatest degradation and that there was an infinite gulf between them and the Spaniards. The laws profited them little, and sometimes were a burden to them, as for example, the laws of their communities. The difficulty of utilizing their products had increased because of the new management under the code of the intendancies, since nothing might be disposed of without recourse to the *junta superior de hacienda*. Separated by law from the other classes, the natives were deprived of the enlightenment and aid which they should have received from communication and contact with other people. The subdelegates tried to remedy the abuses of the *alcaldes mayores*, but since they did not receive any regular remuneration, the remedy was more dangerous than the former condition. If these officials were to depend upon fees, they would perish from hunger; therefore by necessity they had to prostitute their offices, defraud the poor, and carry on commerce. The good bishop said that it was very difficult for the intendants to find suitable persons for subdelegates; thus they were forced to take individuals who were failures in life or lacked talents to subsist in other careers of society.[56]

In the viceroyalty of Peru the viceroy Teodoro de Croix had emphatic views on the system. After he had tried it for several years, he had no use for the new régime and believed that it

---

[54] Branciforte to Alcudia, Sept. 28, 1795, MS, *num.* 169 *reservada*.

[55] Branciforte to the Prince of Peace, Aug. 27, 1796, MS, *num.* 325 *reservada*.

[56] Mora, José María Luis, *Obras sueltas* (Paris, 1837), I, 55, 57.

should be abolished. In a long official letter he made remonstrances to the king against it. He declared that the intendancies had caused many inconveniences and that there was loud outcry in Peru for their suppression. For the good of the country he decided to petition the sovereign to serve his vassals by certain well regulated modifications in the Ordinance of 1782.

Croix maintained that the power of the viceroy had been greatly decreased. In a royal order of October 7, 1788, the intendants were permitted to appoint the subdelegates with the approval of the viceroy. If the viceroy disapproved of the individuals proposed by the intendants he had to report his action to the king through the Minister of the Indies. Croix said that there was a diminished respect for the viceroy among the people, who recognized in their respective intendant a judge invested with all the powers and authority in the four departments of government. They yielded the same obedience to the viceroy only in the intendancy where he resided. He asserted that the people were led to believe that the restriction of the viceregal powers was made to deprive viceroys of a certain imagined despotism, notwithstanding that they had given proofs of fidelity and obedience to the king for more than two and one-half centuries. Although intendants were supposed to be subject to the viceroy and the *junta superior*, the people thought they were not dependent upon the viceroy in anything and looked upon him with indifference. Croix argued that, if this were true so soon after the intendancies were established, as time went on there would develop the most criminal disobedience to the superior government. A few examples of insubordination had already occurred in Guancavelica and Chile and the troops had to be called out to quell them.

He showed that the ecclesiastics did not get along well with the intendants and that their dissensions were most annoying. There was trouble between the intendants and the nuns of Cuzco and Truxillo, the missionaries of the college of Ocopa, and the bishops of Arequipa and Guamanga. The prelates had never before had judges clothed with so much authority as the intendants near them, and the ceremony and etiquette which had to be accorded them was displeasing to the ecclesiastics. They noticed the contrast between the viceroys and intendants. The former by their age, rank, titles, services, and nationality were fit to exercise the honorable functions of vice-patrons, but had been deprived of them. The churchmen regarded the latter as youths without rank, experience, or self control in their conduct. They found still more objection to the lieutenant-assessors of the intendants, whose only merits were that they were the attorneys of the common people before the *audiencia*. Men of desirable degree of learning did not wish to be appointed assessors.

The bishops became more angry at the intendants when they noticed that the lesser clergy tried to win their goodwill for purposes of self-interest. They were less obedient to their prelates, the intendants encouraging them in their disobedience; therefore the bishops feared to have the intendants, as vice-patrons, provide for vacant parishes. Hence parishes were allowed to remain vacant or were served by ad interim appointees, which was not good for the cause of religion. The hope of the bishops for the extinction of the intendancies, or at least of the vice-patronage of the intendants, made them delay from day to day to provide for benefices. The viceroy himself had used all possible means to correct the scandalous disagreements between the ecclesiastics and the intendants, without much success. He had also tried to check the appeals made by the chapters about the performance of ceremonies.

Croix himself thought that the intendants should not be permitted to exercise the vice-patronage, since many of them were not of sufficient uprightness, learning, disinterestedness, and public spirit. He affirmed that the *corregidores* had much less trouble with the churchmen because their authority was strictly subject to the superior power of the viceroys and *audiencias*. At all times the *corregidores* had been obedient and submissive, even though they did have some quarrels with members of the clergy. Whenever bad conduct was found among them they were imprisoned, deposed, or fined according to the nature of the delinquency; therefore offenses were few. By means of *corregidores* directly subject to him the viceroy had been kept well informed of everything that had occurred from Buenos Aires to Lima for two centuries and a half.

Croix believed that the intendants had not given the slightest encouragement to agriculture, commerce, industry, or mining, although this was their special function. The same old agricultural methods traditionally used in Europe were employed in the provinces just as at the beginning. Mining could only be promoted by means of science and wealth, but the intendants were not scientists and refused to invest their money in mining, therefore there was little chance to develop it. He showed how the *corregidores* had formerly aided the miners by furnishing them supplies through *repartimientos*. In his opinion the *cabildos* were more capable of performing the other functions under the department of *policía* than were the intendants. The maps of the provinces made under the supervision of the latter officials were less correct than those of the former.

Croix next asseverated that the intendants had not brought about the expected improvement in the administration of justice in Peru. The chief defects arose from the fact that intendants were not lawyers and resided only in the capital cities of the provinces or in large towns among the Spaniards. People still preferred to appeal their cases to the *audiencia* in spite of the delay. This viceroy did, however, have one good word to say in favor of the intendants. He stated that they and their lieutenant-assessors were more just than the *corregidores* and the lawyers from whom these had received assistance. He also asserted that in the smaller towns the lawsuits were unimportant, their interest centering in a cow, a mule, a measure of maize or potatoes, or a quarrel between two half-drunken Indians. For such cases a legally trained judge was unnecessary, for a severe Indian *alcalde* would suffice. Croix thought that the undue division of the department of justice made many idle judges while their salaries only increased expenses. The capital was the center of the administration of justice for all the viceroyalty and so became the habitation of too many celebrated lawyers; scarcity of cases of course resulted, so they resorted to all the arts of their profession when they did have a case, delaying the process longer than was necessary in order to be able to charge higher fees.

The viceroy complained that the intendants allowed more frequent appeals from the decisions of *alcaldes ordinarios* than the laws prescribed. Since this abuse was general the *audiencia* of Lima sent out repeated circulars ordering the intendants to refrain from permitting such recourse, which belonged only to that body. The intendants evaded these commands by calling appeals complaints and decided them as they saw fit. They set free individuals imprisoned by judges of first instance, and suspended or annulled elections of *alcaldes ordinarios* when the voters had not favored their candidates. By such methods they grievously oppressed the inhabitants of the towns. Occasionally the aggrieved persons tried to prosecute the intendants, but it was very difficult to prove their guilt. Those who had information concerning their conduct were afraid to give evidence and others were won over by flattery. As a result the accusers were often ruined. The members of the *cabildos* could hardly endure the haughtiness of the intendants, who violated all the acts of that body. The honorable members, most needed for the public welfare, became disgusted and refused to attend the meetings. The improvement in administration of justice provided for by official visitations by the intendants had not been realized, and Croix declared that little benefit had resulted from them. An interesting example developed in a tour of inspection made by the intendant of Truxillo. This official made his journeys of visitation to two *partidos* of his intendancy carried in an armchair on the shoulders of Indians after the fashion of the ancient Incas, with no better result than that of taking exercise. Intendants were often contented with any false news about their provinces which subdelegates or other persons gave them.

Croix even declared that the department of finance was not administered any better under the intendants than before. He accused them and their assessors of varying the rules of revenue collection because of their lack of financial experience. They excused some individuals from taxes and punished others, thereby causing discontent among the people and opposition to the payment of dues. They did not realize that there was nothing more injurious than lack of uniformity in tax collection. The intendants imposed their absolute authority, and allowed delays and mistakes to be made by collectors. The viceroy admitted that the solvency of the royal treasury had been improved, but this was not on account of anything that the intendants or their subdelegates had done. It was because of the new system of double entry bookkeeping and the better methods of keeping account.

Croix could not see that intendants had much to do in the department of war, since the troops were few in numbers in Cuzco, Arequipa, and on the frontiers of Tarma. Their work was limited to providing the pay and allowances for the soldiers which the treasury officials as commissaries of war made during the monthly review, hence they were by no means essential in the military department. The viceroy charged too that intendants were slow to put measures into effect and that they sometimes made false reports. For instance, he received an *expediente* in which the intendant of Truxillo falsified the signatures and furnished incorrect documents. When intendants were asked to do something Croix declared that three or four orders were necessary besides summons and many warrants. He advised that the *corregidores* with the title of governors be restored.[57]

Viceroy Lemos, who succeeded the somewhat disgruntled Croix, did not have such pessimistic ideas about the intendancies in Peru. The greatest fault which he found with the system related to the subdelegates. He maintained that industry had not been improved because the administration of the *partidos* was put under the control of those not very effective officials. Rather had it decreased, being confined exclusively to the cities and towns where Spaniards resided. Lemos ventured the opinion that it was impossible for a subdelegate to keep his character pure as a judge with the ridiculous salary of three per cent from tribute collection allowed him by the Ordinance of the Intendants. He therefore recommended that the subdelegates should be paid at least a living salary. Nevertheless he believed that the intendant system, if well regulated, would bring good results to the kingdom. Through the intendants the viceroy might inform himself of the condition of the country, and so qualify himself to take proper measures for its better government.[58]

The much criticized institution seemed to have better success in the viceroyalty of La Plata than in Peru. There many of the evils of colonial administration were corrected and the provinces flourished. Viceroy Vertíz had a favorable impression of the innovation, and worked in harmony with the intendants.[59] In reality the intendants and the four military governors were quite independent in their territories. Their powers were well defined and they did not encroach upon the rights of one another. They

[57] Croix to the king, May 16, 1789, AGI, 146–6–14 (Indiferente General).
[58] *Memorias de los vireyes que hand gobernado el Peru*, VI, 71–72.
[59] *Revista del Archivo General de Buenos Aires*, III, 267–268.

had absolute freedom to defend their districts, and were not subject to any other superior authority except that of the intendant-general and the viceroy. The *audiencias* of Buenos Aires and La Plata did not interfere in matters of administration. They only judged appeals that were submitted to them and took charge of such administrative affairs as were intrusted to them.[60] Levene says that the intendancies decentralized the government which the viceroyalty had unified, forming autonomous nuclei.[61] He thought that this was good for the people as it made them more self-reliant. This is an interesting characterization, placing this great reform in the light of a harbinger of independence.

According to Pelliza, indeed, all that was needed to make the country independent was to replace monarchy by democracy, to appoint American intendants chosen by the people in place of Spaniards selected by the king, and to substitute a president for the imperial viceroy. How easily the transition might have been made is of course only an interesting speculation. The intendants, the same author recorded, had had the good fortune to subdue the barbarous Indians of the frontiers and the pampas. Their military expeditions were not always made with the king's money, but sometimes the people provided it. Under the new régime it was possible for the viceroys of Buenos Aires to devote themselves to the general defense and to improving the country and the life of the people. The Indians were relieved of the abuses which *corregidores* and priests had imposed upon them, and the medieval shadows which had enveloped the creole for so long really began to disperse.[62]

Alexander von Humboldt, a keen observer of conditions in New Spain in 1804, said that the intendancies formed a memorable epoch for the welfare of the Indians, who were freed from many of the petty vexations to which they were subject, due to

---

[60] *Revista del Archivo General de Buenos Aires*, IV, 105–106.
[61] *Historia Argentina* (Buenos Aires, 1913), I, 161.
[62] *Ibid.*, 17, 245–249.

the active vigilance of the intendants. For the first time after centuries of oppression the natives began to enjoy the benefits granted to them by the laws. The noted traveler asserted that none of the twelve intendants of Mexico could be accused of corruption or lack of integrity, but he did not say this about the subdelegates. The latter officials, like the *alcaldes mayores*, vexed the poor by their exactions and showed indulgence toward the rich. The Indians did not hope for protection from them; they hastened to their priests for assistance, since they had more confidence in the ecclesiastics than in the superior magistrates. The result was that the clergy and the subdelegates lived in continual opposition.

The Indians were not allowed to own property; they were obliged to cultivate common lands leased to them by the intendants. The proceeds of their labor entered into the royal coffers and the treasury officials kept a separate account of it which they called the property of each town. The intendants might not dispose of this property in favor of the natives. Finally the Indians got tired of claiming aid from the public treasury because years passed in forming *expedientes* relative to the matter and at the end of the period no reply was made. Hence the intendants regarded the money of the public treasuries as if it had no specified use. For instance, the intendant of Valladolid sent to Madrid about 40,000 *pesos,* which had been collected from the work of the Indians during twelve years, saying to the king that it was a free and patriotic gift which the natives of Mexico made to him to help continue the war with England.

In 1809 the most conflicting opinions, according to the economic interest of the critic, in relation to the intendant system were still expressed. It was said on the one hand that the collection of royal revenues suffered because the treasury officials

---

[63] *Ensayo político sobre Nueva España,* I, 200, 210–211.
[64] *Ibid.,* I, 207–208.

did not have the active functions which they had had under the Laws of the Indies.[65]   On the other hand, José Valiente was a very enthusiastic defender of the system. He pointed out that intendants were under the immediate supervision of the viceroys, *audiencias,* and *juntas superiores,* and that the subdelegates were subordinate to the same authorities, that the administration was very much simplified and systematized, and the execution of the laws facilitated. The government was centralized and energetic. The scandalous abuses of the *repartimientos* and *corregidores* had been forever abolished. Commerce had increased and finances were improved.[66]

In 1816 Viceroy Abascal of Peru spoke of the Ordinance of Intendants as a wise reform, although he was fain to confess that in spite of it communication had not been opened from one town or province to another, and in distant and unpopulated places not even a hut had been provided to relieve the fatigue of travelers. The inhabitants of the viceroyalty had not been educated or instructed in the most necessary arts. He declared that the community funds of each town, which were ordered to be applied to public utilities, such as the upkeep of roads, repair of bridges, and maintenance of elementary schools, had been expended for other less important purposes. He added other stock laments about the deplorable conditions of the country. Many towns lacked buildings suitable for town halls and were without prisons; poverty was general everywhere; agriculture and industry were too unprogressive to support commerce; political and economic conditions were very backward.[67] It seems that the opinion prevailed then as now that legislation alone is capable of relieving economic stagnation.

The intendants and subdelegates were in 1834 made objects of very severe criticism by Señor Escudero. He said that the

[65] *Cedulario,* MS, I, 93.

[66] *Opinion concerning the system of government in America,* Sept. 16, 1809, AGI, 141–5–11.

[67] *Documentos históricos del Peru* (Lima, 1863–1877), II, 6 *et. seq.*

subdelegates had exercised the most monstrous despotism under the cover of their powers, which were unknown and uncertain. Besides, they had to be the blind tools of the wills of the commandants-general, of the judges of the *audiencia*, and of their superiors, the intendants. They had no more will of their own or real power than what they could acquire by the confidence and protection which they knew how to inspire in those officials; hence the support and public prestige enjoyed by them were generally graduated in proportion to the favor that those officials scattered. The gentleman added that the power of such subdelegates was useless and they were nothing more than a ridiculous caricature of the *corregidores*. The intendants themselves were disgusted with their subordinates. Alejo García, the intendant of Sonora, and also the intendant of Durango, dilated on the defects of the subdelegates, calling them the friends of the rich and the oppressors of the poor.[68]

One of the principal defects of the intendant system was the failure to enforce the Ordinances in all their parts. The article which treats of the visitation of provinces by intendants was not strictly fulfilled. Both Croix of Peru and Revillagigedo of Mexico complained of this. The latter viceroy admitted, however, that some intendants met genuine difficulties in making tours of inspection, since their salaries and those of their subdelegates were not high enough to meet the required expenses. Also it was inconvenient for intendants to leave their posts for so long.[69] Again, the intendants in Mexico neglected to draw up regulations for the administration of municipal funds and submit them to the *junta superior* for approval. Malversation of public resources was still common in 1794[70]

---

[68] Escudero, J. A., "Noticias estadísticas del estado de Chihuahua" (Mexico, 1834). In *Papeles varios*, 177, *num.* I, 21–22.

[69] Croix to the king, May 16, 1789, AGI, 146–6–14 (Indiferente General); Revillagigedo, *Dictamen* .... *sobre la ordenanza de intendentes* .... MS, *num.* 402, arts. 248–249; *Instrucción reservada*, arts. 844–847.

[70] *Ibid.*, arts. 154–157.

The king frequently annulled parts of the Ordinance of Intendants when they did not work properly. This caused many doubts and difficulties. In 1787 part of article 11 was annulled, and the right of confirming the election of *alcaldes ordinarios* was restored to all the viceroys. In the cities where there were *audiencias,* and for fifteen leagues around them, the presidents confirmed the *alcaldes.* In small towns viceroys could authorize intendants to do this with later central confirmation. The next year articles 6 and 28 were annulled and the control of municipal finance was again intrusted to the viceroys. This decree was reaffirmed in 1793 and 1803.[71] By 1816 the rights of ecclesiastical vice-patronage were again exercised by the viceroy of Peru.[72]

In 1803 an attempt was made to remodel all the Ordinances of Intendants for the whole of Spanish America. Because of certain defects, violations, unworkable parts, and annulments, these administrative codes had not been so successful as had been expected. Accordingly, the king appointed a council of ministers for the very necessary work of revision. They were to make one general Ordinance for all the colonies, with such additions and variations as seemed necessary. An entirely new document, which consisted of two hundred and twenty-six articles, was drawn up for use in superseding the earlier ones. The wording and arrangement of the articles were entirely different from the Ordinances of 1782 and 1786. The first article combined military and civil control by providing that each province should be under the control of a single person with the title of intendant. The king himself was to appoint the intendants. Articles 2 to 10 treated of the establishment of intendancies in all the viceroyalties. Article 10 fixed the salaries of intendants. Those of Mexico and Peru were to receive 7,000 *pesos,* and those of Santa Fé

---

71 Revillagigedo, *Dictamen . . . . sobre la ordenanza de intendentes . . . .* MS, *num.* 402, arts. 132, 231–238; *Cedulario,* MS, I, 228; *ibid.,* II, 157.

72 *Documentos históricos del Peru,* II, 32. For other annulments of the Ordinance of Intendants see the footnotes of the translation.

and Buenos Aires 5,000. This was a decided decrease in remuneration. Article 11 to 28 dealt with powers of viceroys, superintendents, and *juntas superiores;* articles 28 to 41 with those of intendants of province; and 41 to 54 with those of subdelegates. Articles 54 to 60 considered *repartimientos* and business, 61 Indian *alcaldes,* and 62 to 65 assessors. Articles 66 to 77 took up matters of justice, 77 to 192 finance, and the remainder military affairs.[73]

Perhaps the most notable change related to the subdelegates. Their appointments were to be made directly by the king with the advice of the Council of the Indies. Those officials were to be divided into three classes in order to make promotion possible, as Revillagigedo had suggested. Their salaries were definitely set down for the viceroyalties of Mexico, Peru, and La Plata, but not for Nueve Granada. The highest remuneration was to be 2,400 *pesos* for first-class subdelegates in Peru and Buenos Aires, and 2,200 in Mexico. The lowest was 1,200 *pesos* in Peru and Buenos Aires for those of third class. The salary for the latter officials in New Spain was to be 1,500 *pesos.*[74] Thus an old cause of criticism was removed.

The plan of Viceroy Revillagigedo for dividing the *junta superior* was included in the Ordinance. One part called *"contenciosa"* was to take cognizance of all matters which involved a point of law which needed to be settled by trial.

The other, the *"junta superior de gobierno,"* of which the intendant of the capital was an ex officio member, dealt solely with administrative and financial affairs. The intendants were still of course subject to the higher authority of the viceroys and *audiencias;* therefore the new plan did not provide for any elements of self-government, probably the chief defect. The Ordinance of 1803 lacked the legislative force of that of 1786

---

73 Zamòra y Coronado, III, 379, *et seq.*
74 *Ibid.,* V, 493, *et seq.*

and was never put into effect, on account of certain defects in its military regulations. The Ordinance of 1786 was retained and continued to be used in Spanish America up to the eve of independence.[75]

The arguments for and against the system show on the whole that the minds of the legislators were fixed firmly on raising to its highest pitch of efficiency the practice of colonial administration under the decaying principles of benevolent despotism. There was nowhere visible in the great enactment any appreciation of the need of evolving self-government, or greater well-being, through an evolutionary process of placing responsibility upon the colonial himself. It is trite to repeat that this obtuseness on the part of the governments of Europe brought about the revolutionary era and the emancipation of the New World. The pity is that the new organization could not have been initiated near the beginning, instead of near the end, of the reign of the great Charles III, under whose energetic ministers it might have served the purposes of making a real union of Spain and Spanish America in an effective imperial organization worthy of the great conception embodied in the idea. Such an evolution might have eventuated had the system provided for the elements of self-government. But this was impossible because of the ancient rivalry with England and the dread of revolution in the colonies. The minds of the reformers had moved forward as far as their viewpoint of society and of the grandeur and importance of the Spanish empire would permit. To other hands and other minds the evolution of Spanish American society was to be intrusted.

---

[75] Zamora y Coronado, III, 379.

IV

TRANSLATION OF THE ORDINANCE OF INTENDANTS FOR NEW SPAIN
THE KING

Influenced by the paternal love which all my vassals, even those most distant, deserve from me, and, by the eager desire with which I have tried, ever since my elevation to the throne, to unify the government of the great empires which God has intrusted to me, and set in good order, make happy and defend my extensive dominions of America, I have, as result of very well-founded information and prudent inquiry, resolved to establish intendants of army and province in New Spain. [These intendants, who] are to be granted adequate authority and salaries, shall govern those inhabitants in peace and justice by order of what is intrusted and committed to them by this instruction. They shall take charge of the general administration (*policía*) of New Spain. They shall collect with integrity, zeal, and vigilance the legitimate revenues of my royal treasury as the wise laws of the Indies and the two royal ordinances indicate, which my august father, Philip V, and my beloved brother, Ferdinand VI, published on July 4, 1718, and October 13, 1749.[1]

[1] The intendent system, a French institution, was established in Spain by Philip V in 1718, for the purpose of restoring economic, judicial, and general administration to their ancient splendor; but after a brief trial the intendancies were suppressed. They were reestablished in 1749 by a new ordinance which caused some reforms to be made, and which became the model for the later ordinances of America. The intendant, who took the place of the former governor or *corregidor*, supervised the collection of all the revenues of the treasury, had contentious jurisdiction in cases of contraband or fraud, and in civil and criminal suits of employees of the treasury, and took cognizance of general cases of justice and administration. It was also his duty to improve the administration of municipal finance of the towns, to provide for the distribution of municipal lands and the allotment of funds for the army, and to promote agriculture, industry, and commerce. Later, with the appointment of the Minister of the Interior, and the founding of political governments and provincial deputations, the intendants exercised only the powers relating to the treasury. Escriche, Joaquín, *Diccionario razonado de legislación y jurisprudencia* (Paris, 1869), nueva ed.

I desire that their prudent and just regulations, with the enlargements and restrictions which are expounded in the articles of this ordinance or instruction, shall be exactly observed by the intendants of the kingdom mentioned.

1

In order that my will may have its prompt and proper effect, I command that the territory of that empire, exclusive of the Californias, shall be divided for the present into twelve intendancies. Hereafter, the territory or area of such intendancy, called by the name of the city which must be its capital, in which the intendant will reside, shall be known as only one province. Those [divisions] which at present are called provinces [shall be known] as *partidos*, and they shall keep the names which they have.

One of the intendancies indicated shall be the general one of army and province, and it must be established in the capital of Mexico. The other eleven shall be only intendancies of province. One of them must be established in the city of Puebla de los Ángeles; another in the fortified city of Vera Cruz; another in the city of Mérida de Yucatan; another in the city of Antequera de Oaxaca; another in the city of Valladolid de Michoacan; another in the city of Santa Fé de Guanajuato; another in the city of San Luis Potosí; another in the city of Guadalajara; another in the city of Zacatecas; another in the city of Durango; the remaining one shall be the one which is already established in the city of Arispe and includes the two provinces of Sonora and Sinaloa.

Each of the intendancies mentioned must comprise the jurisdictions, territories, and districts (*partidos*) assigned to them respectively at the end of this instruction, which will be given to the new intendants whom I may choose under their proper titles (which for the present will be issued by the Secretary of State of the Indies). I reserve for myself always and at my pleasure [the right] to appoint to these offices persons of accredited zeal, integrity, intelligence, and good conduct so that I may fulfil my obligations by intrusting to them the immediate government and protection of my people.

2

The viceroy of New Spain is to continue in full exercise of his superior authority and the plenary powers which my royal title and instruction and the laws of the Indies grant him as governor and captain-general within the district of his command, to the high offices of which is added that of president of the *audiencia* and *chancillería* of the capital and metropolis of Mexico. But he shall leave the superintendency and regulation of my royal treasury in all its branches and proceeds to the care, direction, and management of the intendancy-general[a] of army and treasury which shall be created in the capital mentioned. The other intendancies of province, which I order established by this instruction shall be subordinate thereto.

⟨[a] See the royal order of October 22, 1804, concerning the powers of the intendant of Mexico.⟩

3

In order that the supreme power which I have granted and intrusted to my viceroys may in no case or manner be decreased, I desire and command that he [who is viceroy] of New Spain and his successors in that viceroyalty shall place their countersign (*cúmplase*), not only on the titles of the intendants who may be sent to the provinces included in the region of their authority, as they do on the [titles] of their governors, but also on that which is sent to the intendant-general of the army and royal treasury of the aforesaid kingdom.[a] But this latter [official] must also place [his signature] second on the dispatches of intendants of province, as superintendent of my royal treasury, for in everything pertaining thereto they must be subordinate to him, as is provided by this ordinance and was indicated in the preceding article.

For the same reason the before-mentioned superintendent also shall place his countersign on the dispatches forwarded to the intendants of Arispe and Durango. In like manner when they are presented to the commandant-general of the frontier, he shall also place his signature on them, they having first been recorded in the auditor's office (*contaduría de cuentas*) of Mexico, as likewise are other decrees in their turn, and both the latter and the former shall also be recorded in the principal (*contaduría*) of the province to which they respectively pertain.

⟨[a] This is added to by the royal order of October 25, 1787.⟩

4

The superintendency that the intendant-general of army exercises shall be considered as delegated from the general [superintendency] of my royal treasury of the Indies, which resides in my Secretary of State and of the universal Office of the Indies.[a] With the proper object of affording the superintendent-subdelegate some relief in his important duties and at the same time aiding this inauguration of the intendancies by concentrating and unifying the administration of all [of them] as much as the differences between the various towns and provinces may permit, I command the special superintendent-subdelegate to establish at once, with the consent of my viceroy, in the capital of Mexico a *junta superior* of my royal treasury, which he must attend as its president.

This *junta* shall, according to law 8, title 3, book 8 [of the *Recopilación de leyes de los reynos de las Indias*] be composed of the regent of that pretorian *audiencia;* of the *fiscal* of my royal treasury, with a vote in all matters and *expedientes* in which he shall not appear as a litigant; of the senior judge of the tribunal of the accounting-department for accounts, and of the senior accountant or the treasurer-general of army and royal treasury. The members shall take their seats according to the order in which they are named. That official who, according to the rank that belongs to him [is designated first], shall preside over the *juntas* which the superintendent-subdelegate may not be able to attend.

The notary (*escribano*) of the superintendency [of the treasury] shall always be present at the *juntas* in order to legalize votes and decisions not related to the branch of municipal finance (*propios y arbitrios*) and of community funds (*bienes de comunidad*), with the provision that, when necessity demands it, his chief official (*oficial mayor*) shall.act as substitute for him. I completely qualify him for this purpose. Both of them shall enter the *juntas* mentioned without sword or hat, and take their seats on the flat bench placed off the platform at the front opposite [the elevation] occupied by the judge who presides over the *junta*.

⟨ᵃ This refers to the consultative vote of the *junta superior* lately introduced.⟩

5

If on account of absence, illness, or other just cause, any of the members cannot be present at the aforesaid *junta superior de hacienda,* the assessor of the superintendency [of the treasury] may be substituted for the superintendent-subdelegate. The senior judge (*decano*) of the *audiencia* may be substituted for the regent of the *audiencia;* the official who serves in the *fiscal's* office for the *fiscal* of the treasury; for the judge of the tribunal of accounts, his next in seniority; and for the accountant or treasurer-general of army and treasury, his companion. It is to be understood that the assessor of the superintendency shall be seated next after the judge of the tribunal of accounts, and that all the members appointed for each case among those which have been explained in this article and in the preceding one, including the before-cited judges of the royal treasury, according to law 12, title 3, book 8 of the *Recopilación,* shall have a decisive vote concerning all cases whatsoever relating to my royal treasury, although they may not be superior judges (*jueces togados*). The provision of law 17 of the title and book stated, referring to all [the members of the *junta superior*], must always be observed.

6

The *junta* shall be held once or twice each week on the days and hours which the superintendent-subdelegate shall, his important engagements permitting, designate.[a] But if any urgent matter should arise he may convoke other extraordinary *juntas*. In all of these the means shall be discussed, in conformity with this instruction and the orders which I will give hereafter, and the method of arranging the government and administration of justice in my royal treasury according to a uniform system in all the provinces of that empire as much as it is possible [to do so], and in the economic affairs of war.

The aforesaid *junta superior* shall not only take sole charge of the two branches mentioned, but also of those of municipal finance and community funds of the towns. For the direction and cognizance of these I grant it as much authority and powers as shall be necessary, to the unconditional exclusion of all my [other] tribunals, and with dependence solely upon my royal person by the *vía reservada* of the universal Office of the Indies. Contentious matters which arise from the ordinary jurisdiction and spring from *policía* and government, on the appeal of the intendants, their subdelegates, and the other ordinary judges, shall be subject to the respective *audiencia* of the district, as they are by the laws of the *Recopilación* of the Indies.

⟨[a] This article and the following: 10, 28, 29, 31, 32, 33, 34, 35, 44, 45, 47, 48, 49, 50, 51, 52, and 53, which treat of the management and administration of municipal finance and the community funds of the Indians, are annulled by the royal order of February 21, 1788. When the intendancy of Mexico was established, it was doubted whether the intendant should or should not have charge of the treasuries of the communities or societies of San Juan and Santiago which are deposited with the court of the natives (*Juzgado de Indios*). Account was given to his Majesty and in the royal decree cited it was declared that there should be no change in regard to the competence of the aforesaid tribunal of the Indians nor the regulations under which it hitherto had been managed. This royal measure seems to annul the power belonging to the intendants and the *junta superior* relating to the community funds, and it cites the circular of November 11, 1787, concerning the divisions of municipal finance, community funds, and the *censos*.⟩

7

The political governments of Puebla de los Ángeles, of Nueva Vizcaya, and of Sonora and Sinaloa, the *corregimientos* of Mexico, and Antequera de Oaxaca, that of Vera Cruz which must be created, and the *alcaldías mayores* or *corregimientos* of Valladolid, Guanajuato, San Luis Potosí, and Zacatecas shall be united respectively to the intendancies which I am establishing in the capitals enumerated and their provinces. The salaries, which those now receive who are employed in any and all of the offices referred to, must be suppressed, and for the present the service in the intendancy of Guadalajara [must be placed] under the care of the regent-president of that *audiencia.*

I order that the intendants shall henceforth have under their charge the four divisions [branches or causes] of justice, general administration, finance, and war, and I give them all the authority and powers necessary for this, with fitting subordination and dependence in regard to what pertains to the first two branches. The intendants of Arispe and Durango [must be subject] to the commandant-general of their provinces and the ten remaining intendants to the viceroy. All [must be obedient] to the territorial *audiencias,* according to their separate commands, the nature of the cases, and the matters within their cognizance, in conformity with the laws of the *Recopilación* of the Indies as will be explained in the body of this ordinance. For it is my royal pleasure that the jurisdictions established in the *audiencias* shall not be confused, changed, or combined for the purpose of concentrating all [authority] in one person. This measure aims principally to avoid the frequent embarrassments and conflicts which would occur between the intendants and the governors, *corregidores,* or *alcaldes mayores,* if these old offices should remain separate in the capitals and provinces where the new ones are established.

8

With the exception of the intendants of Mexico [City], Guadalajara, Arispe, Mérida de Yucatan, and Vera Cruz, all the rest shall exercise in their provinces the royal vice-patronage according to the laws in their capacity of subdelegates of the respective proprietors; but the conferring of ecclesiastical benefices (*presentaciones eclesiásticas*) shall be reserved for the proprietors as vice-patrons to whom [this right] belongs; also [they shall possess] the absolute use of this supreme prerogative of my crown in the districts of the intendancies where they have their definite residences.

Within the intendancy of Mexico [the patronage] shall belong to the viceroy, in that of Arispe to the commandant-general of the frontier, in that of Guadalajara to the regent-president of its royal *audiencia,* and in that of Mérida and the province of Yucatan to its governor and captain-general. But in the area of the intendancy of Vera Cruz into which the jurisdiction of the governor [of Vera Cruz] does not extend, the exercise [of royal patronage] shall belong as is already provided for his own province, to the intendant of Puebla, just as it shall to the said governor. So also [the patronage] shall be reserved for the governor of Nuevo León within the district of his authority in the same capacity of subdelegate of the vice-patron proprietor (in both cases the viceroy is the proprietor) and with the already expressed reservation in his favor.

9

The remaining *corregimientos* and *alcaldías mayores* of the entire area of the twelve intendancies which are not mentioned in Article 7, including also those of Tixtla and Chilapa, must be suppressed when they become vacant, or when the officials provided by me in both [divisions] have completed their terms.[a]

Meanwhile they shall be subject and subordinate immediately to the respective intendants of their district, and the latter shall subdelegate to them their powers in order that in this manner the government of all the provinces may be at once made uniform and the confusion may be avoided which the diversity of jurisdictions and magistrates always causes.

Although it is my sovereign will that in the extinction aforesaid the *corregimientos* and *alcaldías mayores* of the estate of the Valley of Oaxaca and of Atlixco also shall be included in order to equalize entirely the condition of all my vassals of New Spain, nevertheless the present authorities provided in the offices indicated shall continue, but [they must be] subject to the regulations which are established by this ordinance, until they complete their terms, and until a just compensation is agreed upon for the possessors of the aforesaid estates for their respective rights and privileges.

⟨a This article is suspended and it was ordered by the royal *cédula* of October 15, 1792, that the duke of Terranova should assume the powers that were granted him by the royal dispatch of May 16, 1769, and that the viceroy and the *junta superior* should for the present abstain from acting contrary to what was determined while the matter was being decided in the Council of the Indies.⟩

10

The political and military administrations of Yucatan, Tabasco, Vera Cruz, Acapulco, the New Kingdom of León, Nuevo Santandar, Coahuila, Texas, and New Mexico shall continue. Consequently they must keep the divisions of justice and general administration united to the military authority in their respective territories or districts, except the branch belonging to municipal finance and to community funds of the towns, which must be [under] the exclusive power of the intendants, with subordination to the *junta superior de hacienda*.

It is understood that the jurisdiction of the governor or warden of the fortress (*castellano*) of Acapulco, with the three fortified points pertaining to it, shall, in regard to political matters and justice, remain under the control of the City of the Kings [Lima] and its port. With the purpose of guaranteeing in all that kingdom the attainment of the important purpose set forth in the preceding article relating to the subdelegations [of power] which it provides concerning the two branches, finance and economic matters of war, in the territories under their direct command, I order the respective intendants likewise to issue them for the governors mentioned (excepting those of Yucatan and Vera Cruz) and for the king's lieutenant in the city of Campeche.

11

At the same time that the *corregimientos* and *alcaldías mayores* indicated in Article 9 are being suppressed, the royal jurisdiction must devolve upon the respective intendants as the chief justices (*justicias mayores*) of their provinces, without prejudice to the authority belonging to the *alcaldes ordinarios* which must be exercised in the cities, towns, and villages of the Spaniards, with restriction to their districts or areas.[a] The first year in which this measure shall be made effective, two *alcaldes ordinarios* must likewise also be chosen in the towns having an adequate number of inhabitants (without excepting the capitals of the intendancies or those of the governments which are left in existence) and which at present do not have these officials.

Wherever there is no regular municipal council (*ayuntamiento*) which may perform this duty according to the laws that treat the matter,[2] each political or military governor in his district and the intendants in the remaining provinces shall make these appointments, and both shall conform to the spirit of the laws indicated, and without the necessity of royal confirmation. For (it being expressly understood that law 10, title 3, book 5 of the *Recopilación* is annulled) it is my royal will that the power of confirming the elections which the *ayunta-*

---

[2] *Recopilación*, leyes 1–9, tit. 3, lib. 5, reproduced in the Spanish original.

mientos shall make shall be the duty solely and especially of the governors themselves and of the intendants, according to what has been declared. In each case they shall do this after receiving such reports as shall insure that the aforesaid offices may be assigned to individuals who are judged most suited for the good administration of justice and for the proper security of the revenues of my royal treasury, which must be intrusted to their power according to the dispositions of this instruction.

In one [class] of towns as much as in the other, namely, in those with a municipal council and those without it, only one of the *alcaldes* mentioned shall be chosen in each consecutive year, in order that their offices may be biennial in all the towns, and that the senior *alcalde* may instruct the one newly beginning his duties. It is to be observed that to continue in this office during the second year, he who [receives] the highest vote of those appointed in the first year must remain. I expressly annul the power and the right, in regard to political matters, which the governor, *corregidores*, and *alcaldes mayores* may have had of placing lieutenants in some of the cities, towns, and villages which are indicated in this article.

⟨ª This article is annulled, in regard to the election of *alcaldes ordinarios* for two years, by the royal *cédula* of September 12, 1792, in which it is commanded that they shall hold their position for one year only, this article and the others that provide to the contrary being of no effect. The royal *cédula* is dated September 12, 1799, and is found in the *Gaceta de México*, number 15, April 23, 1800. By the royal order of November 29, 1787, this article was annulled and it was ordered to restore the former observance of law 10, title 3, book 5 of the *Recopilación* concerning the confirmation of *alcaldes ordinarios* and the annual election of the other officials.⟩

12

In each Indian town which is the principal one of the district and in which there may have been a lieutenant-governor, *corregidor*, or *alcalde mayor*, a subdelegate must be appointed.ª He shall have charge of the four divisions [of government], necessarily must be a Spaniard, and shall give bond, as law 9, title 2, book 5 of the *Recopilación* provides, in order that he may administer justice in the towns belonging to the district and keep the natives of it in good order, obedience, and civility. Under a regular title and without fees, only the intendant of the province himself must appoint, for the time of his good pleasure, the subdelegates in those chief towns which may not be [part] of the district of any of the excepted governments. In those which are, the intendant and the respective governor shall come to an agreement, and in the same manner both individuals shall receive information and reports in regard to persons [fit] for the office. Other qualifications being equal, they shall prefer administrators of tobacco, sales tax (*alcabalas*), and other branches of my treasury wherever these officials exist.

But neither the subdelegates cited, nor the *alcaldes ordinarios,* nor the governors who still remain, nor any other person whatever may distribute to Indians, Spaniards, *mestizos,* and the other castes, any personal property, produce, or any cattle, under the irremissible penalty of losing their value in favor of the Indians thus injured, and of paying [a fine of] an equal amount, which shall be applied by equal third parts to my royal chamber of justice, the judge, and the informer. In cases of repeated offense, after the process is drawn up by the intendant, account of it is given to the *junta superior de hacienda,* the litigants are heard, and the crime proved, then the punishment shall be increased to confiscation of property and to perpetual banishment of the delinquents. The execution of this [decision] shall be suspended only in favor of the governors referred to and while the sentence is being submitted to me, and not in the cases of others unless there is occasion for appeal to my royal person.

It is to be understood that the Indians and my other vassals of these dominions consequently are free to trade wherever and with whomever it suits them, in order to provide themselves with everything that they may need. If, besides in the principal towns indicated, the intendant should consider it necessary also to appoint a subdelegate in some other mere Indian town of his province, it may be done as is provided, after consulting the *junta superior de hacienda* and [obtaining] its approval. In such case the *junta* shall so report to me for my information by the *vía reservada* of the Indies.

⟨[a] This was amplified by the royal order of March 28, 1787. Also see articles 77 and 129.

This article is annulled in regard to the sole power of the intendants to appoint subdelegates. The royal order of January 19, 1792, so provides and moreover orders that they shall nominate them to the viceroys or presidents [of the *audiencia*] and that the latter may choose them from those included [on the list] or from others; that they shall give account to the king for his approval, which they also need for the exercise of their duties; that they must serve for five years only; and that they cannot be dismissed without cause nor before the decision of his Majesty.

The count of Revillagigedo knew that with the abolition of the *repartimientos* the provisioning of the towns by private individuals or inhabitants of the towns had been discontinued, in detriment to the poor, to the public, and to the royal treasury; he therefore represented to the king that the aforesaid prohibition had been enforced so rigorously that even sales on credit had been prohibited. He made a distinction between this furnishing of supplies by the inhabitants and the pernicious allotments by the justices. He formed an *expediente* concerning the whole matter and reported to the king, informing him that the prohibition in article 12 should continue with regard to the justices, but not with respect to the merchants or inhabitants. Therefore his Majesty so decided in an official reserved letter of May 13, 1791, directed to his Excellency the marquis of Branciforte, on account of which these *repartimientos* or provisionings have been winked at by succeeding administrations. Royal permission has even been granted in order that certain such contracts might be carried out, although they were in opposition to the opinion of those who were ignorant of this royal order.

The royal reserved order of May 13, 1791, and another of June 13, 1799, were annulled by the royal *cédula* of April 7, 1800, in which notwithstanding any public or reserved royal order, it is commanded that article 12 shall be inviolably observed. And since it is provided in that decree that his Excellency the viceroy shall take cognizance exclusively of the *repartimientos*, an *expediente* was drawn up on the initiative of the natives of San Miguel el Grande, and the civil *fiscal* requested that account should be given to his Majesty with a transcript of the *expediente* and other official documents concerning the declaration of the legitimate judge who must take cognizance [of the matter]. Until the present, that is, January of 1806, no determination has been reached and the viceroy continues to take cognizance by virtue of his position. By the royal order of April 30, 1788, the decision was confirmed in the *junta superior de hacienda* that the *alcaldes mayores* may collect debts for *repartimientos* they have made.⟩

13

Notwithstanding this measure for appointing Spanish judges in the chief Indian towns, which was set forth in the preceding article, it is my royal will to preserve for them for their welfare the right and ancient custom wherever it exists, of choosing every year among themselves the governors or *alcaldes* and other public officials which the laws and ordinances allow for their purely economic control; and [these officials] shall exact from the natives the royal tribute which they pay to my sovereign government in acknowledgment of the vassalage and great protection which this affords them. But this shall not be put in charge of other natives than those whom the intendants or their subdelegates have, according to practice, seen fit to appoint as such governors or collectors for the exaction mentioned and the greater security of my treasury in this particular.

In order to avoid the disturbances, lawsuits, and tumults which frequently arise among those natives on account of their election of officials, I command the Spanish judge always to attend and preside over their *juntas*. If the judge is absent or lawfully hindered [from being present], he shall appoint [some one] for this, provided that he also is a Spaniard. In no other way may they hold elections or shall that which they decide in them be valid.

14

After these elections of the Indians are made at the accustomed time and in the form provided herein, the subdelegate or the *alcaldes ordinarios* shall give account of them in a report to the intendant of the province or to the respective governor, if they should be held in some one of the districts in which governors still exist, in order that he may approve or amend them. [The intendant or governor] should prefer those who know the Spanish language and are most skilled in the commendable vocations of agriculture or industry; and, by the means which he may consider most gentle, he should try opportunely to influence the natives also to heed the aforesaid conditions for the elections mentioned. When the elections are thus decided by the intendant or governor, he shall hand his decisions to the judge, who must carry them out without permitting any levying of dues upon the Indians. It is to be expressly understood that any practice or custom contrary to this measure shall be annulled.

In order that the very important purpose of encouraging the natives to devote themselves to agriculture and industry and to speaking Spanish may not be dependent solely upon the means here ordered, the intendants, their subdelegates, and the *alcaldes ordinarios* respectively shall protect in every way those who are most efficient in both matters.

DEPARTMENT OF JUSTICE

15

The intendant-general of army and treasury, and each one of the intendants of province, must have a lieutenant-lawyer who shall exercise for them jurisdiction over civil and criminal litigation in the capital of their particular territory. At the same time he shall be an ordinary assessor in all the business of the intendancy, exercising the authority of its superior official in [case of] his non-appearance, illness, and absences while visiting his province, or from any just cause. It is to be understood that the assessor of the intendant-general must possess the same power in everything relating to the superintendency of my royal treasury which the intendant exercises, and he must substitute for him in his absences, illnesses, or incapacity.

In order that the said lieutenants may have all the qualifications which their offices require, they must be examined and approved by my councils, *chancillerías,* or *audiencias.* They shall be appointed by me with the advice of the Council of the Indies, which shall propose for each lieutenancy three persons of learning and known probity, so that I may choose from among them him whom I regard most fit for my royal service (if this is not done without consultation as I do with the first ones).

16

As it is very possible that at some time both the *intendant-corregidor* of a province and his lieutenant-assessor may be lacking either through death, illness, or absence, I declare that in any of these cases the senior of the two principal judges of the treasury of the province shall in the interim perform the duties and functions of the intendant. The lawyer [*letrado*] whom this official chooses [shall exercise] the powers of the lieutenant-assessor. It is to be understood that in the first of the cases cited, that regarding death, they both shall do this only in the interim until my viceroy, with the consent of the super-intendent-subdelegate, shall select persons of entire satisfaction and accredited ability and learning, who shall perform the duties respectively of the intendancy and *corregimiento,* and the lieutenancy ad interim.

But if the intendant-general of Mexico and his lieutenant should die, it is my sovereign will that the senior judge of the tribunal of accounts shall substitute in the first office, and in the second he whom the viceroy with the advice of said senior judge shall choose as assessor ad interim. Account must be given to me concerning the former and the latter vacancies by the *vía reservada* of the Indies in order that I may approve them.

17

Inasmuch as the exercise of the powers and functions of the intendant and those of the accountant or treasurer of my royal treasury are incompatible in practice; and also since the just discharge of both, on account of the different places and the identity of the time within which respectively they must function [is impossible], whenever, in observance of that which is provided in the foregoing article because of any one of the two cases alluded to, it may occur that the exercise of the power of intendant in any province shall devolve upon the senior of the principal judges of the treasury, I desire and order that this official shall appoint a person of his confidence, who may either belong to the subtreasuries or may not, who shall with the authority [subdelegated from his superior] while the latter serves as intendant, attend to the dispatch [of matters] concerning the local treasuries. He shall bestow upon such subordinate sufficient power for the purpose stated, since the responsibility which belongs to the *contador-judge* or treasurer must be his in the affairs which concern him.

18

In order that the aforesaid lieutenants may perform the duties of their offices decently and with perfect freedom, I assign to them the salary of one thousand *pesos* from the funds of the municipal finance, besides the fees indicated in the schedule (*arancel*) ; to [the assessor of] the intendant-general another thousand *pesos* from my royal treasury, and to each one [of the assessors] of the remaining intendants, as the tax assessors, five hundred *pesos*. I command that the latter shall serve for five years, or for the greater length of time that the intendants, by whom they should be appointed, may continue in office, or for the term that I shall consider it fitting to prolong for them. [The intendants] cannot remove them without previous justification, the cognizance of just causes, and my decision or that of my Council of the Indies. But they may be suspended by the *junta superior de hacienda,* if upon prior examination of the cases which the intendants shall have drawn up, ground shall be found for this, account of everything being given to me.

19

Appeals and recourses by litigants from the decisions or sentences of the aforesaid lieutenants as ordinary judges must be heard by the *audiencia* of the district in accordance with the laws of those kingdoms. If pleas of recusation are entered against them, such pleas must be drawn in conformity with the royal *cédula* issued as a general instruction for such cases on November 18, 1773.[3] The intendants shall observe the same practice in cases and affairs under their inspection when their lieutenants are challenged in their capacity as ordinary assessors, for they are never to be deprived of their cognizance [of such cases] since they have titles from me, and are responsible for their decisions.

20

The *intendant-corregidores* must preside over the municipal councils of their capitals, and the public meetings of these.[a] When they cannot attend, because of absence, illness, or other obstacle, their lieutenants shall do it; and in the absence of both [of these officials], the *alcaldes ordinarios,* if they exist, or he who, according to law, privilege, or custom, may perform the duty. Afterward account must be given to the intendant, if he shall be in the capital, concerning what was discussed in the town councils (*cabildos*) in order that, if he finds no serious objection, to the injury of the public or to the harm of any individuals who may demand rightly to be heard, he may arrange for its fulfillment.

⟨[a] In a superior order of January 13, 1808, this was ordered observed by the *cabildo* of Vera Cruz, because of it having been said that it was not in effect. This superior order was protested before the king and is pending, but meanwhile the aforesaid article referred to is being observed in the port mentioned.⟩

[3] See below in the original under number 2 the royal *cédula* cited.

21

Likewise the *intendant-corregidores* and their lieutenants shall consider carefully and make a special study of all the Laws of the Indies which prescribe the wisest and most suitable rules for the administration of justice and for the good government of the towns of those dominions of mine. They also shall examine with particular attention that which is established in the rules of those kingdoms, and what is provided in the absence of such laws; in each case they must conform with that which is provided in this instruction. The judges, affording an example of their proper observance, must efficaciously see that all other persons, Spaniards as well as the natives and the castes, shall respect and keep the aforesaid laws with obedience and due punctuality.

22

Among the cares and duties of the intendants that of the establishment and maintenance of peace in the towns of their provinces is the most urgent.[a] They must prevent the justices from acting with partiality, passion, or vengeance; for this purpose they shall interpose their authority and remedy abuses against the public welfare and my vassals which result from enmities. In these cases they may summon their lieutenants, subdelegates, *alcaldes ordinarios,* and other inferior judges, in order to notify them of their obligation and to exhort them to fulfil it. If this does not suffice, they shall give account with proof to the higher tribunal which may be competent [to handle the case] according to the nature of the matter, so that it may reprimand them and remove the disturbances, which the abuse of power by the justices and other persons who stir up in the towns envy, hatred, and discord, to the serious injury of their functions, usually causes.

⟨[a] The royal *cédula* of August 24, 1799, agrees with this article. In article 4 of the decree it is said that *alcaldes ordinarios* are free from *residencias,* because the chief justices of the provinces, who are the intendants, must be very much on the lookout concerning their actions.⟩

23

Also with similar vigilance, the intendants shall pay attention to the prompt and regular dispatch of the cases and matters under their cognizance, and [shall see that] litigants are not troubled by delays, nor made to pay more fees than those due according to the schedules. If, through truthful information, they shall find that the inferior judges of their provinces cause extortions in these matters, they shall warn them of their negligence or abuse. When this measure does not suffice to check them, they shall inform the proper superior judge with accompanying proof in order that they may be properly punished.

24

When judges are sent by my Council of the Indies to conduct *residencias* as later provided for in this instruction, or when judges of commission or inquiry are dispatched by *audiencias* to the cities, towns, or villages of the provinces, if they are not sent against the intendants in their capacity as *corregidores*, the latter shall be on the lookout whether the said judges comply with what is provided in the laws and their instructions. They must inform themselves accurately whether crimes deserving punishment are overlooked or tolerated by them on account of complaisance or interest, or whether cases are delayed purposely and take more time than they need; and, if [judges] receive exorbitant salaries or dues, the intendants must exhort them to restraint and moderation, and if this does not suffice they shall give account to the *fiscal* of the Council of the Indies in matters pertaining to *residencias,* or to the *audiencia* of the district in affairs concerning commissions which emanate from that body.

The same procedure shall be observed with respect to the treasurers (*receptores*) of the *audiencias* and to any other judges who exercise delegated jurisdiction in their provinces. As the intendants must inform themselves of the abuses which exist in the towns of their territory, they may instruct the aforesaid judges of *residencia* or inquiry concerning them, with entire caution and secrecy. For the same reason, these and other commissioners shall have the obligation of communicating and presenting their commissions to the *intendant-corregidores* of the province where they are assigned, since the authority and jurisdiction which they possess must be evident to the latter, and for the free exercise thereof it is essential that the intendants shall offer them their services and the assistance provided by law.

25

As long as the *corregidores* and *alcaldes mayores,* who until now have been appointed by me and by the possessors of the estates of the Valley of Oaxaca and of Atlixco respectively, shall continue to serve (these offices being finally suppressed according to provisions already noted) the intendants shall see that the visits they make to the towns within their jurisdictions shall not be made without previous notice. In case of permitting [the visitations] for proper reasons which the intendants may explain to them, it must only be [done] with the needful order that they shall not burden the town revenues by illegal dues, or cause any expense to the inhabitants and natives, whom they must pay for the beasts of burden and supplies that these shall furnish for them. They also shall be warned not to cover up the misdeeds of the ordinary justices by agreement or for any other consideration.

26

The intendants themselves shall be obliged continually to visit their provinces in the seasons which best permit this. Every year they shall perform [this duty] in the territories and districts which they can visit and examine so that, by the serious reflection [with] which preferred magistrates must do it, they may study how to increase agriculture, promote commerce, encourage the industry of the people, favor mining, and, finally by whatever means they may possess by their own judgment and the powers that are granted them, procure the happiness of those vassals, which is the object of my care and royal attention.

27

The intendants must perform these visitations without imposing any burdens upon the towns and with the purposes explained in this instruction and in the laws of title 2, book 5, of the *Recopilación* of the Indies.[4] Only in case of being entirely prevented from making [the visitations] themselves, shall they send commissioned subdelegates in their entire confidence, with specific instructions concerning what shall be done for the public welfare and for the relief of persons who complain, or have been injured by the inferior justices or the powerful men who commonly oppress the poor and helpless.

28

With the purpose of uniformly regulating the government, management, and distribution of all the municipal funds of the Spanish cities and towns, and of the communal funds of the Indian towns of that empire, I intrust the inspection of both [branches] solely to the *junta superior de hacienda* with the jurisdiction granted it in article 6, annulling expressly any other conflicting measure even though it may have been approved. I command that the accounting department of this division shall continue in the capital of Mexico as the visitor general of that kingdom established it by my order in the year 1766.

I reserve for myself [the right] to appoint the accountant (*contador*) and necessary officials, in order that they may keep

---

4 *Recopilación*, leyes 15–20, 22, tit. 2, lib. 5, contained in the Appendix of the original.

the most accurate account and calculation of these public funds, and that through the same office the *expedientes,* orders, and measures, which the aforesaid *junta superior* may decide by common consent, may be issued. Although there is in the capital of Mexico a commissioned judge of the royal *audiencia* with the name of superintendent-judge of municipal finance of that city and of the drainage of Huehuetoca, from the present moment he must cease [to serve] in those employments, since I order them to be united to the intendancy general as its exclusive privilege.

⟨a This article and the 6th are annulled by the royal order of September 14, 1788 (see article 69), published in a proclamation (*bando*) of September 15, 1783; and the royal circular order of November 11, 1787, which is cited in the foregoing order, is inserted in the *Gaceta de México* of April 22, 1788.⟩

29

In order that the same *junta superior* may establish with due understanding a general rule in regard to the administration and management of the said division [branch] in all the towns of the kingdom, it shall ask the intendants for as much information as it considers necessary.ᵃ Upon the examination of this it shall communicate its measures and resolutions to them by means of the general accountant of municipal finance, who shall be the secretary of the *junta* in everything respecting this separate division, and correspondence shall be conducted through him in so far as it may concern the same.

⟨ᵃ See article 6.⟩

30

In order that the said general accountant of municipal finance may perform properly the aforesaid duty of secretary of the *junta superior,* he must attend all the [meetings] which are held by it in order to treat of that which concerns the branch mentioned. When circumstances and necessity demand it, his chief assistant [whom] I completely qualify for this purpose, shall substitute for him. In order to avoid doubts and even disputes about the manner of attendance of the accountant at the meetings indicated, I command that he shall enter and attend them with his sword and hat; that he shall take his seat after the last member of the *junta,* on a chair without arms in case [the members] occupy those which have [arms] or are seated on benches with backs; that he shall be called *"merced"* by all the members, whether they be regular appointees or substitutes, and that without depriving him of the capacity of secretary of the general accountant, he shall have because of such [power] an informative vote. In the use thereof and of the knowledge of everything concerning the branch mentioned, which he may acquire through his office, he may and must explain to the *junta* orally when asked by that body, or any of its members, or of his own volition whatever he may consider conducive to the best results in the resolution which may be agreed upon notwithstanding the fact that he may as such accountant have done this already in writing in the case in hand. The same procedure is to be understood with regard to the chief assistant when he substitutes for his superior, except in the matter of his seat, for he shall take the same one which is by article 4 assigned to the notary of the superintendency of my royal treasury and its *junta superior.*

31

As soon as the intendants take possession of their offices they must ask each one of the Spanish cities, towns, and villages, and each of the Indian towns of their provinces for an exact account, signed by the justices and notaries of the *ayuntamiento,* wherever they exist, concerning the municipal finance, or the community funds which they enjoy, concerning the grant and origin of them, the perpetual or temporary dues that they pay, the necessary or extraordinary expenses to which they are subject, the surplus or deficit that occurs every year, and concerning the actual location and custody of, and the accounting for these funds. They shall order that the inferior judges and notaries shall be responsible for the certainty and exactness of this information.

32

Likewise in the capitals of the provinces, by their own efforts
or by means of their lieutenants, and in the remaining territories
and districts by the *alcaldes ordinarios* and subdelegates, the
intendants shall inform themselves very minutely concerning
the municipal taxes (*arbitrios*) which the towns possess, whether
they have royal power for this, for what motives and with what
purposes they were granted them, and whether the cause continues or has ceased. In the latter case or in one [in which] the
time of the concession and its extension, if such there be, may
have expired, they shall report to the *junta superior* in order
that such municipal taxes may be suppressed. They shall do the
same when these are still to subsist, first making investigation
whether it may be fitting to alter or change their imposition upon
different articles, so that the burden of the community may be
decreased.

33

After very careful examination of all the information mentioned in the two preceding articles, and of their supporting
documents, which the intendants shall require when they think
necessary, they must draw up a provisional ordinance (*reglamento*) for municipal finance or the community funds of each
town. They shall modify or exclude the items of expenditures
which seem to them exorbitant or superfluous, although these
may have been determined upon and permitted by former approved ordinances or regulations. They shall transmit [the or-
dinance] signed with the order that it shall be observed in all its
parts until [there may be] a new measure. They shall address a
copy of it, with the account given by the justices and the proper
report concerning the reasons and motives which they have had
in mind, to the *junta superior de hacienda,* so that with complete
knowledge of the subject that body may approve or modify it.

The said *junta* shall give account to me by the *vía reservada* in order that [the ordinance] may obtain my confirmation, or my sovereign pleasure may be determined.

Since it is not my royal will to vary the purposes which the laws of book 6, title 4, of the *Recopilación* give for the use of common funds of Indian towns, and in part they are very different from those which have been and must be given for the municipal finance of Spanish towns, I order that for the formation of the required ordinances, for mere Indian towns and their community funds, including their land-lease revenues, the thirty-eight laws of the above-mentioned book and title shall be observed, in so far as they may not be contrary to what is provided by this instruction.

34

In the special ordinances mentioned the parts concerning expenditure must be divided into four classes. The first [shall consist] of appropriations for traveling expenses assigned to justices, members, and subordinate officials of the municipal councils, and salaries of the public officials, namely, the doctor or surgeon where he is present, and the school teachers, who necessarily shall be appointed in all the Spanish and Indian towns of a sufficient number of inhabitants. The second [shall include] the returns of the *censos*, or other dues which legitimately shall be paid by the towns themselves, being imposed by royal authority or converted into a common fund, and their continuance being justified. The third [shall comprise] votive offerings from festivities and voluntary alms, and the fourth the necessary, or extraordinary and incidental, expenses which may not have a fixed quota. It is to be observed that for these last items the intendants shall assign the annual gratuity which may seem suitable according to the conditions and capacity of the towns. When [the amount] does not suffice they shall make it known [by giving] proof of the urgency and showing that the assigned funds have been exhausted. The intendants may issue warrants for the expenditure in Spanish cities and towns of not to exceed forty *pesos*, and in Indian towns twenty *pesos;* but if the sum should be greater they must report to the *junta superior* and await its decision.

35

When the aforesaid ordinances are approved by that body after the intendants remit them, the general accountant of municipal finance shall send them back, retaining a copy of each one in his office, and taking care that another must remain in the principal accounting-offices of the province. The originals shall be sent to the respective towns for their observance and prompt fulfillment, so long as nothing to the contrary is determined and ordered by me.

36

For this purpose there must be established in each Spanish city, town, or village, including the capitals of the provinces, a municipal *junta,* under the charge of which the administration and management of these matters must be placed.[a] It shall be composed of the *alcalde ordinario* [having] the first vote of seniority, who shall preside over it; of two councilmen (*regidores*), and of the attorney-general (*procurador-general*) or *síndico,* without a vote, in order to promote that which may be most useful to the community. Where there are more than two *regidores,* it is provided that they must alternate in this office year by year, with the purpose that they all shall be instructed concerning the importance of the office and concerning economic administration.

The corporation of the *ayuntamiento* may not intermeddle in this matter nor under any pretext embarrass the measures of their municipal *juntas,* since [these bodies] must put up for public auction annually the collectorships of the branches of municipal finance, as will be provided in the following article, in order to sell them to the highest bidder without allowing overbidding or other blameworthy procedure. In case of the lack of lessees [the *juntas*] shall administer the funds with proper integrity and legality.

⟨ᵃ This article is annulled by vote of the *junta superior* of January 9, 1805, in which it is declared that the subdelegates are the persons who must preside over municipal *juntas* and not the *alcaldes ordinarios*.⟩

37

Nothing is so important to the public interest as accuracy in the leasing of the revenues of the towns, and the greatest care concerning the public supplies (*abastos*), since the communities are interested that the former shall be auctioned at a just value, and that the second may possess the greatest advantage of prices. As it is indispensable to avoid the combinations and monopolies which usually occur within and outside of the *ayuntamientos*, the *intendant-corregidores* shall be vigilant concerning this, and take care that the municipal *juntas* which the preceding article establishes in the capitals of their provinces shall perform with fidelity and disinterestedness the obligation of being present with their lieutenant-assessor in the usual public place, or in the one which may be assigned [to them], in order to supervise and conduct the auctions of the revenues, also of the supplies, wherever these [branches] are established, after publishing [the sales of office] for thirty days and dispatching their legal notices (*avisos*) and summonses to the towns, as is fitting, and posting edicts, so that [the matter] may come to the attention of everybody. They may allow any bid and over-bids when assured of their free proffer, but the *regidores*, their relatives or intimate friends may not be connived with to the injury of the community, nor shall they by means of their authority make any profit from a decreased value of the taxes, or from any increase in the cost of that which must serve for the maintenance of the towns.

38

The intendants shall demand this same procedure of the other justices and municipal *juntas* of the cities, towns, and villages of their provinces, in order that the measure may be applied uniformly, and that the abuses which contribute to the decay of justice shall be suppressed. But if their orders and advice are not sufficient, they shall give account to the *junta superior de hacienda* and to my fiscal, included in it, concerning what may pertain to the municipal finances, and to the viceroy or commandant-general of the frontier respectively, in regard to that which may relate to the supplies, so that he may provide a remedy, and according to the cases punish those who may commit or conceal these injurious misdeeds.

39

Inasmuch as the municipal *juntas* mentioned may consider that the leases of the branches of municipal finance, in their entirety or in part, can be made more advantageously for a longer time than that of a year, they shall refer [the matter] to the intendant of province and, he, expressing the grounds and causes which he may have in order to make modifications in this matter, for which I grant him full faculties, must report to the *junta superior de hacienda,* but the contracts must not exceed five years.

40

The members of each municipal *junta* must appoint annually at their own account and risk a bonded steward (*mayordomo*) or receiver, who shall have charge of precisely all the funds of municipal finance, and of their exact account and calculation.[a] One and one-half per cent of that which he collects, not of the sums remaining on hand from one year to another, shall be assigned to him for his responsibility and work, with the indispensable proviso that the revenues must be placed monthly in the strongbox with the three keys, which latter must belong to the *alcalde-presidente* of the *junta*, to the clerk of the *ayuntamiento*, if there is one, or, in his lack, to the senior *regidor*, and to the steward of the revenues. For no motive may they intrust [the keys] to one another. It it to be understood that if on any day of the month the other two key-bearers may wish to propose to place in the strongbox, because of their importance or other reason, any funds in the possession of the steward it shall be done, and the said steward shall have no power to resist their request.

⟨[a] At present they give bonds under a decision of the *junta superior* of the year 1797. By this is meant the steward or depositor of the funds of municipal finance.⟩

41

At the end of the year the steward or depositor shall make up his report, restricting it to precisely the debit which may be shown from the leases of revenues and their collection, and to data concerning the special funds provided for in accordance with the regulation or with the later orders of the intendant or of the *junta superior*. [Each disbursal] must have been authorized by formal warrant of the towns, which must in turn hold lawful receipts from the persons interested. In order to facilitate the examination and approval of these accounts they must be drawn up by exact rule in conformity with the mode and method determined in the ordinances, and with the models which the general accounting-office must send with them by means of the intendant, according to article 35.

42

The steward must submit this annual account to the municipal *junta* some time during the month of January of the following year. If a balance shall result from his account, he shall deposit it in the strongbox of the three keys, in the presence of the members of the aforesaid *junta* and of the persons who shall compose the new *junta,* also of the steward or receiver who shall be appointed. After the accounting has been made, it shall be certified by a notary if one is present, and a formal attestation shall be added, which shall be signed by the members of the retiring *junta* declaring that the public revenues have produced no other proceeds. The *junta* shall then present this certificate to the town council in the presence of the advocate of the community, in order that said council may assent to or add to the account, to which it shall affix its decree of approval or its exceptions to any items. When [the report] is returned to the *junta* the latter shall without delay send the original with the supporting vouchers to the intendant, leaving in its archive complete copies of everything for the following administration, a memorandum of this being attached at the end of the aforesaid original.

43

With the account indicated, and the proper security, there must be sent also to the capital of the province subject to the order of the intendant the amount which, according to its credit and debit, shall remain as a surplus and shall be considered as cash on hand. Only that quantity shall be left in the treasury which the ordinance may permit for meeting the expenditures designated by it, until the first receipts or collection of the proceeds of the year are being made. This transaction [of transferring the funds] shall be completed by an authentic record set forth at the end of the above-mentioned account.

The intendant shall give order that these funds transmitted in this manner be received into the principal treasury of the province where, under proper account and calculation, they shall be kept entirely separate and guarded in a coffer which must be placed in the office cited, and be destined only for these public funds. This strongbox shall have three keys, one of which the intendant himself [shall possess] and the judges of the royal treasury, the accountant and treasurer [shall have] the other two. The latter official shall, under the supervision of the former, make up for each city, town, or village its regular account of that which belongs to it from the aforesaid funds and of what amount is being paid out from them under decisions of the *junta superior de hacienda,* and consequent orders of the intendant, for the purposes which article 47 of this instruction provides and for the other reasons for which such money shall be spent according to the laws which treat the matter;[5] he shall also indicate what sums pertain to the four and two per cent which article 51 mentions, since these latter sums must be taken and discounted from these funds on hand.

44

The Spanish subdelegates whom the intendants must appoint in the principal Indian towns indicated in article 12, for the purpose of attending to the direction and management of the lands and other property of their communities and of the remaining towns of their jurisdiction and cognizance, and for keeping custody, account, and calculation of the funds that these may produce annually, shall likewise observe rules similar to those which are provided for the municipal *juntas* mentioned. Since the aforesaid lands are worked either in common by the Indians of the respective community or state, in conformity with law 31, title 4, book 6, of the *Recopilación,* or, this law not being observed, are in whole or in part leased or administered with the other properties under control of the aforesaid inferior judges, who intervene directly with the native governors or *alcaldes* themselves, these said subdelegates shall take very particular care to collect these proceeds, place them in the local treasury of three keys established in the chief town where they reside, and

---

[5] *Recopilación,* leyes 4, 10, tit. 13, lib. 4.

draw up at the end of the year the certified account of the revenues and expenditures in the form provided, in orded to send it with the surplus fund, if there be any, to the intendant. They shall make evident by a document or a credible process the personal presence of the before-mentioned officials of the Indian community. In order that the latter may be informed for themselves as to the good regulation and security with which the proceeds from the common funds must be managed, the governor or *alcalde* and the senior *regidor* shall have the two keys of the coffer containing their funds. The third key must always remain in the possession of the Spanish judge and the said coffer must be kept in the domicile of the officials (*casas reales*) of the principal town of his residence, or in some other well protected place.

45

The examination and closing of these accounts shall be the duty of the principal accountants of province, whether they be [accounts] of municipal funds or those of Indian communities; and as soon as they receive them, the intendants shall transmit them to the aforesaid accountants with the proper decree in order that, if they find the accounts correct they may make a record of the fact and, with the approval and authorization of the intendants themselves, send them to the municipal *juntas* or to the subdelegate-judges of the towns; but if the aforesaid accountants find any revisions [necessary in the accounts] they shall attach them by using half-width sheets (*pliegos*) to the margin, expressing in each case the motives therefor. They shall transmit [the amended documents] to the municipal *junta* or to the subdelegate who sent them with the order to correct them within the time which the intendant shall designate, and with notice that if this is not done, the revised parts shall be excluded, and that action will be taken to recover the sums in question.

46

When the accounts are closed in one or other of the methods designated, the intendant shall send to the *junta superior de hacienda* an abstract of each one, certified by the principal accountant of his province, with a statement either concerning the branches [of municipal finance], their income, the expenses which they may have incurred, the funds that remain in the coffers, and [those which] are still due from debtors, and of the first or second contributors separately, or concerning the balance which the steward of the revenues may find so that in whatever cases may occur, the *junta superior* may act with sufficient information. If at any time [that body] should deem it proper that the general accounting-office of the branch [of municipal finance] should review these special accounts, it shall ask the intendant for them with the supporting records; it shall command that [the accounts] be returned after examination, so that they may be deposited in the archives with the other documents in the accounting-office of the province.

47

The amount which each town may possess as an annual surplus from the proceeds of municipal finance, or from the community funds, shall, after meeting the obligations determined in its special ordinance, be invested in the purchase of lands and the imposition of rents which, becoming sufficient for paying their public debts and providing for the communal necessities, will permit that the *arbitrios*, which always are burdensome to the public, be suppressed. In case there are no *arbitrios* nor *censos* to pay from the *propios* or community funds, the surplus mentioned shall be applied to encourage manufactures useful to the aforesaid towns and their provinces; such establishments being first proposed by the intendants and approved by the *junta superior* for any one of such investments.

48

Notwithstanding that the period of the concessions of some municipal taxes may have expired, the *junta superior de hacienda* may with just cause permit its continuation. Also it may do this in the cases of those established by common agreement, if the towns are well provided for thereby, or are obliged to tolerate them because of the lack of municipal funds. However, under these circumstances of failure of revenue to meet their obligations, the towns shall make it known to the *junta superior* by means of the intendant of their province, and shall propose a tax which may be less burdensome to their inhabitants so that, when the need is recognized, the concession may be granted. In either of the two cases the *junta* shall temporarily put into practice whatever it may determine, giving account to me by the *via reservada* of the Indies, in order that it may obtain my approval, or that I may decide what may be most to my sovereign pleasure.

49

All the documents concerning this branch [of finance] must be drawn up and formalized by the respective intendants of the district, whose orders the municipal *juntas* and the inferior justices shall obey without excuse or delay. In order that administrative measures may be more clear and expeditious, the intendants shall not issue them by means of notaries but by means of the principal accountants of the province, who shall write out the orders decided upon in view of the documents which must pass through their offices, because the accounts and papers in regard to this department must be deposited separately from others in the archives;[a] [the latter officials] must dispatch said orders without demanding dues, fees, or any other emoluments from interested parties.

⟨ a Orders of the intendants by means of accountants.⟩

50

When the municipal *juntas* and inferior justices shall consider themselves aggrieved by the measures of their respective intendants, although these may emanate from the *junta superior de hacienda,* which circumstance shall always be expressed in them whether it be in regard to the revision of accounts, the renewal of funds, the increase or the reduction of the items designated by the ordinances, the proposing of new taxes, or any other matter relative to the administration and control of these branches, they may make their appeals, with due moderation and proper proof, directly to the *junta superior* itself, or by the hand of the intendant of their province in order that, when it is informed concerning the grounds and causes which the offended persons explain, it may take the action it considers just.

51

Since, for an establishment of such importance and utility to the aforesaid towns, it is necessary that the intendants have the immediate and respective aid of the accountants and principal treasurers of their provinces, and the latter may have that of the subordinates needed to help them in the dispatch of what pertains to the said branch, and in keeping account and calculation of it according as each has been indicated, I command that from the total income of the municipal funds every year four per cent shall be deducted in the Spanish cities, towns, and villages just as is done in these kingdoms [in Spain], and only two per cent from the communal funds of Indian towns; and that the total amount shall, under the supervision of the chief accountants of the provinces, be deposited separately in the principal treasuries of the provinces, in order that from this fund traveling expenses and moderate salaries, which the intendants shall determine with the approval of the *junta superior,* may be paid to the accountants, treasurers, and officials; likewise that, clerical expenses [may be met] which are legitimately caused in the dispatch [of matters belonging] to the same branch. Monthly payment of each of these expenses must be preceded by a report which the accountants shall form concerning the first, and a certified account concerning the second which must follow, and the corresponding decree of the intendant at the end of all these.

52

The said principal treasurers of province must draw up annually the respective account concerning the proceeds and distribution of the four and the two per cent, showing the traveling expenses which have been assigned to them and to the chief accountants, for salaries of the officials appointed to dispatch [matters] of the branch mentioned, and for the office expenses which may have been caused in it. When the account has been examined and compared by the head accountant of the province with whatever annotations he may make, and after the intendant has placed his authorization on it, the latter shall send it to the general accounting-office of municipal funds in order that, when it is inspected in that office, the *junta superior de hacienda* shall be informed of the results, and with its approval issue the suitable certificate that the account is closed. The surplus that may remain after paying the expenses and salaries referred to shall be at the disposal of the aforesaid *junta superior* to meet the expenditures of the general accounting-office.

53

Also at the beginning of each year the intendants shall send to the *junta superior de hacienda* an individual statement, certified by the chief accountants of the province, which shall set forth what sums the revenues, municipal taxes, and community funds of all the towns of their districts contain, with a declaration of the incomes, imposts, and balances from them, the *censos* which may have been redeemed by composition, and the taxes (*arbitrios*) which may have ceased or have been granted again, in order that the aforesaid *junta* may command that concerning all moneys there shall be formed by the general accounting-office of these branches another general statement for each of the provinces and with the same distinctions. It shall submit this to my royal hands by the *vía reservada* of the Indies and to my supreme Council of the Indies, explaning to me at the same time whatever may occur to it for the general welfare of my vassals, and, from its experience in this matter, what it may find needing amplification or reform, in order to perfect the administration and management of public funds in that kingdom.

54

The faithfulness and uprightness of the clerks and notaries not only influence public affairs, but also the honor, life, and possessions of my vassals. Consequently they must be persons of good character, integrity, and pure motives. Everything fitting whereby they may perform the duties of their offices, and whereby the judicial records and papers under their care may be kept in safe custody, and all falsification, insertion, or omission may be avoided, is provided in the royal laws of these [Spanish] dominions and of those [of America].[6] This being the case the *intendant-corregidores* shall heed with special vigilance that in their provinces and districts the rules determined by the laws and *cédulas* already issued, or which shall be dispatched concerning this subject, shall be observed and kept inviolable, and they are admonished that they will be held responsible for any tolerance or negligence, and no excuses shall be accepted from them.

---

[6] *Recopilación*, tit. 8, lib. 5.

55

Likewise the intendants shall see that the pecuniary penalties and fines imposed by the *alcaldes ordinarios* and their subdelegates, whether they may pertain to my royal chamber of justice or to the public cause, shall not be concealed or misapplied. [They shall see] that an accurate account of this branch is kept, and that it conforms entirely with the provisions of the laws of the Indies[7] and the ordinances that treat of this matter. They shall correspond with the regents of the respective *audiencias* about it, since they are subdelegates of this branch in the district of the tribunal, according to article 57 of the instruction which, under date of June 20, 1776, was given them by me for the exercise of their duties.

56

Although, as is provided, the intendants must give account to the viceroy or to the general commandant of the frontier respectively, and to the higher tribunals of that kingdom, according to the nature of the cases and the difference of authority, concerning everything that occurs in this department worthy of remedy, at the same time I wish them to inform me by the *vía reservada* of the Indies concerning any serious matters that may arise and which they may think worthy of my royal attention. They must state whether they have rendered account, or not, to the said superiors and to the tribunals, and [must mention] the measures taken by them if any have been taken, in order that my decision may be communicated to them by the said *vía reservada*.

---

[7] *Recopilación*, ley 29, tit. 25, lib. 2.

DEPARTMENT OF POLICÍA

57

To the faithful administration of justice and the other matters provided in the preceding article, should be added the care of everything pertaining to police and the greater advantage of my vassals by such means as may secure an exact and local knowledge of that kingdom, and the desirable ends which I have sought by this ordinance. In order to facilitate them I command the intendants, by means of engineers of entire competence and intelligence, to make topographical maps of their provinces, on which their boundaries, mountains, forests, rivers, and lakes shall be marked and designated. The engineers whom [the intendants] commission for this purpose shall carry out their commands with as much accuracy, punctuality, and clearness as possible.

58

Through the said engineers and their individual reports [the intendants] shall inform themselves particularly and separately concerning the climate and quality of the lands which each province contains; concerning the natural productions in the mineral, vegetable, and animal kingdoms; concerning industry and commerce, external and internal; concerning their mountains, valleys, meadows, and pasture grounds; concerning the rivers that may be joined, enlarged, and made navigable; at how much cost [this may be done] and what advantages may result for that empire and for my vassals from doing so; where it shall be possible and convenient to open new canals useful for the irrigation of tillable lands, and to erect mills; in what condition their bridges are found, and concerning those which it is best to repair or reconstruct; concerning what roads may be improved and shortened to prevent roundabout journeys; concerning what measures must be taken for their security; in what places timber is found useful for the construction of vessels, or rare woods to trade in Europe; and concerning what ports are spacious enough to shelter ships, and which for the same [reason], it may be fitting to fortify for use or to close on account of harmful conditions; so that with these reports and the personal visitations of their provinces which the intendants must make, each one may be informed of the state of his territory, of the quality of the lands which it possesses, and of the means of improving them, in order to give me and my supreme Council of the Indies annually all the knowledge conducive to the preservation, development, and happiness of those dominions.

59

With all the solicitude and careful attention which justify my confidence in them [the intendants] themselves must seek, and by means of the subordinate judges ascertain the inclinations, manner of living, and customs of the inhabitants subject to their government, in order to correct and punish idle and troublesome persons who, far from serving for the good order and administration of the towns, cause disturbances and scandals, disfiguring by their vices and laziness the good appearance of the state and preverting well disposed individuals. It is not to be understood that under this pretext a case [based] on groundless accusations must be made, nor that [the intendants] may intermeddle in order to examine the manner of living, character, and domestic or private habits [of the people] for such a course of action cannot produce tranquility, good example, or wise public administration. This watchfulness must not be exercised to the injury of other citizens, since in this particular matter the vigilance and care that he who rules shall exercise must harmonize with the prudence which must also be inseparable from him.

60

With the intention indicated and in order that the virtues of the good may flourish, the intendants shall see that in the towns of their provinces vagabonds, or other people without employment and application to labor, shall not be permitted. They shall cause those [belonging to] this class, if they shall be capable and of the proper age for bearing arms or for seamanship, to be assigned to the fixed regiments of that kingdom, or to the service of warships and merchantmen which may come to their ports of the north and south, and in default of these, to public or royal works for the time that they may judge best according to the circumstances of the cases.

If they should be useless for these purposes, or beggars by profession, they shall cause them to be collected into permanent or temporary workhouses, where they may be employed in proportion to their strength. But when they are proved to be turbulent subjects, not dependable, and of bad manner of living, they shall impose upon them the penalties established by the laws of the Indies,[8] that is, subject them to the work of the mines or *presidios* in the manner of condemned criminals, or to those occupations that correspond to this and which are permitted by the said laws.

61

It shall be the worthy object, and the special duty of the intendants not only to encourage and extend in the territories of their respective districts most adaptable to it, the cultivation of the valuable *grana fina* or cochineal which formerly was raised in abundance in many provinces of that empire but today is confined to the province of Oaxaca, by effectively aiding the Indians who shall devote themselves to this very useful occupa-

---

[8] *Recopilación*, all the laws of tit. 4, lib. 7; ley 4, tit. 5, lib. 7; ley 10, tit. 8, lib. 7.

tion in order that they may trade freely in the aforesaid kingdom, or on their own account send it to Spain if they wish, as is permitted by law 21, title 18, book 4 of the *Recopilación;* but also they shall see that these natives and the other castes of the common people shall apply themselves preferably to the sowing and cultivation of hemp and flax, according to law 20 of the same book and title. If, in order to attain such important purposes, the intendants shall need to make distributions of royal lands or of private domain, I will grant them the power whereby they may do this, but they must give account with vindication [of their action] to the *junta superior de hacienda.* But it must be understood that, with respect to the landed properties of individuals, only those which, on account of indolence or the absolute incapacity of the owners [to work them], are left uncultivated [may be so reapportioned] and the *junta* shall arrange that their value must be paid from the public funds. In regard to unoccupied or royal lands it shall be done without injury to the community property and the commons (*exidos*) which, according to the laws,[9] each town or municipal organization shall necessarily have. The lands of the second class cited shall be allotted by the intendants in pieces of ground suitable for married Indians who do not have them in their own right or that of their wives, under the condition that such allotments may not be transferred, in order that the children and descendants of such Indians, of both sexes, may succeed to them.

Since it is my royal will that all the natives shall enjoy an adequate endowment of landed property, and that the lands apportioned for the purposes provided, whether bought with public funds, or waste or royal lands, shall pass [into the control] of those who desire them, whether they be Indians or members of the other castes; but they shall have only the right of possession (*dominio útil*) since the direct ownership is reserved for my royal crown and for the public funds respectively,

[9] *Recopilación,* leyes 7, 13–14, tit. 7, lib. 4.

the intendants must be careful that both races cultivate them for their own profit, and they shall make them realize and understand how much advantage and utility will result to them from this pious measure of mine. Those who do not apply them-selves to using properly the lands allotted to them shall have them taken away (as I command to be done without hesitation) and given to others who will obey my order.

62

Likewise it shall be very fitting that [the intendants] try to encourage the large crops of cotton which are raised in all hot and temperate countries, and the wild silk that is produced in the mountains of Misteca and other places of that kingdom. In order that this product, and the coarse and the fine-washed wool, treated of in law 2, title 18, book 4, of the *Recopilación,* and raw and spun hemp and flax may be brought to Spain as raw materials of much utility for national commerce and manufac-ture, I grant them all the same freedom from export and import duties as is enjoyed by the cotton of my dominions of America.

63

With similar attention and care, and by whatever means pos-sible, the *intendant-corregidores* must cause the landholders and natives of their provinces, after availing themselves of the run-ning and underground waters for the irrigation and fertility of the lands, to promote agriculture and the sowing of grains, especially that of wheat, and aid these by exemption from royal dues which are levied upon flour in its transportation from Vera Cruz and the other ports of that kingdom. [They shall provide] the farmers, in proportion to their means with horned and wool-producing cattle for working and cultivating their estates, and see that they apply themselves to raising mules and excellent horses, of use for my royal service, and also to the increase of horned cattle. Likewise, with special vigilance they shall maintain the preservation of the forests and woods. Most of all, they shall devote themselves to the protection of industry, mining, and commerce, as [they are] the branches which directly contribute to the wealth and happiness of those dominions of mine [in America] and these [of Spain].

64

Likewise the intendants shall see that all the judges and subdelegates of their provinces repair the bridges well, and mend the public roads of their respective districts for the public welfare, and that they do not permit the farmers to interfere with them by placing their milestones and landmarks for this purpose. The [judges] shall punish offenders with suitable fines and penalties, besides obliging them to make amend for the injury at their own expense. If they shall need greater widening [of roads], new bridges, or highways to facilitate travel, they shall give account with sufficient proof to the intendants in order that, after the latter inform the *junta superior de hacienda,* what is fitting may be decided, in case that the towns of the territory where these works or repairs shall be made cannot bear the cost [of them], according as law 53, title 3, book 3 of the *Recopilación* provides.

65

The intendants shall also see that, for the greater convenience of travelers, the justices of their territory shall cause to be set up, in all the places where two or more roads or paths meet, a raised and permanent signpost with a placard which reads, "road to such and such a place," in order that those who may pass by, either coming or going, may go on with certain knowledge and without misgiving of losing their way. For the same reason it must be mentioned on the placard whether the highways are for beasts of burden or for carriages.

Inasmuch as through a noticeable and damaging abandonment, the use has almost disappeared in New Spain of carriages with two wheels and of the long narrow carts which were very common, and which facilitated the transportation of goods, merchandise, and products at moderate prices, the intendants shall apply themselves with the greatest attention to encourage the reestablishment of cart-transportation in their provinces. They must be equally heedful that the subordinate judges devote themselves also to this important matter, and promote it among the *hacendados* and the inhabitants of their particular jurisdictions.

66

Since travelers are also discommoded by the lack of inns and what is needed in them, the *intendant-corregidores* must, according to law 18, title 2 of book 5, and law 1, title 17 of book 5 of the *Recopilación* of the Indies, see that in all the towns and places of travel there shall be inns and lodging houses of sufficient capacity, with an adequate store of provisions, clean beds, and other things, necessary for the proper entertainment, comfort, and ease of travelers at as low a cost as possible, so that without charging them excessively innkeepers may be repaid for their care, expenditure, and outlay for supplies. In order that there may be hotels and taverns in the necessary places of travel where they do not exist, [the intendants] shall inform the *junta superior de hacienda,* and this [body] shall decide that they be built with the surplus from municipal funds, or by assessment of costs among those who receive the benefit according to law 1, title 16, and law 7, title 15 of book 4 of the *Recopilación.*

67

The *intendant-corregidores* shall themselves, with great vigilance and by means of the subordinate judges of each town, see that the provincial *alcaldes* or those of the *Santa Hermandad* and its mounted police where they exist, fulfil exactly the obligation which the laws impose upon them of inspecting the country and forests in order to keep the roads safe and the commerce of travelers free. For this purpose [the intendants] shall warn them under the proper penalties and [hold them] responsible for whatever violent attack or robbery may be committed within their districts, if they themselves or their mounted guards do not visit frequently the highways and uninhabited places in order to prevent [these evils]. The intendants shall proceed in this [matter] with the vigilance which common safety requires, and effectively aid the judges of the tribunal of *La Acordada* which is established in that kingdom [to deal with] thieves and other public transgressors.

68

With similar care the intendants shall provide that the justices of all the towns of their provinces shall take great pains to keep them clean and beautified, and see that the streets are level and paved; also that they shall not permit lack of symmetry in buildings that may be newly erected, in order not to disfigure their public appearance, especially in the populous Spanish cities and towns. If any edifice or private house should threaten to fall into ruins, they shall oblige their owners to repair them within a suitable time, which they shall assign to them. If they do not do this the intendants shall command that it be done at the cost of the said owners.

Likewise when [public] works and new houses are constructed or old ones are torn down, they shall see that the streets are kept wide and straight, and the plazas as large as possible. In the same manner if the proprietors of houses that are in ruins do not rebuild them, [the intendants] must oblige them to sell their plots of ground at a just appraisement, in order that the purchasers may put this measure into effect. In the case of entails, ecclesiastical possessions, or other permanent foundations, their income shall be held judicially in trust until a new imposition [of taxes].

69

The intendants shall see that the houses in Indian towns are built in good style. They must take care that royal buildings, wherever they may exist, those of the community, and other edifices are kept in repair. With respect to large Spanish towns the intendants must show similar solicitude, and they shall provide that the capitals [of provinces] be inclosed within walls, as this facilitates very much their better government, public administration, and protection. For this [work] they shall propose to the *junta superior de hacienda* the means which they consider least burdensome to the communities, in case there are not sufficient funds from the surplus of municipal finance, so that it may decide upon proper measures, or, according to the circumstances of the case, consult me.

70

Likewise the intendants shall take heed that in none of the towns under their command any church or other public building shall be constructed until drawings of their plans, of their façades, and courts have first been presented to them in order that, after submitting these to the *junta superior,* this [body] may have them examined by engineers or architects. When [the plans] are corrected by these men in so far as is required and is conducive to the greater stability and durability of the work, as well as to its beauty, proper arrangement, and in other respects as they may professionally advise, [the architects] shall also suggest the means which they may judge most suitable for the attainment of the projects formed, with regard to the expense that they may desire to incur, or which the persons or divisions [of finance] are able to bear which pay the cost of them, after which the approval of the aforesaid *junta* shall be obtained.

Since, as is generally observed, there is total neglect of the repair of churches, whereby a considerable burden falls upon my royal treasury, as much through not attending to these repairs promptly as because it is almost always necessary for [the treasury] to defray the great expenses inevitable in such cases because the dues from burial and other [ecclesiastical rites] which by canonical laws are assigned for the material construction of temples and matters relating thereto such as for the dwellings of priests, wherever they exist, are not administered and employed as is fitting—[since this is so] the intendants shall with the advice of the ordinary justices of their district devote themselves to inspecting and regulating this important matter, in order that what is proper may be done in regard to it, and take care to aid opportunely with the funds indicated the rebuilding which the said edifices may need.

71

Every four months the *intendant-corregidores* shall give account, respectively to the viceroy or to the commandant-general of the frontier, and to the intendant-general of army, concerning the scarcity or abundance of the products which there may be in their provinces, and concerning their current prices in order that, with specific information concerning the condition of the provinces in this respect, and uniting the duties of my service and of the public welfare which are under the care of each one, they may by common consent and at an opportune time, provide for the supply of their necessities, or for the production and commerce (which must always be free) of their surplus commodities, to the end that the farmers, encouraged by the increase of prices, may not decrease sowings nor abandon their useful occupations.

72

The [intendants] must inquire about the condition of the public granaries (*pósitos*) of the capital and other towns of their provinces where they have been established. If they shall find them in disuse or abolished, they mush investigate the reason and order that they be restored, maintained, and administered according to their ordinances. But if there are no such regulations they shall draw them up in conformity with the laws regarding the purposes of their establishment which are well explained in law 11, title 13, book 4 of the *Recopilación* of the Indies. They shall then submit [the new ordinances] to the viceroy or to the commandant-general of the frontier with the information which they may think convenient in order that, after the opinion of the *acuerdo* of the *audiencia* of the territory is expressed concerning them, he may correct them if they need this, approve them temporarily, and in the same manner command that they be put into effect until my confirmation is obtained in consultation with my supreme Council of the Indies, to which tribunal the viceroy himself, or the commandant-general as the case may be, shall send [the ordinances] for this purpose.

73

In ªconsideration of the advantages which accrue to the principal cities and towns from having public granaries (*alhóndigas*) in them for public supplies, and in order to remedy the abuses that hucksters and retailers [middlemen] of wheat, flour, and other grains cause, I authorize the *intendant-corregidores* to establish these storehouses in the large towns for the use of the communities, if they think best. I [also command] them to draft ordinances suitable for their control and administration according to law 19, title 14, book 4 of the *Recopilación* of the

Indies, and send them with the proper report to the viceroy or to the commandant-general of the frontier.

After [the ordinances] are examined by the *acuerdo* of the *audiencia* of the district in its turn so that it may regulate them in whatever may be required, and when they are temporarily approved as the law cited provides, the former or the latter official shall order them put into effect as amended. He shall then send them to my supreme Council of the Indies so that, after I have been consulted about them, my royal confirmation may be obtained, or [that body] may order what it considers best. The intendants must investigate the actual condition of the public granaries already founded, if they exist in some towns, and cause their ordinances to be observed exactly, or revise them, and in the manner provided submit them for my sovereign approval if they lack this necessary confirmation.

⟨ª Granaries.⟩

74

The proper title and ratio of money are of interest to society and to the state, and as this is therefore a matter which deserves the first consideration, I command the *intendant-corre-gidores*, [either] themselves or by means of their lieutenants and subordinate judges, to take heed constantly that the gold and silver coins which are current in those dominions of mine may not be defaced or counterfeited, and that the precious metals which the mines and placers produce may not be falsified. For the purposes expressed, and with the assistance of a notary who shall certify to them and to their results, the intendants shall make as many investigations and charges as they may think fitting; they shall also cause as many customary visitations of silversmith's shops, stores, and other public workshops as may be convenient.

DEPARTMENT OF FINANCE

75

The duties which the *intendant-corregidores* must perform in their provinces have been explained in general, as have those which they shall cause the subordinate judges thereof to fulfil in the administration of justice and political and economic control, on which depend the development and happiness of the towns. They shall keep the following rules in regard to the third department under their cognizance, which pertains to my royal treasury.

76

The general management of my royal revenues, which are already or shall be established within the area of the aforesaid kingdom, and that of as many revenues as may pertain now and always to my royal treasury whatever form they may have, shall hereafter be under the exclusive supervision and cognizance of the intendants, with all that is subsidiary, dependent, and connected therewith, regardless of whether the branches are administered for my account, or may be leased, or placed under the system of collection by contract with political entities. I order and declare furthermore that the contentious jurisdiction, granted by law 2, title 3, book 8 of the *Recopilación* to treasury officials for the collection of revenues and the funds of the branches of my royal treasury, must be understood to be wholly conveyed and transferred to the intendants in their respective provinces,[a] to the absolute exclusion of the judges of the royal treasury who must restrict themselves to this simple title hereafter, especially those of accountant and treasurer, although they shall always be subject as hitherto to bonds and to the joint responsibility in regard to whatever applies to them, and they shall be subordinate to these new magistrates as their immediate chiefs and superiors.[b]

The obligation however, which today resides in the treasury officials, of administering and collecting what belongs to the branches of my royal treasury under their charge, shall continue in the care of the aforesaid officials, and they shall exercise all the coactive economic powers conducive to good administration and collection, with the difference that in the cases in which it may be necessary to proceed judicially against debtors to the treasury, they must try them and prosecute the claims as representatives of my royal exchequer before the proper intendant or subdelegates,[c] in order that in the use of the jurisdiction which is declared theirs [the latter] may issue suitable orders according to law.

⟨[a] Many doubts concerning the terms in which the coactive power mentioned in this article must be understood have been set forth in numerous *expedientes;* decisions on them were rendered by the *junta superior* and his Majesty approved them in the royal *cédula* of November 20, 1796.   [b] See articles 88 and 145.   [c] Also see article 118 in which administrators of revenues are discussed.⟩

77

Therefore,[a] in order that this may be done and the orders and provisions of the intendants relative to this department and that of war may be executed in all the area of this province by duly authorized persons, the intendants shall, in the capitals of the political and military governments which still exist (except those of Yucatan and Vera Cruz) as well as in the other inferior cities and towns of numerous inhabitants, and more especially where there is a royal treasury, even though it be merely a branch office, appoint subdelegates for disputed matters only, in the two departments (causes) mentioned.

It is to be understood that in the capitals and districts of the governments mentioned, the said subdelegation [of powers] must devolve upon the governors themselves, as is provided by article 10,[b] and that in the places indicated and in their respective territories it must not in any case devolve upon the *alcaldes ordi-*

narios,[c] much less upon the accountants or treasurers or other administrators of any branches of my treasury; but it must be intrusted to private individuals of the best reputation, and of the necessary qualifications, after information concerning them [is obtained] from persons who. can give it with proper knowledge. Wherefore I declare that the military governors as subdelegates of the respective intendants must be subordinate to them, and that the powers of the said subdelegates and of those which are by article 12 ordered established with reference to the two departments mentioned, shall extend only to the faculty of drawing up or receiving summaries from subordinate clerks of my revenues and preparing the same for judicial decision, in which form they must be submitted to the intendant of the province, in order that, with the advice of his assessor, he may pronounce that which is justly fitting.

⟨[a] See articles 145 and 12. [b] This seems contrary to article 12. [c] The governors of the New Kingdom of León and Santander, by virtue of this article are placed in the condition of subdelegates of the intendants of San Luis Potosí in that which pertains to the departments of finance and economy of war, as also do those of Coahuila and Texas, by the superior order of December 1, 1789, which his Majesty approved by the royal order of July 6, 1790.⟩

78

With regard to the exercise of jurisdiction over civil and criminal litigation in the affairs and business concerning my revenues, the intendants must take cognizance exclusively, with absolute prohibition of all other magistrates,[a] tribunals, and *audiencias* of that kingdom, except only the *junta superior de hacienda.*[b] They shall also decide all cases in which my treasury may have some interest or might receive injury, or which belong to any one of its branches and revenues which may be administered or leased, both with respect to collections and also all their incidentals;[c] so that none of the intendants, including the intendant of Mexico for that province, may permit any recourse or appeal by litigants, except to the said *junta superior,* in the cases and matters in which such action is appropriate; nor may this body admit recourse or appeal from its own resolution save only to my royal person by the *vía reservada* of the Indies.[9] It must be observed that the superintendent-subdelegate must not be present when a measure which he has issued as intendant of the province under his immediate care is being discussed on appeal in the *junta;* neither shall the assessor of the superintendency [of the treasury] attend if the decision has been pronounced upon his advice. In such cases another judge, from the tribunal of accounts, may meet with the aforesaid *junta.*

⟨[a] See article 145. [b] Royal order of January 20, 1778; it is the fourth of those collected by Señor Beleña. [c] The credits of the treasury enjoy the privilege of judicial attraction, even in universal judgments, although the persons concerned enjoy the privilege of the *fuero.* The royal order of September 19, which inserts the decree of the same date, is conclusive and decisive.⟩

79

[a]Although the revenues from tobacco, *alcabalas, pulque* powder, and playing cards are to continue to be controlled exclusively in New Spain by the superintendent-subdelegate of my royal treasury and by the officials whom I have appointed for their better administration and management, I command that the intendants shall in their respective provinces, whether themselves or through their subdelegates, take cognizance in first instance of all cases and contentious matters which may arise in the aforesaid branches, allowing appeals to the *junta superior de hacienda* according as is determined for them and for other officials of my royal treasury. Consequently it is to be understood that what is ordered in this matter by special ordinances concerning the said revenues is annulled. In regard to administrative and economic matters concerning them, the intendants shall aid as much as possible all measures which the superintendent-subdelegate or the respective general managers may

[9] This cannot be done now except through the Council of Orders [*sic*]; according to the royal order of January 11, 1791.

promulgate, by maintaining proper relations with those [officials] concerning whatever may come up in this connection.

⟨ᵃ For the understanding of this article the *junta superior* declared in a vote of July 3, 1788, that the decision of any point of justice in matters concerning the treasury, even though there is strictly speaking no contradiction of the declaration of the court, is the exclusive right of the justices. See also the circular concerning the *alcabalas* of January 29, 1790, and article 6 of the proclamation of October 11, 1788. In explanation of this article it was declared by the *junta superior de real hacienda* of October 4, 1787, with the approval of his Majesty in the royal order of June 11, 1788, that the securities of the *alcabalas* and their incidentals belong to the administration of the branch, as an economic and gubernatorial matter.⟩

80

ᵃIn order to prove fully and pass sentence in cases of fraud which may occur against the said rents of tobacco, *alcabalas*, *pulque,* powder, playing cards, and other revenues which pertain to my royal treasury, and in order to impose the confiscations and fines, the intendants and their subdelegates shall, in the part which respectively belongs to them, observe punctually the rules determined in the special ordinances and instructions of each branch, as well as in the *reglamento* or guide (*pauta*) dated July 29, 1785, formed by the general accountant, which I approved and ordered observed by my royal *cédula* of February 21 of the present year [1786].¹⁰ They shall impartially impose upon smugglers and defrauders the penalties established in the ordinances and instructions indicated and in the royal laws, for the purpose of checking and correcting this class of delinquents, for they are common enemies as usurpers of the funds of the state, which are intended for the benefit, use, and defense of all vassals.ᵇ

⟨ᵃ Confiscations. This has been added to, as far as the guide for confiscations is concerned, by the royal order of April 21, 1786, transcribed on the last sheet of the aforesaid guide. ᵇ See articles 139 and 240.⟩

---

¹⁰ The *cédula* and the *reglamento* which are cited are found in Appendix, number 9, of the original.

81

[a]The intendants shall also be the sole judges in any cases that may arise within the area of their provinces concerning sales, compositions, and distributions of the royal lands or private domains. The owners and those who seek new landgrants shall allege their rights and make their petitions before the said intendants in order that, after these papers are drawn up legally by an advocate of my royal treasury whom they shall appoint, they shall decide them according to law with the advice of their ordinary assessors; and they shall permit appeals to the *junta superior de hacienda*, or, if those interested do not enter any recourse, [the intendants] shall give account to the *junta* with the original proceedings when they judge them to be in condition to issue a title, so that when the proceedings are reviewed by that body, it shall return them or issue the said title if there be no objection; or, if correction does occur, before issuing it, command them to do the things which are noted as being deficient and ordered done.

By means of this process they may obtain without new difficulties the proper confirmations, which the aforesaid *junta superior* shall give in due time. This body must act in the matter, as must also the intendants, their subdelegates, and other officials, according to what is provided in the royal instruction of October 15, 1754,[11] in so far as the said instruction is not contrary to the present rule—and without disregarding the wholesome provisions of the laws which are cited herein, and law 9, title 12, book 4 of the *Recopilación*.

⟨[a] This article is changed by the royal *cédula* of March 23, 1798. See the additions to this same article in its corresponding manuscript, or in the *Gaceta de México*, number 11, of October 22, 1798.⟩

---

[11] See Appendix, number 10, in the original.

82

The intendants must not intermeddle in cases concerning confiscation of estates situated in their provinces, of which my viceroy, commandant-general of the frontier, the *audiencias*, or other tribunals shall take cognizance, without a special commission or order from them while the properties mentioned are held sequestered. But if they shall be confiscated on account of a sentence that was commanded to be executed, it shall be the special duty of the intendant to take action for the alienation and collection of their income, also to take cognizance of all the petitions and lawsuits which may afterward arise concerning the confiscated properties. For this purpose my *fiscales* shall draw up for them an authentic instrument in regard to seizures, in order that they may provide for the collection in accordance therewith. The intendants shall always be subordinate to the superintendent-subdelegate of my royal treasury, or to the *junta superior* thereof, if the case on account of its nature pertains thereto, in conformity with the declarations in this instruction.

83

Likewise the intendants shall take cognizance of cases concerning prizes, shipwrecks, vessels seeking refuge, and unclaimed property of any kind, for the purpose of making investigations and for making collections and applying these to my royal treasury, after taking the necessary measures prescribed by law and giving an account to me by the *vía reservada* of the Indies, in order that I may thereby inform the proper tribunals, so that they may communicate to the aforesaid intendants the decisions which may be fitting.

84

In like manner the fulfillment of my royal *cédulas*, which may be sent to any judge of revenues, and of the orders, patents, and dispatches issued in their favor, belongs to the special duty of the intendants, in order that [such *cédulas*] may be put into effect; so also does the duty of seeing that the prerogatives and privileges which pertain to them on account of their positions shall be observed for all the subordinate officials and employees of the respective revenues.

They shall command the subordinate judges of their provinces to observe and fulfil these strictly. They may entreat and demand, if it shall be necessary in my royal name, the captains-general, governors, and commandants of my troops to give authority and aid to their measures; for it is my royal intention that they shall favor the said measures promptly with the greatest activity so that they may have due effect, and that the injurious consequences may be avoided which might result to my royal interests from any dispute, embarrassment, or delay in lending these aids, by obstructing the course of measures useful to my service.

85

For the same purpose it is also my sovereign will that, if any case occurs which concerns the defense of their special competence in the two departments of finance and war on account of impediment or conflict which any other tribunal may cause, the intendants shall report this to the *junta* mentioned so that with its superior authority it may correct the situation and put into effect provisionally whatever it may decide. It shall give account to me by the *vía reservada* in order that I may approve its action, or take fitting measures for the better direction of matters concerning my royal interests.

Therefore, for this purpose and that of providing my vassals with prompt remedy for any grievances which they may experience in the revenues and affairs relating to the two departments cited, I grant the aforesaid *junta* the necessary jurisdiction and powers, to take cognizance of, briefly and summarily with the

hearing of my fiscal, and decide cases appealed from the intendants. When its measure is passed it shall advise me thereof by
sending the proceedings, if any of the litigants should demand
this. But when there may be conflict or doubt about the powers
of the said *junta superior de hacienda,* the viceroy shall decide
it according to the exact spirit of this instruction, and that which
he may decide shall also be put into effect temporarily, and
account be given me by the *vía reservada* of the Indies.

86

In order to avoid causing conflict of jurisdiction concerning
the privilege (*fuero*) that belongs to judges and subordinate
employees of my royal treasury, I declare, since it is inherent
in the rank and honors which are granted to intendants of army
and to those of province by article 302 of this instruction, that
they all must possess, and their wives, children, and servants
shall enjoy, the military privileges (*fuero*) in the cases and with
the exceptions with which it is granted by the various articles
of titles 1, 2, and 11 of treatise 8 of the General Ordinances of
the Army dated October 22, 1768, and by later declarations[11]
to soldiers, their wives, children, and servants.

The *junta superior de hacienda,* to which I grant the necessary jurisdiction and powers for this, and which it may subdelegate to the persons whom it may consider fitting for [giving]
evidence in the cases, shall have cognizance exclusively in first
instance concerning civil and criminal lawsuits [of persons having the military privilege], with appeals to my royal person by
the *vía reservada* of the Indies. Likewise it may take cognizance
of their wills according to article 20 of the before-cited title 11,
and subdelegate this power for such hearing in such cases and
for such persons as it sees fit; with the proviso that all matters
and cases relative to the intendants which may arise from the

---

[11] See Appendix 11 of the original for the articles of the military ordinances and declarations mentioned.

ordinary royal jurisdiction and from the department of general administration of which they shall have charge as *corregidores,* must be understood to be excluded from the aforesaid military privilege; for in regard to these matters that which is provided by article 6 of this instruction must be observed.

87

Likewise, I declare that inasmuch as the functions of commissaries of war are granted by virtue of article 282, to the general accountant and treasurer, also to the chief treasury officials of provinces and to those outside of the capitals, with their prerogatives and uniforms, they all must and shall therefore enjoy the military privilege in the precise terms expressed by the preceding article. Also officials and other subordinates who may be employed or retired on salary, whether in the treasury and the general accounting-office of the army in Mexico City or in the principal provincial ones, since they must exercise military functions in their districts, shall likewise enjoy this privilege.

The respective intendants, since they are the natural political and military chiefs, shall have exclusive cognizance in first instance of all their civil and criminal cases, providing that they shall not lose the aforesaid [military] *fuero;* also [they shall take cognizance] of their wills according to article 19, title 11, treatise 8 of the ordinances cited, with appeal from their measures to the *junta superior de hacienda* and from those of that body to my royal person.

In order to remove every cause for conflict concerning the cognizance of matters which may relate to any of the persons for whom the military privilege is declared by this article and the foregoing one, I command that what is determined by my royal *cédula* of April 3, 1776,[12] shall be observed exactly and to

---

12 See Appendix 12 of the original for the article of the military ordinances which has been cited.

the letter, and that in the cases in which the said *cédula* orders
that the Council of War shall be consulted, this shall be done
(on account of the distance across the sea, and even when conflicts may occur between any of my royal *audiencias* and the
aforesaid *junta superior*) in the same manner and for the same
purpose by command of my viceroy of Mexico before another
junta which he shall form [instead of the Council of War] and
over which he shall preside in his apartment. The intendant-
general of army and the regent of that pretorian *audiencia* shall
also be members of the said *junta,* and it shall decide, by a
plurality vote and according to the *cédula* mentioned, the case
or doubtful matter about which it may be consulted, since I
grant it sufficient authority, jurisdiction, and powers for this.

88

[a]All the other judges and subordinates employed in the management, administration, and protection of my royal revenues
shall enjoy the inactive privilege (*fuero pasivo*) of treasury
officials only in civil and criminal matters and cases growing
out of or concerning their positions. Consequently I declare
that as a general rule in all lawsuits of this kind the intendants,
under whose command [these officials] shall serve, shall be sole
judges and as such have cognizance; but in common crimes,
general actions, measures of administration and good government, agreements and private business of the judges and subordinates referred to, they remain subject to the ordinary royal
jurisdiction.[b]

In those cases in which the intendants, either themselves or
through their lieutenants, shall proceed as *corregidores* against
employees of the revenues, it is to be observed that this shall be
done with subordination to the *audiencia* of the territory, to which
they shall allow appeals of litigants. [c]In those suits in which
they shall act in the capacity of intendants in matters of the

revenues or details concerning them, they shall do this only under the *junta superior de hacienda*, to the absolute exclusion of other tribunals. I command the former and the latter officials to maintain reciprocally the good relations which are fitting for my royal service, and that with good faith the matters pertaining to their respective cognizance shall be submitted to each other according to this instruction. It must be understood that otherwise they will incur my royal displeasure.

⟨ª What is provided in this article is ordered to be understood as applying to employees and subordinate officials of the powder revenues, by royal order of May 18, 1792, in which the doubt presented by the *junta superior* about the suit against Miguel Algarin, an employee in the branch of powder, for the payment of a debt, was decided. In the royal order of June 8, 1804, it is declared that notaries of the royal treasury do not enjoy the privilege which this article grants. ᵇ See article 91. ᶜ The circular concerning *alcabalas* of January 13, 1781, and articles 76, 77, and 91 must be borne in mind.⟩

89

ªIf, for the prosecution of cases or for other purposes of my service, the ordinary royal jurisdiction should need the declarations or reports of subordinate officials of my royal revenues, whether they may enjoy the military privileges or may have only those of a minister of the treasury, the judge must first apply in writing to the intendant concerned and his order must be obtained so that the declaration may be acquired legally and without difficulty; this written request need not be sent, but shall indeed be dispensed with in criminal cases arising from overt acts; and in other judicial actions in which the proper administration of justice might thereby be put in jeopardy, [the request] shall also be deferred until after the steps shall have been taken which secrecy demands. Thereupon, the request shall be sent to the intendant, to the end that my royal service may be cared for as circumstances require.

The same procedureᵇ shall be observed reciprocally by the intendants whenever their jurisdiction may require that subordinates of the ordinary royal jurisdiction should make declaration or give judicial information, with the distinction of cases that has been indicated. But in extrajudicial matters all shall be obliged, without waiting for the order of their superior, to give in good faith the information which may be asked by another official for his administration; with the proviso that when, in the cases which come up before the ordinary royal jurisdiction, under the circumstances herein prescribed, it may be necessary to take declarations from judges or subordinates who in conformity with articles 86 and 87 enjoy the military privilege, or when it is necessary to ratify those which they have given, the notaries must go to do this at said officers' homes even when [such notaries] are members of the chamber of justice of any of my royal *audiencias* or *chancillerías*, for this I have determined and commanded as general rule in the royal order of October 30, 1773.

⟨ª The circular of this superior government of February 19, 1803, commands that this article and the following one shall be observed, and provides that when the crimes of the employees are trifling the arrests that are imposed upon them shall merely be confinement within the precinct of the city or to their homes, without prejudice to their obligations in the regular hours [of work].

ᵇ Concerning this matter there is also the royal order of July 14, 1790, in which the provisions in the ordinances of tobacco, in this Ordinance of the Intendants, and the practice in Spain is ordered observed, namely, that they cannot be made prisoners for debts. The reason for this is that in order to pay them they cannot do so in any other manner than with a third or a fourth part of their salaries. For there could be no percentage deducted [from their salaries] however much these might be if they were taken prisoners, hence [the practice] originated that they should be restricted if at all to their homes or to the capital without ceasing to perform their duties.⟩

90

In suits and cases in which judges and subordinate officials of the direction, administration, and protection of my royal treasury are subject to the cognizance of the ordinary royal jurisdiction under the preceding articles, they cannot be arrested by that jurisdiction without a report thereon being made before or afterward, according to the different cases explained in article 89 concerning declarations, to their immediate superiors, so that these may put other individuals in their places and that my royal service may not be endangered; or, for this purpose, what is ordered by article 93 may be observed, if circumstances demand.

91

[a]I wish and command also that all employees in the direction, administration, and preservation of my revenues shall be exempted from and relieved of public and municipal offices in order that they shall not be occupied by them or be distracted from their duties, which they must attend to punctually and properly. But this exemption must not be extended to the royal and municipal fees which shall originate on account of their persons, estates, contracts, rents, or the lawful commerce which they may have and enjoy beside their salaries. Likewise I desire that whatever other immunities and prerogatives may belong to them respectively, and may be granted them by the ordinance or special instruction of the branch in which they serve, may be observed for the aforesaid employees.

⟨[a] Law 14, title 1, book 5 of the *Recopilación de Castilla* exempts married men from the duties of public councils for the first four years. This article and 88 in regard to commerce, trade, and profits of employees are annulled by the royal order of August 4, 1794. It appears with other *cédulas* relative to the matter in the *expediente* marked F. P. N. 15, sheet 1ª, law 1ª, and with the court decisions (*autos acordadas*) 2 and 4, title 14, book 6.⟩

92

Likewise it is my will that neither the ordinary judges nor any others shall prevent persons employed in safeguarding my royal treasury from using any offensive and defensive weapons which have not been expressly prohibited by my special orders and the decrees (*bandos*) of that government [of New Spain], because it is always understood that they are acting officially as do the other judges and ordinary bailiffs (*alguaciles*). For I am confident that the intendants, under whose order they serve, will not permit them to use daggers, poniards, or knives, these being prohibited as dangerous and highly prejudicial to public safety. They shall also seriously admonish subordinates not to misuse other weapons by making a show of them. The intendants shall correct and punish those who disobey their orders concerning this matter, for that which is granted them on account of their positions in order to fend off or restrain defrauders must not be used to intimidate those who are not such, nor to scandalize the public.

93

[a]Inasmuch as experience has shown the very serious inconveniences that commonly occur to my royal treasury from imprisoning persons intrusted with the collection [of the funds] of any of its branches without providing properly for the security of their moneys and papers, and for drawing up their accounts, I command that[b] for no occurrence, of whatever kind, not even in criminal cases and other matters excepted in article 89, may any judge, not even the intendants themselves, imprison any individual who may have charge of funds of my royal treasury, without first, except if it is night, conducting him to the royal subtreasury or wherever he may have the respective funds and papers under his care; there he himself shall produce the keys, and in his presence the money and effects which he says belong to my treasury shall be counted.

As the official himself may indicate, the papers, books, accounts, promissory notes, or other securities which he may have concerning the same matter, shall be examined and an inventory made with entire separation, so that he may not afterward allege concealment or falsification of any funds, nor that freedom and means of giving a certified account have been denied him, or [make it possible] that any one else should give it from the books and documents inventoried in his presence. After this first duty has been attended to the intendants shall take the keys, which they shall not receive from him before [this]. If the arrest should be made at night [the procedure] must be observed on the next morning in preference to any other, with the proper precautions to prevent flight.

Everything shall be made secure and put under the care of a person who shall be responsible, and shall continue the commission. The official arrested shall be conducted wherever may be fitting and the case which has given occasion for the imprisonment shall proceed without delay in closing the account because of it, [this being done] by the individual himself if the case and the circumstances shall permit, or by his guarantors, or by any person who may be officially appointed if neither he nor his bondsmen do it. In this manner and in no other may keys and papers be taken from those who have control of the funds of my royal treasury, under penalty that he who may do to the contrary shall be responsible for the results just as the one employed or commissioned and his guarantors would be, for there are means of providing for the security of persons [serving the treasury] and for the administration of justice without lack of due respect for my royal treasury.

⟨[a] Precautions for the imprisonment of inferior officials of the royal treasury. [b] The royal order of October 11, 1784, if found in Beleña, the last *foja*, order 519, likewise the circular of January 13, 1781, concerning *alcabalas*.⟩

94

In order that what is determined in articles 86, 87, 282, and 302 concerning the rank, honors, and legal privilege which the intendants of army and province, and the judges of the royal treasury (accountants and treasurers) shall have and enjoy, may not cause doubts concerning which of the insurance funds (*montes pios*) each shall recognize and contribute to for the purposes of their establishment, I declare that the intendants of army as well as those of province shall be understood to be included in the *monte-pio militar* just as are these intendants of my kingdoms [of Spain]. They shall be incorporated in it under the contribution and percentages which its particular ordinance provides in just proportion to the salary that they receive.

[I announce] also that because the ministers of the royal treasury, the general accountants and treasurers, and of the principal ones of the provinces and those outside of the capitals of all of the area of New Spain, are included in the *monte-pio de ministerio* which is established in that kingdom according to the royal ordinance which I was pleased to issue on February 7, 1770, for its administration, and have consequently contributed sufficiently to its funds, I desire that no change be made in this arrangement notwithstanding the practice observed in Spain with regard to accountants and treasurers of the army and commissaries of war.

95

In the capitals in which there are notaries of the royal treasury, which offices are salable and transferable in the dominions of the Indies, the intendants shall be served by them for the transaction and dispatch of all matters belonging to my revenues of whatever kind, unless in some of them, as happens in the case of tobacco, there may be special notaries. But where these officials have not been named the intendants may choose notaries of their confidence who, under the condition of being removable, shall serve them and perform their duties with integrity and legality without other salary, wage, or emolument than the fees assigned them from the general schedule of that kingdom.[a]

However, when these are not sufficient to pay them for their work [of forming] *expedientes* for the poor and official documents, the intendants shall propose to the *junta superior,* by means of the superintendent-subdelegate, the recompense or expense account which shall be allowed them from my royal treasury. When the amount which it considers just is determined by that body, it shall advise me concerning its opinion by the *vía reservada*, suspending the payment until my royal approval [is obtained]. The records of whatever business the intendants may transact with reference to my revenues through any of the notaries indicated must be kept permanently in the intendancies in rooms specially designated for this purpose, and must not be removed from these offices to those belonging to the said notaries, even though the latter may be notaries of my royal treasury.

⟨ᵃ Even though they may be royal appointees if there are not enough public notaries or regularly named ones; or in which case [clerks chosen by the intendants] must be preferred. This was decided by the *junta superior* of May 8, 1792, and by the royal order of February 2, 1793, which approves and explains it.⟩

96

The fifteen proprietory subtreasuries which at present have been established in the kingdom of New Spain, and are located in Mexico City, Pachuca, Cimapan, Acapulco, Guanajuato, San Luis Potosí, Guadalajara, Bolaños, Sombrerete, Zacatecas, Durango, Chihuahua, Rosario, Vera Cruz, and Mérida de Yucatan, must remain for the present in the condition of so many treasuries and accounting-offices of the royal treasury. Besides these I command proprietary treasuries to be formed also in the cities of Puebla de los Ángeles, Antequera de Oaxaca, Valladolid de Michoacan, Arispe, and Campeche; but with the difference that those of Mexico City must be the general depositories of the army and the royal treasury of all the kingdom. The subtreasuries of the capitals of the remainder of the twelve intendancies, in which they must be situated as is provided, shall be classified as the principal exchequers of intendancy and province. Those in the list named which are within the area of each intendancy but outside of its capital, even though hitherto they may have considered others as their central establishment [shall be regarded] as subsidiary and subordinate to those of the capitals respectively.

At present the other inferior treasuries, which likewise have been founded within the boundary of some intendancies and are administered by lieutenants subordinate to the proprietors of their same districts, shall continue under the name of minor treasuries. But as a consequence of this new establishment perhaps it may be useful and necessary to erect in addition some other subsidiary proprietary treasury either minor or subordinate, or to transfer some of those in both classes already created to some other place than that in which they are situated, or finally to change the present immediate dependence of all or part of the minor treasuries, giving them into the jurisdiction of some outside depository (*foranea*) which has just been erected, or to. the principal ones of the province. Therefore for the greater advantage of the income of my treasury, it shall be the special duty of the intendants to observe with profound reflection that which it shall be fitting to do in their respective districts concerning the matters mentioned. This they shall accordingly propose to the superintendent-subdelegate in the terms they may deem best under the circumstances in order that, after it has been discussed and decided by the *junta superior de hacienda*, the latter may command it to put into effect, and shall give account to me by the *vía reservada* so that I may grant my royal approval, or determine what may be my sovereign pleasure.

97

The position of royal factor which exists in the treasury of the capital of Mexico shall be suppressed as soon as it becomes vacant. The functions, which the various laws of the *Recopilación* of the Indies[13] and the instruction of the treasury officials of the year 1573 recommend for this office, shall be transferred to the ministers of the royal treasury (the accountant and treasurer) according to law 38, title 4, book 8; with the difference

---

[13] *Recopilación*, leyes 34, 35, 37, tit. 4, lib. 8; ley 21, tit. 7, lib. 8.

that all those duties which are entirely relative to the warehouses must devolve upon a general guard of these, a position for whom I command to be established and whose appointment I reserve to myself. He shall receive the annual salary of 1,200 *pesos*, and, under sufficient bond, he shall have the immediate responsibility for whatever may enter into the aforesaid magazines, and the obligation of keeping account of that which he may receive and pay out by orders of the treasury officials mentioned, so that at the end of the year, or whenever it may be necessary, it may be compared with that which those [officials] likewise shall keep. The above-mentioned general guard of arsenals shall, without lessening the absolute responsibility which he is declared to have, appoint and keep an adjutant or lieutenant who shall receive from the general treasury each year the salary of 500 *pesos*.

98

[a]Since there is at present in each of the treasuries of Cimapan, Sombrerete, and Chihuahua only one treasury official, I command that another one shall be added to each of them, in order that all the proprietary treasuries and accounting-offices may be administered as is fitting by two different individuals. The subtreasuries of this kind to be created in the cities of Puebla, Antequera, Valladolid, Arispe, and Campeche, as is provided in article 96, must be established in the same manner, with the subordinate officials and salaries which the *junta superior de hacienda* shall consider necessary for the discharge of their special business. [This must be done] on the initiative of the respective intendants through the superintendent-subdelegate, and with the aid of the reports to him by the accountants commissioned for the establishment of the method of the account and calculation ordered by the general accounting-office in its practical instruction of April 27, 1784, and required of them by article 34 of the instruction given them for the management

and administration of their office under date of August 1, 1785. This [measure] shall be put into effect temporarily until my sovereign approval may be obtained.

In all the other accounting-offices and treasuries, in the principal ones of the province as well as those outside of the capitals, the number and the salaries of their subordinates, likewise the percentage or salary which must be paid to the lieutenants who administer the minor or subject treasuries, shall be regulated by the same methods, with due heed to their particular conditions. That which the *junta* may agree to put into effect in this matter must be suspended until account is given to me by the *vía reservada*, and I may approve it, or decide what may be my royal pleasure.

⟨ᵃ This article and 100, 211, 234, 235, 236, 237, and 244 are annulled, in regard to observance of the practical and provisional instruction for the general accounting-office of the Indies prescribing the method of accounts by system of double entry, by virtue of the royal order of October 25, 1787, in which, with the exception of certain points which remain in force, it is commanded that the method of accounts given in the instruction of September 30, 1767, continue without change.⟩

99

The ministers of the royal treasury, that is the general accountant and the treasurer of Mexico City, and the principal treasury officials of Vera Cruz, shall receive the same remuneration of 4,000 *pesos* which those with the title of treasury officials in the first, and in the second those [called] ministers of the treasury enjoy, who at present administer both treasuries. Each of the chief accountants and treasurers of province of the remaining intendancies shall receive a salary of 3,000 *pesos*, except those of Mérida and Arispe, who for the present shall continue with only 2,500 *pesos*. It must be understood that, not only are any traveling expenses which may be paid to those who now serve in the aforesaid appointments in the capacity of treasury officials, but also all the fees they may receive on account of the branches [of finance] and the special matters under their charge, shall be included in each of these salaries mentioned, with absolute prohibition against exacting emoluments or any dues under any motive or in any case.

The accountants and treasurers of the subtreasuries (*foraneas*) at Acapulco, Pachuca, Cimapan, Sombrerete, and Bolaños shall have the same salaries which those who at present administer them as treasury officials receive. The officials of the subtreasuries of Chihuahua and Rosario shall receive 2,200 *pesos*, and those of the one ordered to be created in the city of San Francisco de Campeche 1,800 *pesos*. It must be understood with regard to all the subtreasuries referred to, that while the respective intendants are taking cognizance of the conditions of each one, they shall propose to the superintendent-subdelegates the increases or reductions in the salaries mentioned which they consider just and fitting, in order that, when [these] are discussed and agreed upon in the *junta superior de hacienda,* that body may give account to me by the *vía reservada,* and I may decide in view of this what I may think best.

100

In the branches [of finance] which are under the charge of the aforesaid ministers of the royal treasury, and in which they must exercise the coactive economic authority reserved to them by article 76, all their duties and functions which belong to them in the capacity of accountants and treasurers for whatever may be connected with the administration or collection of the revenues, the guarding of the funds that enter into their possession, or their distribution in payment of charges, shall be common to each of them just as hitherto they have been for the treasury officials.

Likewise the obligation of rendering an account at the end of the year, and of keeping the books within that time shall be their joint official responsibility. They shall observe in these matters with the greatest accuracy all that which the practical and provisional instruction of the general accounting-office cited in article 98 of this ordinance and approved by me on May 9, 1784, prescribes. But there shall be an exception to this common responsibility in the branch of municipal finance, for in it the aforesaid ministers must respectively exercise the special and peculiar duties of accountants and treasurers as was indicated in the articles that treat of the said branch.

⟨ª See article 98.   Joint responsibility.⟩

101

Because of the joint responsibility and the reciprocal exercise of the functions which the preceding article determines it follows as law 19, title 28, book 8 of the *Recopilación* requires, that what must be paid from the subtreasuries of my royal treasury shall not be paid by warrants of the judges who administer them, because they must know, on account of their offices, according to law 20 of the same book and title, what payments are or are not just. As nothing may be drawn from the subtreasury without the attendance of both judges, the drawing up of warrants which must be sent to the same persons as issued them would be as unprofitable as useless. It is therefore my will that in the future the aforesaid law 19 shall be observed punctually, and that all other statutes which ordered the use of the said warrants shall be expressly understood to be annulled.

102

I also wish and command that the provisions of laws 1 and 2 of the aforesaid title 28, book 8, and those which are determined by other statutes of the *Recopilación*[14] shall retain in all their force and strength the particular regulation that neither the superintendent-subdelegate nor the intendants nor any other

---

[14] *Recopilación*, ley 132, tit. 15, lib. 2; ley 57, tit. 3, lib. 3; ley 6, tit. 7, lib. 3; leyes 11, 13, 15, tit. 28, lib. 8.

person, without exception because of dignity or rank, shall draw upon my royal treasury without my special order. When they do to the contrary, the accountants and treasurers shall not pay such warrants, without first doing that which laws 3 and 7 of the same title and book command for them. In this case the responsibility shall be upon him who shall issue the warrant, and the result shall be charged against him, or by the auditor's office against the minister of the royal treasury, if they cannot show that they have duly complied with the obligation which the two laws cited impose upon them. Exception shall be made from the prohibition and rules stated for payment of those expenses which are incurred under the decisions of the *junta superior de hacienda* in the cases and matters which it is permitted by this instruction to decide, and in other matters in which, in conformity with the spirit of certain of the collected laws,[15] it may and must do this.

103

For the payment of all salaries, pensions, or other expenditures, which I may consider best to command to be met by orders, patents, *cédulas*, or dispatches, they must first be presented to the superintendent-subdelegate in order that, after he has put his order upon them and commanded a memorandum thereof to be made in the auditor's office and by the respective ministers of the royal treasury, the latter shall make their payment as is fitting, and the former may have the necessary evidence of their origin for guidance in the making up of its accounts.

It is to be noted that whenever the said payments have to be made by some one of the treasuries belonging to another intendancy than that under the immediate charge of the said superintendent, my *cédulas* or orders from which they originate, with the superintendent's countersign mentioned and the memoran-

---

[15] Found among those cited under the said number 14 of the Appendix in the original.

dum by the auditor's office, must be presented to the intendant drawn upon so that he may submit them with his order to the proper ministers of the treasury, in order that, after making the necessary memorandum, they may pay what is authorized according to the conditions and terms specified in the documents presented, without need of another order from the intendant or the superintendent-subdelegate.

104

When the payment is authorized by a decision of the *junta superior de hacienda* a transcript of the decision with its proper counter-signature shall be sent by the president of that body as superintendent in the manner prescribed in the preceding article, after a memorandum has been made by the auditor's office, to the judges of the royal treasury to whom the duty of putting it into effect belongs. It is to be understood that extraordinary expenditures of this kind must always be provisional pending my royal approval, and that the ministers of the treasury in paying them shall not be obliged to make the memorials or replies which the before cited laws 3 and 7, title 28, book 8 of the *Recopilación* order, neither shall they be held responsible in such cases.

105

Extraordinary expenses of the kind indicated in matters relating to each intendancy must be agreed upon by a provincial *junta* of the royal treasury which shall be formed in its capital to discuss them and to ascertain the causes that require them. It shall be composed of the intendant, his lieutenant-assessor, the chief ministers of the royal treasury, and of its attorney general, who shall have a vote in the cases wherein he may not act as a litigant. In respect to their seats, these officials shall keep the order in which they are named.

The intendant shall by a transcript give account of what may be decided upon to the *junta superior* of Mexico City through the superintendent-subdelegate as its president, in order that when the matter is investigated and examined in the *junta* with due attention and as the laws recommend,[16] it shall determine what it may deem most fitting, and consequently the proper order may be issued, so that the payments in question may be made under the prescribed rules by the respective treasury, or may be disapproved in case the said *junta superior* so determines.

⟨ª See article 297.⟩

106

If, in meeting any of the payments which are ordered made, either when they originate by my command or from the deliberations of the *junta superior de hacienda,* any doubt in regard to the method of putting them into effect should appear to the ministers, the accountant and treasurer, they shall submit the difficulty to the intendant and he shall decide it; or if the matter should give occasion, and its seriousness deserve, the intendant shall consult the said *junta superior.* In this case the aforesaid ministers of the royal treasury shall not be held responsible for the injury which may result from such a decision if noticed by the tribunal of accounts, but the intendant, or the *junta superior* shall be so held responsible if they have given the order.

This same procedure shall be followed in the suits of litigants to whom the ministers of the treasury may refuse to make payments because of doubts or the lack of necessary evidence which should be presented to them. In such case the persons interested shall have recourse to the intendant of the province, who shall hear the arguments of both parties, and make a decision by which the aforesaid ministers must abide. Such payments must be validated in the court of accounts upon the decision or order of the intendant.

---

[16] *Recopilación,* ley 132, tit. 15, lib. 2; ley 57, tit. 3, lib. 3; ley 6, tit. 7, lib. 3; leyes 11, 14, 15, tit. 28, lib. 8.

107

In case a just motive shall occur to the superintendent-subdelegate or to one of the intendants for suspending any payments which may be in process, he must give notice in writing and, in the said manner as provided for completing such transactions, warn officials of the royal treasury upon which the order is drawn not to continue them; he must then give suitable advice to the tribunal of accounts for its guidance in the action which may be taken in regard to them.

108

Each intendant may issue a draft and order the transfer of the funds of my royal exchequer from one treasury to another in his province to the places where they may be required for the needs of my service. Generally only the superintendent-subdelegate shall have power [of sending resources] from the treasuries of one province to those of another. He shall communicate his orders for this purpose to the respective intendants so that they may arrange for their fulfillment, it being understood that in any one of these cases the ministers of the royal treasury transmitting shall be obliged to make these remittances under the provisions of law 12, title 6, book 8 of the *Recopilación,* and that the proper credit item of the remitters shall be the debit item of the recipients. The latter shall balance their account by the letter of consignment and the former by the order indicated, duplicated by the bill of lading of the conductor and the receipt or voucher of the treasury to which it is consigned.

109

Nothing will prove so conducive to the end that the branches of my treasury and the other divisions of the political government may be directed and managed with justice and prudence, and that they shall be regulated and unified according to an intelligible and certain method in the provinces of that empire, as the "General Account Book of my Royal Treasury" which law 1, title 7, book 8 of the *Recopilación* mentions. It was suggested on account of its importance by Don Francisco de Toledo, viceroy of Peru, and following him it was ordered to be begun and kept by a royal *cédula* of February 12, 1591. It was again commanded by various other later laws, but until the present time nothing has been done about it.

Wherefore it shall be one of the chief and special cares of each intendant, without sparing activity or fatigue, to make the aforesaid "General Account Book of my Royal Treasury" relating to his province, maintaining complete subordination to what is provided for it in the five following articles, and in laws 18, 19, and 20, title 14, book 3 of the *Recopilación.* When it is completed the intendants shall each send without delay a copy of it to the superintendent-subdelegate, who shall cause a general book of the kingdom, in triplicate and authorized in due form, to be made by the tribunal of accounts (in the archives of which the others must be deposited) as quickly as possible from all the books submitted. He shall leave one copy under the charge of his superintendency [of the treasury] and send the other two to my royal hands and to the general accounting-office of the Indies by the *vía reservada,* so that in all the offices referred to and in each intendancy respectively this important information may be possessed.

110

The said "General Account Book of my Royal Treasury" must contain a fundamental report concerning all the branches of revenue entering [the exchequer] established within the district of each treasury; [first] those that form the common total sum [of the funds] of my treasury and are used to meet the charges and expenditures to which it is subject in the Indies, as [for example] the import and export duties (*almojarifazgos*), tributes, sales taxes (*alcabalas*), and other similar duties; [second] those special revenues the proceeds of which, although they belong to me, have some particular destination in these kingdoms or in America, like those of the *mesada*,[17] ecclesiastical vacancies,[18] Bulls of the Crusade (indulgences), court fines (*penas de cámara*) and others of this kind; [and third] those which may be called alien [i.e., non-royal] because of their origin and purpose, and only enter my treasuries because of the special protection that I give them, such as the deposits, the estates of deceased persons (*bienes de difuntos*), pensions for widows and orphans (*monte-pios*), and some municipal funds.

111

A separate account and report must be given in the aforesaid book concerning each one of the branches mentioned, using as many pages for this as are necessary, and leaving some blank in order to set down the changes which I may think it suitable to make in each one. The origin of all the divisions of finance must be explained in so far as this can be ascertained—that is, the law, royal *cédula,* or order by virtue of which [the revenue] is collected, on what articles or persons, how much on each one, and in what period of time, what special charges it has against it in particular besides the common and general costs of collection, what origin and purpose these special charges have, and what the destination of the net proceeds may be, if the law, royal *cédula* or order, or any later decree or custom declared this; and finally, the variations which [these branches] may have undergone since their origin or establishment with regard to the objects taxed and the quantity collectible up to the present time.

---

[17] One month's salary contributed to the government.

[18] Salaries attached to church positions which reverted to the crown in case of vacancies.

112

Likewise account must be given of the real estate belonging to my royal patrimony, as [for instance] the mines, houses, or estates of any kind. There must be a statement in each account, if it can be ascertained, of the cause, purpose, or antiquity of the land or the mine possessed, the special charges levied on it, what the revenue is either by administration or leasing, and what their ordinary proceeds are for the year, or for five years.

113

The fixed charges must be indicated with the same detail. They shall be divided into classes, first that of the royal treasury, second political adminstration, third ecclesiastical matters, fourth military affairs, fifth permanent pensions, and sixth temporary pensions. The origin and purpose of each one of the aforesaid pensions shall be declared, and the different ancient or modern coins in which they were granted shall be reduced to the *pesos* or *reales* of the silver money current in the Indies. This also must be done with the various kinds of ducats mentioned in the royal *cédula* or circular of September 15, 1776.[19] According to the resolution therein made the ducat of the Indies shall be valued at 11 *reales* and one *maravedí* of their current money, or at 375 *maravedis*, which is the same thing, and the *peso* assayed in conformity with law 9, title 8, book 8 of the *Recopilación* [shall be worth] 450 *maravedís* of the same kind.

The number and kind of positions in each of the departments referred to, and their respective annual salaries, shall also be stated. Finally all the information [shall be furnished] which may contribute to afford a well founded and exact knowledge concerning what must be the material object of the duty, obligation, zeal, and activity equally of the intendants, who have

---

[19] See Appendix, number 15, in the original.

general charge of administration, and also of the ministers of the royal treasury on whom the collection and distribution, or control [of the funds] in detail may belong, with the functions connected with and declared to pertain to this ministry.

In order that those who at present perform these duties, and those who shall succeed them later may promptly find in this book the information which they must frequently seek in it for their guidance, an index of all the branches, expenses, and separate funds which occur, shall be placed at the beginning, indicating the sheet wherein each item may be found. For this purpose the whole book shall have its pages numbered, the name of it shall be placed on the first sheet, and shall be legalized with the solemnity which law 1, title 6, book 8 of the *Recopilación* provides.

⟨[a] By royal order of August 19, 1791, which is on the 31st *foja* of the *expediente* concerning the half-annate for the privileges of being an *oidor*, this is commanded to be observed for the directors of tobacco.

[b] The 450 *maravedís* make a *peso*, 5 *reales* and 8 *maravedís*.

[c] For the equivalence of the coins see article 254 and the royal order to which it refers.⟩

114

When I consider it best to order that any of the above enumerated branches be permanently or temporarily suppressed, that their collectible quota be increased or diminished, that any fixed charge shall be abolished, increased, or decreased, that any rural estate be alienated or sold, or in a word, that any notable change be made in the matters which may be expressed in the book mentioned, the fact shall be noted in the proper place, citing the royal *cédulas* or orders which command this, and the page of the book where, according to law 30, title 7, book 8 of the *Recopilación*, it must be copied. The ministers of the royal treasury who have charge of administration in detail shall annotate this same thing in their manual of account, in order that the date on which the variation began to affect the account and calculation may be evident therein.

115

For the more prompt and reasonable accomplishment of what is ordered in the six preceding articles, and so that in the meantime the intendants may continue to give with due knowledge the orders which may be fitting for the aforesaid proposed ends whereby my royal treasury may be directed and managed with an exact and uniform method, it is necessary that special information concerning the origin, progress, and final condition of all the rents and dues pertaining to it, be obtained immediately. For this purpose I command the tribunal of accounts of Mexico, and the other ministers of the accounting-offices, treasuries, and any other offices of the royal treasury, without the least excuse or delay, to give and submit to the intendants as many reports, accounts and certified copies as they shall ask for, without withholding *cédulas,* orders, or other documents.

In order to avoid delay when the intendants may need to have recourse to the tribunal of accounts and other offices of the capital of Mexico, they shall inform the superintendent-subdelegate, so that he may order that what they request shall be promptly dispatched. In these matters he must have all the authority needed and the power which I grant him of presiding over the tribunal of accounts referred to whenever he may consider his attendance necessary, and of exercising exclusively all the other powers which were bestowed upon the viceroys respecting the same tribunal by the various laws of the *Recopilación.*[20] He shall take heed of the conduct of the ministers and subordinates who compose it, and cause them to perform their duties with integrity and due exactness.

---

[20] *Recopilación,* leyes, 3, 4, 23, 25, 34, 41, 44, 52, 53, 62, 64, 66, 67, 68, 73, 74, 76, 89, 91, 101, 102, 104, 105, 108, title 1, lib. 8; leyes 5, 6, 9, tit. 2, lib. 1; ley 78, tit. 15, lib. 2, as indicated in the Appendix of the original.

116

In regard to the rents which are administered for the account of my royal treasury, the intendants shall provide carefully for the exactness of their collection, and for the greater increase of their proceeds if this may be obtained with justice and honesty. They shall observe the disinterestedness and integrity with which ministers of the royal treasury (the accountants and treasurers), the other administrators, whether general, chief, or private persons, and other subordinates to whom their collection is intrusted, may proceed, that they may avoid the many injuries which are brought upon my royal treasury, with no less grievances to the people, from [doing] the contrary. If the intendants should need aid from their superiors so as to restrain and punish employees, they shall report to the superintendent-subdelegate, and observe the orders which he may communicate to them.

117

If any branch or revenue of my royal treasury may be leased in whole or in part, the intendants shall take care to prevent the irregularities and acts of violence whereby contractors commonly oppress the people by obliging them to make exorbitant payment, which the former regulate according to ambition and not to the capacity of the contributors, whom they afflict in the collections with exactions and expenses which the people are not able to bear. Since the most effective means of preventing these injuries will always be to prefer collection by a well ordered system of administration, as I have commanded in regard to the revenues of *alcabalas* and other dues, and by the equitable contracts or the system of collection by the towns where the system of administration cannot be established, I order the subordinate judges and tax-gatherers of ·the tributes and other royal dues which those vassals pay me, to collect them at the proper times, so as to avoid the burden of expenses and the arrears from one year to another which generally result from the carelessness of administrators or the negligence of the said justices.

118

ᵃThe intendants shall also see very particularly that administrators, receivers, or collectors of the revenues of my royal treasury in their district shall pay into the respective treasuries what they ought, at the time designated. They shall at the proper time effectively call to account the justices and other persons responsible for their exaction. They shall inform themselves every month through the ministers of the royal treasury of their territory concerning the condition of the collections, in order to take opportunely the necessary measures against those who resist or defer payment.

⟨ᵃ See articles 129 and 130.⟩

119

Experience has proved everywhere that relieving the people from writs and attachments has produced very advantageous results, for [when they are oppressed] all they spend in securing delays and paying salaries is withdrawn from their principal profits. In consideration of this fact the intendants shall try to avoid as much as possible the issue of writs, except in very necessary cases, [granting] moderate daily salaries and definite terms to judges. They shall send out only one minister for all kinds of unpaid levies so that he may demand their payment at the same time with least injury to debtors. In these cases they shall respect the privileges of the Indians and the months of delay [in making payment] granted to farmers in all my dominions, which in Spain are the months of June, July, and August because their crops so require. ᵃSimilarly the intendant shall designate in his province, but with the approval of the *junta superior de hacienda,* those months which may be best for the same consideration and purpose.

⟨ᵃ Law 25, title 21, book 4; and law 25, title 13, book 8 of [the *Recopilación* of] *Castile.*⟩

120

With equal attention the intendants must ascertain secretly and reservedly how the justices conduct themselves in the assessment and exaction of the sums which the towns under the system of collection by contract, if there be any such, pay to my royal treasury from the branch of *alcabalas* or other divisions of revenue. They also shall inquire whether the contribution is levied on the inhabitants with due consideration for the property, contracts, business, and profits of each one, and whether they lease or administer the public markets honestly wherever they are found, in order that the profits therefrom may serve the common welfare by being applied to the payment of the town's revenue contract in such part as they may, in case they have no other preferred use.

121

In order that all those who feel aggrieved concerning these assessments under the system of collection by contract by the towns may have recourse to the intendants, the latter must take cognizance of their complaints and give proper orders to the respective justices so that the abuse may be corrected. When the latter officials do not obey what is commanded, or when they allege circumstances of fact which require an examination or proof, the intendants shall intrust the proceedings to their lieutenants, the subdelegates of the districts, with power of appointing experienced persons who shall revise the assessments, in order that, the injustice being shown, they may correct it. But if this process should be maliciously delayed by the justices, the intendants shall, through fines, compel them [to obey], causing everything to be done at their expense, and that the injury of the litigants shall be indemnified.

122

The intendants must never allow more than the net total of the taxes to be assessed. They shall prohibit all abuse or increase under pretext of dues for notaries, salaries of tax-assessors, or any other expenses, since it is the duty and obligation of justices, or of persons commissioned by the towns under the system of collection by contract, to make the collection, transfer, and deposit [of the funds] in my royal treasuries, with such remuneration as has been assigned them for this. This amount shall be the only one which may be included in and added to the assessments, and in no case may it exceed five per cent.

123

In consideration of this compensation from the taxes granted by the towns to their judges or tax-gatherers, when [these officials] are found to be in default, attachments shall be issued against them, their goods, and their guarantors, but not against the communes or first contributors. The intendants shall warn collectors in advance by legal notices and written orders, so that they may not pretend ignorance or for any reason delay levying the taxes. For if they levy the assessment in due time they can pay the treasury within the term specified.

124

If, however, it may be recognized that the delay is caused by the absolute incapacity of the towns [to pay the taxes] on account of some unusual event, and not from the negligence or complaisance of the justices in the measures which they shall be obliged to take for the collection of the royal tributes and other taxes which are under their control, the intendants shall inform themselves concerning the condition of the said towns and the reasons by which these arrears are caused. If necessary they shall dispatch a person in their confidence to investigate conditions summarily and accurately, so that, if they find the delay to be unavoidable, they may so advise the *junta superior de hacienda* in order that this body may grant the extension of time which it may consider fitting, according to the circumstances and to what is commanded concerning this matter in article 141.

125

In case the intendants find that in their provinces any revenues from road tolls, bridge tolls, fishing tolls, or any others that belong to my royal treasury or to the public use have been concealed or misappropriated, they shall take cognizance thereof and [draw up] the proper reports in order to give account to the *fiscales* of my Council of the Indies, or to the *audiencia* of the district, as is fitting according to the nature of the cases. At the same time they shall inform me by the *vía reservada* concerning what they may discover in these matters, in order that I may command that adequate orders be given, or that proper legal action be taken.

126

When the intendancies are established, the royal tributes of their respective districts must necessarily be collected in the principal and subsidiary treasuries together with all the other ordinary revenues of my treasury, as at present is done by the treasuries of Guadalajara and Zacatecas with the tributes pertaining to the kingdom of Nueva Galicia; and this earliest tax of those dominions must immediately be placed under the exclusive inspection and cognizance of the intendants as superiors of their provinces, of their subdelegates therein, and of the subordinate justices, as judges of this revenue with the same entire jurisdiction as in the other divisions of my royal treasury.

In consideration of the foregoing, I command that, at the same time that the intendancies are being established, the jurisdictional faculty in the collection of the afore-mentioned revenue which the *contaduría general* established in Mexico City has exercised and does now exercise, shall cease. Nevertheless, this office shall continue with the title of general accounting-office of assessments (*retasas*) but only with the use of the functions that as such shall pertain to it, and which will be stated farther on.

[a]Inasmuch as the business of the aforesaid office is largely diminished by this measure, and its superior official will be relieved of his present duties of giving accounts and bonds, it is my sovereign will that the *junta superior de hacienda* in consideration thereof shall reduce the number of positions which the said *contaduría general* now has to what it may consider sufficient, and that when the unnecessary offices and individuals who serve in them, also the employees in other similar positions are suppressed, it shall justly regulate the salaries of those who must continue [to serve] as likewise that of the accountant. It shall give me account of everything by the *vía reservada* in order that I may approve it or decide what shall be my royal pleasure.

⟨[a] Suppression of offices.⟩

127

In order that the observance of that which is commanded by the preceding article may in no way embarrass the proper accounting and calculation [of the funds] of the said branch of my royal tributes, I declare that the governors, *corregidores,* or *alcaldes mayores* who are in office at the time of the establishment of the intendancy to which the districts under their command may pertain, and who have deposited in the treasury the moneys corresponding to the first or second third of the year's tributes under their charge, must also do this with the remainder or remainders, in the same place and manner as they did before with either period; so that the new method of making deposits in the treasury of the territory must be begun by each governor, *corregidor,* or *alcalde mayor* with the first third of the year respectively, in order that in this way the accounts may not fall short and they may be submitted complete to the general accounting-office, which shall include them in its report.

128

Inasmuch as by the new regulations, when the intendancies are established, the royal tributes must be collected by the respective subtreasuries of my royal treasury in the manner above provided, it is obvious that the deposit of funds both in the principal treasuries of the province, as well as in the subsidiary ones, will increase in proportion as the collection is augmented in each district by the proposed system of collection. I therefore command that, in view of and in due proportion to the increase which the new measure may create in the annual deposit in each treasury, the respective accountants and treasurers shall increase their bonds under the same conditions of joint responsibility and other requirements as those by which treasury officials have been obliged to give and did give bonds in conformity with the laws to which these employees are always subject, as has been said.

129

The collection of my royal tributes, their transfer to the principal treasuries or subsidiary ones of each intendancy, and the deposit [of the funds] in them, during the periods when the *corregidores* or *alcaldes mayores* are completing their terms of office, must be the precise obligation, responsibility, and risk of the *alcaldes ordinarios* in the cities, towns, and villages where those officials exist, or in which they may be established as provided by article 11. It must be understood as one of the duties of the office that they shall be held responsible with their person and property jointly for the payment, if this should be delayed on account of their carelessness or neglect.

The subdelegates whom the intendants shall, either themselves or by the advice of the political and military governors
appoint, shall have the same obligation in the chief Indian towns
of the district according to article 12,[a] with only the difference
that the subdelegates shall give bond to the satisfaction of the
ministers of the treasury of the territory, both with respect to
the aforesaid revenue, as well as to any other which they must
collect. Let it be understood that the said subdelegates, the same
as the *alcaldes ordinarios*, must deposit the tributes in my treasuries by thirds according to the practice in those provinces, and
that all these officials must collect the sum to which this amounts[b]
from pure Indians, through the respective native governors or
alcaldes themselves, since the subdelegates are required so to
exact this as was explained in article 13. They must also pay
the amount by thirds in the capitals of the districts; but the
aforesaid subdelegates and the *alcaldes ordinarios* themselves
must collect the tributes of the other castes liable thereto from
the first contributors. Also the total collection which these
judges transmit to my treasuries shall be under the care and
charge of the ministers of the royal treasury.

⟨[a] See the circular of the superior government of June 9, 1793, concerning the various matters relative to these securities. [b] See articles 118
and 230.⟩

130

Since the provisions of the preceding article for the *alcaldes
ordinarios* and subdelegates which it mentions, as well as for the
ministers of the royal treasury (the accountants and treasurers)
make it necessary that rules be given them for the most exact
collection and accounting of my royal tributes in so far as these
officers are respectively concerned with them, I order the general accountant of assessments to send without delay to the intendants copies of the ordinances and instructions of this revenue
in order that, after complying with the part that pertains to
them, they shall transmit them to the principal accountants and

treasurers of the principal and subsidiary treasuries, and to the ordinary justices and subdelegates of their districts who are obliged to collect the tax mentioned.

The intendants shall see to the punctual observance of these instructions in so far as they are not contrary to what is provided by this ordinance, with the understanding that the rules prescribed by the said ordinances and instructions for the general accountant of tributes shall apply to the ministers of the royal treasury when there may be occasion for this, since the latter do not have jurisdiction; they shall also apply to the *alcaldes ordinarios* and subdelegates in everything that they prescribe respecting *corregidores* and *alcaldes mayores*, whose duties are similar.

131

Since, for the new system that is established for the management, cognizance, collection, and receipt [of the funds] of the branch of the royal tributes, it is essential that the intendants shall immediately obtain all the instruction necessary concerning its condition with regard to their provinces, and that correspondingly appropriate information shall be furnished to the principal and subsidiary accounting-offices and treasuries, also to the subordinate justices and subdelegates for the most exact fulfillment of the part belonging to them, therefore I wish and command that the tribunal of accounts, the general accountant of assessments, the governors, *corregidores, alcaldes mayores,* and others concerned shall submit to the respective intendants without excuse or delay complete transcripts of the last registers, computations, and rates of tribute payers, of the measures taken regarding them and of all other appropriate documents by which the latter may become familiar with the present administration of the branch, the most recent condition of its revenues, and of its favorable credits and debits, so that after communicating all which concerns them of this to the principal and outside treasurers, to the *alcaldes ordinarios*, and to the subdelegates, the intendants may order the latter to proceed to the collection and the former to the proper accounting [of the funds]. The intendants shall aid all these officials as much as they may need and is fitting.

132

ªFor the collection, transfer, and deposit of the tributes which the *alcaldes ordinarios* and the subdelegates already mentioned must make, according to the lists or registers of persons paying the tax, and to the rates which are given them for this, and under the responsibility and other securities defined in article 129, I command that the remuneration of six per cent of the total amount which enters into the respective treasury shall be paid to them. It is to be understood that they must leave one per cent of this for the Indian governors or *alcaldes* who collected the tribute from the first contributors. The five per cent left shall be for their own benefit because of their responsibility and work in the collection. The duty of the aforesaid Indian tax-collectors consists only of making the deposits in the chief towns where the respective subdelegates or *alcaldes ordinarios* reside, and of [seeing] that the first contributors obey by paying their quota in their towns, as law 44, title 5, book 6 and law 10, title 9, book 8 of the *Recopilación* provide.

⟨ª The note which is set down in the following article belongs to the present one of 132. In *expediente* G. S., number 4, page 66, which was sent to the accounting office of the *Provincias Internas*, appears the vote of the *junta superior* of May 31, 1794, concerning the securities which governors shall take as the first step, in regard to which the circular order of the 15th of the same June was dispatched to the intendants.⟩

133

In order that the branch of tributes may be regulated justly and fairly, for my treasury is greatly injured by the inequality with which they are exacted, and by the many abuses which governors, *corregidores*, and *alcaldes mayores* have introduced in their collection, they having been responsible for the collection and deposit of the tributes in the treasury without a salary or any remuneration, it is my will that it shall also be the duty and care of the intendants to make correct tax lists of all the inhabitants of their respective provinces; especially shall they see to the very important matter of making visitations every five years, either themselves or by means of their commissioners and subdelegates of the utmost responsibility, for the enumeration and computation, or matriculation of the tribute payers, keeping separate the Indians, Negroes, free mulattoes, and the other castes who without exception must pay tributes according to laws 1, 2, and 3, title 5, book 7 of the *Recopilación*, although they may be domestic servants of the viceroys, magistrates, ecclesiastical prelates, or of any other privileged or influential persons. For all these must deduct the tributes from the wages they pay to their servants as members of the tribute-paying classes, and cause the amounts to be paid to the tax-collectors of this branch.

134

Since the many and habitual frauds, which likewise have been experienced up to the present time in the formation of reports of visitations and the consequent enumeration [of the people], and in the registers and rates of the tribute payers, have been no less prejudicial to the just revenues, and since the care of my *fiscales* or the vigilance of the courts have not been able to remedy them, it is necessary in order to check them at the root, to determine the most exact and suitable rules for carrying on the said proceedings. For this purpose, I command the superintendent-subdelegate of my royal treasury to draw up the ordinance which he may think best, after acquiring all the information that may be conducive thereto, and keeping in mind and consideration the laws of the *Recopilación* which treat of this subject; [he shall also bear in mind] the formal instruction composed of twenty-eight articles issued by the superior government of Lima on July 24, 1770, which I approved by a *cédula* of May 25, 1772, for the guidance of the inspector-judges (*jueces revistadores*) within the area of that kingdom; the royal provision consisting of twenty-three articles, decreed and printed, which my royal *audiencia* of Mexico has customarily issued for the completion of the said enumerations of the tribute payers; the memoranda of Don Josef Antonio de Areche, when he was my civil *fiscal* in the above-mentioned *audiencia*, drawn up for the guidance of the attorneys of my royal treasury in the enumerations mentioned; any other instructions or rules which may have been in practice; and finally, whatever is provided by this ordinance in regard to this tax and its collection.

When the superintendent-subdelegate has drawn up the regulation as he is directed, he shall carry it to the *junta superior de hacienda* in order that, with the advice of its *fiscal*, [that body] may correct the measure in so far as is required, and transmit it to the tribunal of accounts, to the general accounting-office of assessments, and to the intendants of province; the latter [shall send it] to their commissioners or subdelegates, so that they may observe and obey it temporarily in the part which pertains to each of them, while the said *junta* gives account to me by the *vía reservada* with a copy of the aforesaid ordinance. It shall explain to me what may occur to it and seem best concerning the ordinance, in order that I may condescend to approve it or decide what will be my sovereign pleasure. For the time being this my will is, that until the new ordinance mentioned is sanctioned and transmitted, the rules hitherto established, in so far as they are not contrary to what is determined hereby, shall be observed in the making of visitations, enumeration of [the people], and in assessing the rates of the tribute payers.

135

As soon as the intendants have finished the computation and levy of rates on the tribute payers, either themselves or by means of their judges of commission, at the same time that they submit the original documents to the *junta superior* for the purposes which will be specified, they shall send complete transcripts of those of each district to the ministers of the royal treasury, whose duty it is to liquidate the account. They shall also give duplicate documents to the *alcaldes ordinarios,* subdelegates, and the native governors or *alcaldes* who are responsible for the collection of the tax, in order that they may each one put them into effect according to the new registers and as of the date thereof (as I have resolved by general rule notwithstanding that which was determined by law 62, title 5, book 6 of the *Recopilación* which I expressly annul in this matter) without delaying to take into consideration that which, in view of the aforesaid original accounts and rates, the *junta superior de hacienda* may decide.

To [this body] I intrust the revision and approval of those documents with the sanction of my *fiscal* who is included in the *junta,* and of the general accounting-office of assessments. The sessions (*acuerdos*) of my royal *audiencias* are prohibited [from doing this] for the just purpose of avoiding habitual delays and hindrances, and of relieving those tribunals of the accumulations of business that occur in them.

136

In the review of the documents concerning enumeration and visitations of tribute payers which must, upon petition of my *fiscal,* be given by the *junta superior* to the general accounting-office, an exact statement must be included of the legitimate contributors of every class in each capital of the district according to the new register; of those who shall be exempted; of the *caciques*, widows, and unmarried who are excused; and of the net sum which, with deduction of the former and the latter, each chief town must pay; and finally a general resumé embracing all those balances and a comparison thereof with that of the preceding tax register [must be made], so that with the same separation of classes the difference may be shown concerning the number of tribute payers, whether of decrease or increase, in order that, the proceedings being returned to the *junta superior de hacienda* after this operation, that body may approve the list and its rates, declare exempt those to whom [this privilege] may belong, and command that the tribute payers included in the register shall pay the quota assessed to them, and certify that the increase or decrease in their number which appears is correct. Finally, the documents shall be returned to the accounting-office of assessments (where they must be deposited in the archives) in order that, in conformity with the same list and its said approbation, this body may form for each district, showing each chief town separately, a similar register with the respective items which shall be inserted in the order or decree of valuation that the *junta superior* must issue certified by its notary. When a memorandum is taken by the auditor's office this [list] shall be submitted to the intendant to whom it belongs, so that, after giving a copy of that part which concerns it to each chief town, he may transmit a copy of that which may concern them to the *alcaldes ordinarios*, subdelegates, and ministers of the royal treasury of the territory; but the original shall be left in the notary's office of the intendancy for future guidance.

137

In all the provinces (without changing the just privilege which the Tlaxcaltecs possess) the tribute and royal dues which the Indians must pay from eighteen years of age, when they begin to pay tribute, until fifty, as law 7, title 5, book 6 of the *Recopilación* commands, shall be reduced to the uniform amount of sixteen *reales* of New Spain money, without including in the said sum the other *real* which they pay for judges and hospitals, which must be collected under the same conditions which are provided for the tribute; and no difference shall be made whether the Indians be unmarried or married, although they may be under the authority of their parents, when once they have reached the age of eighteen, in order that they may not feel restrained from matrimony, to their own great injury, to that of the population, and of good order, as they do now with the misused inducement of remaining half-tribute payers while they are not married.

Only the ligitimate *caciques* and their oldest sons, women of any condition, and Indian governors and *alcaldes* while they are serving as such, shall be exempted from both taxes according to laws 18, 19, and 20 of the same title and book of the *Recopilación*. Likewise the tribute of Negroes, free mulattoes, and of other castes of their class must be exacted justly. Their tributes shall be fixed at the moderate rate of twenty-four *reales* for all, both for the unmarried and the married after they reach eighteen years of age.

138

The *intendant-corregidores* shall not only provide that vagabonds of the tribute-paying class shall enter a useful occupation, or be placed under the service of well-known masters, who shall pay their tributes by deducting it from their salaries according to law 3, title 5, book 7 of the *Recopilación;* but they shall also see that it is exacted from all persons without tolerance to the contrary. In observance of laws 9, 10, and 13, title 5, book 6 of the *Recopilación* likewise those who work in the mines, although they may be forced to labor in them, as well as those who are employed on farms, in workshops, pack-trains, and other occupations in Spanish towns shall also pay tributes.

139

With similar exactitude the intendants must take care that the exemption from tribute, which I have just granted to the free castes (*pardos*) who serve in the bodies of provincial militia of New Spain, shall not be extended under any motive or pretext to those of the same class who are enlisted in the flying and urban companies, as is declared by the general proclamation (*bando*) of the viceroy of that kingdom in fulfillment of my royal instructions and orders given for the formation of provincial troops.

140

The *alcaldes ordinarios* and also the subdelegates who must collect the tributes from first and second contributors and deposit them in my royal treasuries according to article 129, shall be charged or debited, during the five years that intervene between one visitation and enumeration and the next, with the exact number of tribute payers shown on the list, whether before or after it is approved by the *junta superior* as is provided in article 135, and according to the respective quotas of their levy. It shall be the responsibility of all these officials to transfer [to the treasury] the sums that result from the proper collection. For since it is my royal will that the very serious inconveniences shall be checked which are experienced in the method of judicial proceedings, depositions upon oath, and other legal acts which have been provided to set forth that tributaries may have died, absented themselves, have reached the class of those exempt, etc., I wish and command that, it being understood that the proceedings indicated are expressly annulled and of no effect, the number of [these diminutions] shall be fairly considered to be compensated for by adding to the prior number those who during the period have begun to pay tribute, either on reaching the age of eighteen (for although they may be married before, I grant them freedom from tribute until that time, [by] extending the provision of law

9, title 17, book 6 of the *Recopilación* to all the area of the kingdom of New Spain for the sake of marriage), or because they may have come to live in the province, district, town, or place after the tax list in force was formed. But if the increase of new tributaries or the decrease of the old ones should be so perceptible that the report of the treasury or of the collectors ought in justice be heard, although the five years of the aforesaid tax list are not yet completed, then the intendants may make a judicial investigation by means of examinations and second assessments as laws 54, 56, 57, 58, and 59, title 5, book 6 of the *Recopilación* provide.

141

[a]In cases of public calamity on account of general or local epidemics from which the Indians and other castes of the common people habitually suffer, or of the lack of rain sometimes experienced in those provinces of New Spain, the intendants shall inform the *junta superior de hacienda* with adequate proof, as provided in article 124, in order that, after noting the circumstances of the case, it may grant the people delay in the paying of tributes. The *junta* should not grant the rebate or total remission of these, but when it may consider the causes just which have occurred for the one or for the other measure, it shall consult me about the matter by the *vía reservada,* the delay being conceded meanwhile, in order that my approval may be obtained or I may decide what I think most fitting to prevent the evils frequently experienced when the tribute payers from some flourishing provinces move into others which are afflicted with scarcity of crops or with diseases, for the sole purpose of freeing themselves from the tax.

⟨[a] According to the spirit of this article the *junta superior* decided in the case of the house of Aristaga Bazán of Vera Cruz to delay payment of the revenue of 37,000 *pesos* which were due from it to the branch of secular revenues (*temporalidades*). until such time as this estate might become recuperated and it could be seen what its arrears might be, at which time it might be decided whether it should be freed from paying revenues or whether these might be diminished. This was in the year 1816, when injuries caused by the insurrection were alleged.⟩

142

Some persons, in order to be exempt from the just dues of the *alcabalas* which are paid in the Indies at the moderate rate of six per cent, and four per cent on the enemy frontiers, fraudulently grant, bestow upon, or transfer their possessions and wealth to their children or ecclesiastical relatives, thereby violating the laws of these dominions [of Spain] and those [of America], and causing great injury to my royal treasury. In order to prevent such frauds, the intendants, their subdelegates, and subordinate justices must take heed of them with special vigilance, and the former must give a correct account of them to the *junta superior de hacienda,* so that it may inform me and I may apply a fitting remedy [for them] by the use of my supreme power.

But in the meantime they shall publish proclamations in their provinces that no clerk or notary shall, under the penalty which law 30, title 13, book 8 of the *Recopilación* of the Indies imposes, draw up the legal documents for such gifts or transfers, although they may be under the name of sales, without proper license therefor being first obtained or that of the respective subdelegates, so that this may be done. These officials shall, each in his case, obtain for this purpose the information which they may think best and thereupon provide or represent, the subdelegate to the intendant, and the latter to the *junta superior,* what may seem just to them according to the circumstances of the events, always keeping in mind law 10, title 12, book 4 of the *Recopilación* of the Indies, which is one of the fundamental statutes of those kingdoms.

143

[a]By article 8 of the concordat celebrated in the year 1737[b] between this crown and the Holy See it was agreed that from the date of the concordat cited, all the property which under

whatsoever title, any church, religious establishment, or ecclesiastical community might acquire and should therefore fall into
mortmain, should from that time and forever with their income
also, be subject to all the royal taxes and imposts which laymen
shall pay, except the possessions of the first foundations, and with
the condition that these said estates which may be obtained in
the future shall be free from those dues which ecclesiastics pay
for apostolic concessions. Although the observance of the concordat has been required and has been put into effect in these my
dominions of Spain, hitherto the extension thereof to those
of the Indies has been omitted.

But since it is my sovereign will that the aforesaid provisions
shall be fulfilled in all those kingdoms, I command that it shall
be put into effect in New Spain with reference to those estates
that under any title shall fall into mortmain from the date of
this ordinance on, and that consequently not only the *alcabala*
shall be collected from the commodities which they produce, but
also all the other dues which may be paid to me from estates
pertaining to seculars. What is ordered in the preceding article
respecting clerks and notaries must be observed in order that
none of the acquisitions indicated may be concealed when they
occur, and this resolution must be made public by proclamations
which the intendants shall order promulgated in their respective
provinces.

⟨ᵃ Mortmain. ᵇ On September 26th.⟩

144

Since the collection of the above-mentioned revenue of
alcabalas in the capital of Mexico and in that kingdom generally
is the duty of special administrators, and as this means has been
preferred, in compliance with my royal orders and instructions,
to that of special [private] leases, it is my royal will that [the
same method] shall continue in the future because of the advan-

tages which are experienced for my royal treasury and for my vassals from its practice. In this consideration I command the intendants, with the advice of the general managers of this revenue appointed temporarily for its uniform regulation, to devote their attention, authority, and active measures to the same end, and to watch the conduct of all employed in its collection and safe-keeping.

145

[a]In order that administrators of *alcabalas* and other revenues may not lack sufficient authority and power for the best performance of their duties, I wish them to exercise all the coactive economic prerogatives fitting for their effective collection under the same conditions that are declared in article 76 respecting the ministers of the royal treasury. As is stated therein, contentious jurisdiction shall be reserved for the intendants, although they, either because they do not have subdelegates in the respective districts, or on account of the distances and difficulty in regard to appeals,[b] may delegate to the aforesaid administrators as much [of this jurisdiction] as may be needed to prepare the cases for the status of a sentence, in order that they may submit them to the intendants.

But I except the superintendent-administrator of the customhouse of Mexico City and of the districts united to it from this limitation; for, because very large sums from the *alcabalas* are collected in this customhouse, it is fitting and it is my sovereign will that his administration shall be free from embarrassment in the territory within which it is exclusive. In it he shall exercise the authority and powers which were granted him by the ordinance formed for the said customhouse, and dated September 26, 1753; but in the exercise of his faculties these shall be limited to procedure only in first instance against creditors and debtors under the *alcabala*, and to taking cognizance in proper form of the cases in which this tax may be disputed or when the legitimate indebtedness thereunder shall be in any manner doubted. [He shall be subject] in all this to the restrictions and amplifications which may have been provided by later royal orders, but after the *alcabala* is paid he may consent to appeals from his definitive sentence to the *junta superior de hacienda.*[c] But in all other respects his authority and powers as set forth in the ordinance cited must be considered expressly annulled, and what is provided in this instruction must be observed.

⟨[a] How must business be encouraged? See the decision of the *junta superior* which drew up the circulars of July 12, 1792, and January 29, 1790. [b] See article 77. [c] Royal order of September 27, 1778, found in Beleña, folio 3, order 26.⟩

146

[a]The royal tax paid on *pulque* is collected at the aforesaid customhouse and also in that of the city of Puebla upon its entrance into either capital, as is the tax paid by the *pulque* shops where that beverage, which is regional, is sold and is permitted to the Indians by law 37, title 1, book 6 of the *Recopilación.* I therefore command that this branch, formerly a monopoly, shall always be administered in those two cities, and that the same shall be done in all the other districts of their provinces and of the others wherever the *maguey* plant and the use of *pulque*, which is extracted from it, have been extended, in order to avoid by this means the harmful abuses and disorders which contractors who collect it according to their own interests and greed regularly cause in disturbance of the public tranquility.

In order that there may be the same payment of this tax in all districts according to its origin and establishment, and that the compounds and harmful mixtures which are made with *pulque* may be avoided as much as possible, since they destroy the health of the natives, for which reason the law cited prohibited them, I also command the intendants and subordinate judges to watch and visit with great care the *pulque* shops, and cause them to observe punctually the ordinance published on

July 9, 1753, the proclamations, and other measures that have been given heretofore and those which may be issued in the future concerning this matter. They shall equalize the tax generally fixed, and try to suppress the drinking-shops (*tepacherías*) in which various beverages very harmful to the Indians and other castes of the pople are made and secretly consumed.

⟨ᵃ *Pulque.*⟩

147

Although what is ordered in general concerning this third department [of finance], and that which in particular is provided for the revenues from tobacco, tributes, *alcabalas,* and *pulque* may be considered to be sufficient, in order to make the collection, management, and distribution [of the funds] of my royal treasury uniform in all the provinces of the kingdom of New Spain under the proper rules which are defined in the laws of the *Recopilación, cédulas,* instructions, and ordinances of their special branches in so far as these are not contrary to what is provided by this ordinance, I consider it fitting also to explain my royal intentions concerning each one of the other revenues of which my treasury there is composed, and concerning which as yet no specific statement is made in this ordinance.

148

ᵃThe monopoly and manufacture of powder, which formerly were leased, with great abuses and public dangers, at present are under profitable administration for the account of my royal treasury. I desire that they shall always continue under this same method according to the ordinances of this branch promulgated in Mexico on May 20, 1767, in so far as is not contrary to what is provided by this ordinance, in order to insure the defenses of my dominions and the advantage which my vassals experience from the excellent quality and abundance of such a commendable commodity.

I command the intendants, ordinary justices, and magistrates employed in the protection of my revenues to pursue, arrest, and punish the secret manufacturers of powder and those who bring it into the kingdom as contraband. Since the intendants must exercise contentious jurisdiction in this revenue according to article 80, they shall impose upon both classes of offenders the penalties established by the ordinances mentioned, and they all shall take care that the special rules defined in them concerning dealers in saltpetre, sulphur, and fireworks, shall be observed.

⟨ᵃ Gunpowder.⟩

149

ᵃThe monopoly of playing cards also is and must continue to be administered according to its special ordinances published on April 23, 1768, except that the intendants must exercise contentious jurisdiction [in it] as in the other branches of my treasury, in order to prevent by this just means the serious inconveniences and disorders which prevailed under the former contracts which my glorious father and lord Philip V by his royal order or circular issued in the year 1744, commanded to be abolished. Since the management and directive economic control of this revenue are united to those of tobacco and powder in the factories and administrative offices of the provinces, and as the union of their respective revenue guards, which has been established, is very useful for the aforesaid three branches and for that of *alcabalas,* I command that it shall continue wherever this may be possible, as was provided by my viceroy and approved by me. The sum which proportionally corresponds to their annual proceeds shall be charged to [the account of] each revenue so that a sufficient amount may be produced to pay its cost, and in order that all those employed as revenue guards may likewise take heed of the frauds which are committed to the injury of these revenues and to [that] of the other dues of my treasury.

⟨ᵃ Playing cards.⟩

150

[a]The royal dues of fifths (*quintos*) from gold, silver, copper, and other metals, which the placers and mines of these dominions [of Spain] and the others of America produce, always received the first consideration of my glorious forefathers. Since my father and lord Philip V in the year 1723 reduced that tax in the kingdom of New Spain to the tenth (*diezmo*) to the general benefit of the state and the nation; and since I also, influenced by the same causes, have decreased the dues on gold to three per cent, and the price of quicksilver and powder for the benefit of the miners, and have, in order to encourage and ennoble their very useful industry, granted them other very valuable and unalterable favors set forth in the royal ordinances which I thought well to issue under the date of May 22, 1783, for the direction, management, and administration of the important corporation of mining of that kingdom; I therefore desire the intendants to pay special attention not only to patronizing and protecting the aforesaid organization in the provinces under their control, but also either themselves or by means of subordinate judges, to see to the most exact observance of everything which I have commanded by the ordinances cited; namely, that neither perquisites, recompenses, or fees shall be charged to miners in the royal accounting-offices and treasuries, nor in the administrative offices of the monopoly for quicksilver and powder which they may need, not even under the title of fees for officials or notaries; that intendants shall punish offenders severely, besides [imposing upon them] the penalty of making restitution, and of repaying double or quadruple the amount in cases of repeated offense; and that the quicksilver which they request for cash, or under security to pay for it within the time that they shall be allowed, shall be given in small quantites to the poor who are engaged in the mining industry, without charging them interest or extra price for it.

⟨[a] Fifths.⟩

151

Inasmuch as it is provided in article 13, title 3 of the Ordinances of the Corporation of Mining, that the tribunal of appeals therein commanded to be set up in each province for the purposes of its organization shall be composed, among other individuals, of the most competent judge there may be in the province, who shall be appointed by me, I therefore declare it my sovereign will that the performance of the duties of this very important office, and consequently the presidency of the aforesaid tribunals with all the authority and powers granted by the ordinances, shall belong to the intendants in their respective provinces, except in those of Mexico City and Guadalajara, by virtue of what is prescribed for both capitals by the said article.

With the just purpose of avoiding the uncertainties and abuses which mining would experience if, on account of the great distance and expense its members should be compelled to carry on long deferred litigation, I command that in the towns of Chihuahua and Rosario, and in all other places very far distant from those in which their respective intendants reside, their subdelegates shall in like manner exercise the aforesaid judicature of appeals for them. In their absence, illness, or incapacity the senior judge of my royal treasury and of the respective subtreasury [shall do this.]

152

ªWith the just aim of preventing the concealment and fraudulent removal of gold and silver in bullion which poor miners sell to dealers and exchangers of these metals, in evident violation of the laws which prohibit the acquisition of and trade in these metals before the fifth is deducted, I command that in all the principal and subsidiary and minor treasuries of the provinces which have mines in current operation, there shall always be kept the money considered necessary for the purchase of and proper payment for the gold and silver which the miners may bring to sell. In order that their value may be paid promptly at the current price and with due knowledge of the fineness of the metals, the intendants shall, with the advice and consent of the *junta superior de hacienda,* through the superintendent-subdelegate, provide that, wherever it has not been done, the office of melter and assayer of the present subtreasuries shall be incorporated and united to my royal treasury as soon as possible.

They shall also see that [those positions are filled] by faithful and efficient individuals who receive fixed salaries, in order that the shipments of silver and gold may be smelted and assayed as soon as their owners present them, in their presence and that of the ministers of the royal treasury, as is commanded by law 11, title 22, book 4 of the *Recopilación.* It is to be understood that the appointment and approval of assayers must be preceded by the indispensable examination which law 17 of the same title and book provides for and which must be conducted by the chief assayer of the kingdom.

⟨ª *Recopilación,* ley 2, tit. 24, lib. 4.⟩

153

Deputy and special judges were established in my dominions of the Indies for the management, administration, and collection of the funds of the revenues from quicksilver, stamped paper, half-annates,[21] and fees for titles of nobility (*lanzas*), and the practice still exists in New Spain. But considering that these divisions of the general control of my royal patrimony, besides the burden which they place upon its net proceeds, prevent in no small degree a knowledge of its actual income and do not prevent great negligence in the collections, I have resolved that the aforesaid branches shall be united to the general organization of the administration of the other divisions of my royal treasury.

21 A half-year's salary contributed to the crown once in five years.

Consequently I command that the superintendent-subdelegate of the exchequer shall have under his care generally, and the intendants particularly in their respective provinces, directive and economic cognizance of the four branches mentioned under the special rules that will be indicated in this instruction, and that they shall exercise in these the contentious jurisdiction which is granted to them with regard to other branches of my royal treasury by article 78.

⟨ᵃ Stamped paper, half-annates, and *lanzas*.⟩

154

The quicksilver for the extraction of gold and silver is brought to New Spain from this kingdom [of Spain] and sometimes from Peru. It shall be under the control of the ministers of the royal treasury, the general accountant and the general treasurer, who must keep account of this branch of my treasury under the supervision of its general accounting-office established in Mexico City. For the present this office must continue, under the understanding that the *junta superior* [shall immediately take action] concerning the number of its members and of the subordinate officials of the aforesaid branch, and concerning the salaries of both, according as present conditions and a prudent economy of my royal treasury shall demand. It shall put its decision into effect and give me account in order that I may approve its measures.

Considering that an abundant supply of the said article is as useful as it is indispensable for the working of metals which are not smelted, the superintendent-subdelegate shall take care to order that the treasuries of those provinces shall be provided with the quantities that the mining camps situated in them may need. Their intendants shall see that quicksilver is never lacking in the various magazines and other places where it is needed, and that the ministers of the royal treasuries, whether principal ones or subsidiary, under whose charge [the mercury] must respectively belong, shall inform them within sufficient time in order that they themselves may notify the aforesaid superintendent-subdelegate, so that he may fittingly command that the necessary remittances [of the metal] shall be made.

155

Under date of January 15, 1709, an instruction which was then considered opportune was issued for the direction, control, and management of this branch; and afterward various *cédulas* and royal orders were promulgated successively for the same purpose as conditions and the period required them, and it has been administered under these rules until the present. But since these orders should necessarily be altered to accord with what is declared by this instruction, and it being for the same reason fitting to avoid confusion by reducing the numerous rules which shall be in force in the future to one formal ordinance, I command the superintendent-subdelegate to draw up the ordinance immediately, keeping in mind for this all the present *cédulas* and royal orders which have been indicated, the instruction cited, and that which has been decided by this ordinance in the matter and in the ordinances of the important organization of mining which were mentioned in article 150; he shall also take the advice of its royal tribunal, of that of accounts, and that of the general accounting-office of the said branch. When [the ordinance] is thus completed, he shall submit it to the *junta superior* so that, after it is examined by [that body] in the presence of the *fiscal*, the *junta* shall revise it in so far as it may think fitting, and authorize it to be put into effect provisionally, until account is given me by the *via reservada* with a transcript of the document itself and of everything which was considered in connection with it, when I may condescend to approve it according to my sovereign will.

156

As has been said, the branch of stamped paper in New Spain is under the direction of a special judge. The [paper] is sold in Mexico City by its particular treasurer, who is paid the high rate of eight per cent on its annual proceeds, and its issue is generally intrusted in the greater part of that kingdom to the *corregidores* and *alcaldes mayores* as [part] of their duties, without any remuneration for this. But since these positions are to be suppressed as is provided by article 9, and as experience has shown the great abuses which my royal treasury and the public credit have hitherto suffered in the use and consumption of stamped paper, because great distances and other reasons have made the rules useless which the laws of the *Recopilación* of the Indies and various later measures prescribed for both purposes; and inasmuch as the remedy of these abuses is as essential to my treasury as to the welfare of my vassals, I command the well tried method for the aforesaid branch which has been observed since the year 1770 in the district of the *audiencia* of Guadalajara in conformity with a measure of the general visitation, shall be extended to all the other provinces of the aforesaid kingdom. The issue of stamped paper shall generally be the duty of the administrators of tobacco, with the moderate compensation or rate of four per cent on its proceeds, and under the surety of bonds corresponding to the value of what is intrusted to them, to which the respective ministers of the royal treasury must certify; in like manner the latter officials must be obliged to receive the stamps which are assigned for the consumption of their district, to keep account of them, to distribute them among the administrators mentioned, and collect from these officials the net proceeds.

As had been said already, the direction of this branch in general and the duty of commanding the general accountant and treasurer of the royal treasury, under the proper account and calculation, to receive the stamped paper that is sent to New Spain for the consumption of that kingdom, shall remain under the charge of the superintendent-subdelegate. He likewise must provide that the aforesaid ministers shall send to each one of the other intendancies as many reams of paper as they may consider necessary in view of the probable use of it, in order that they may distribute them among the treasuries; and the latter shall do the same among the administrative offices of the tobacco monopolies which may be in their territories, under the rules and securities provided, as also shall the said intendant-general of Mexico do for those establishments of that capital and province under his immediate control.

It shall be the duty of the intendants and subordinate judges to take heed that law 18, title 23, book 8 of the *Recopilación* shall be observed generally and exactly in regard to everything else which that law prescribes and may be contrary to what is provided herein. [They shall also see] that in its fulfillment all my vassals shall use the paper authorized with the proper stamp in all judicial proceedings and public contracts, no judge or magistrate being permitted to validate the simple and common paper [for such cases] under any motive or pretext; for only in the rare case of absolute lack of any of the stamps may each intendant in his province with advice of the superintendent-subdelegate authorize the necessary utilization of ordinary paper; and since the office of treasurer of the branch mentioned has been alienated from my crown, I likewise order that said office shall be abolished immediately and shall be incorporated to it, and the amount of the said proceeds which the owner has expended must be restored to him.

157

In order to assure as is fitting the proper and punctual observance · of everything provided in the foregoing article and make it possible besides for the superintendent-subdelegate to receive from the intendants of the province and transmit to my royal hands opportunely the information needful in order to arrange for the shipment of paper stamped with each denomination, which must be done for each biennium by taking account of the surplus from the preceding one as has been repeatedly commanded, he shall draw up the instruction and ordinance which he may deem best after he has heard the opinion of the tribunal of accounts concerning it. When his report has been examined and revised in so far as may be necessary by the *junta superior de hacienda* with the attendance of the *fiscal,* that body shall command it to be put into effect in the interval while account is being given me by the *vía reservada* with the [required] tran- script, and I may be pleased to approve it or decide what may be my sovereign pleasure.

158

The royal dues from *lanzas* and half-annates, the regulation and collection of which are likewise intrusted exclusively in that kingdom to a judge of commission, have their particular and separate accounting-office in Mexico City. Since in observance of my sovereign resolution contained in article 153 of this instruction, both branches and their special tribunals must in future be under the charge of the superintendent-subdelegate and of the intendants of province respectively, I command that the latter and the former, as also the special accounting-office mentioned, which must continue for the present, shall be directed and guided in their management by the particular rules for the imposition and collection of the aforesaid revenues in all my dominions of the Indies, which shall be prescribed in the special ordinance that I have ordered to be drawn up, and which will be issued in due time.

159

[a]The revenue from salt mines was one of the most important dues which the Indian emperors enjoyed. Although, under such an ancient right, and by the preeminent one of my royal

crown to all the salt produced in my dominions, it was commanded in law 13, title 23, book 8 of the *Recopilación* that the salt mines which could be administered without harm to the Indians should be monopolized, this has not been done with certain of the many salt pits that exist in New Spain but these ought to have been placed under the workings of said law, leaving to the Indians the free use of only the few deposits that they need and may work under the moderate rate which they must pay for the license.

With the just purpose that the equitable rule which the above cited law gave concerning this branch may be observed in all that empire, I wish the intendants to observe it and cause it to be observed in their provinces. They shall preserve for the Indian towns which work the salt the permission to take it out under the fitting or ordinary payment of the license tax which belongs to my royal treasury. I [desire] that the other salt mines, of which the natives do not avail themselves, shall be administered as pertaining to my supreme prerogative. The intendants shall always bear in mind the great importance of an abundance of salt, and shall see that it is sold at reasonable prices in that country, because it is a very necessary commodity for all the inhabitants, especially for cattle-raisers for their cattle and for miners for washing and working metals.

⟨[a] Salt mines.⟩

160

[a]The tax from the grant of licenses to grocery stores (*composición de pulperías*) is one of the revenues under my royal patrimony in both Americas. It was established by law 12, title 8, book 4 of the *Recopilación*, which assigned a license fee of from thirty to forty *pesos*, that all stores which shall be opened and established above the number of those [allowed] by ordinance must pay for the privilege which is granted to them of engaging in purveying provisions to the people. The purpose of

this permission is to avoid the monopolies which may develop among the permitted grocery stores which the municipal councils of the cities, towns, and villages may establish, restricting the sale to the public of the most necessary commodities, like bread, oil, wine, vinegar, and other things of this kind which ordinarily are sold in such shops. Therefore, in order to attain a worthy object for the public utility, it is necessary that this branch of industry shall be left free, so that any one of my vassals may seek in it his own sustenance, that at the same time cheap provisions of good quality may be furnished to the community, and also that the privileged exemption which the law cited grants to such supernumerary grocery stores may be preserved to them. This law was therefore renewed by the royal *cédula* of February 5, 1730.[22]

Wherefore the intendants in their provinces, in the capacity of *corregidores* and chief justices thereof, shall designate exactly in every ordinary village (*lugar*) that is raised to the status of a city or town, the required number of grocery stores permitted by the ordinance, and no more. For all others which it may be desired to establish they shall give the proper licenses, and, under their authority as intendants, shall command a report to be made by the respective ministers of the royal treasury, in which the individuals to whom they may be granted shall be indicated. The [intendants] shall cause them to give bonds to the satisfaction of the said ministers, as the collection of the annual amount of thirty or forty *pesos* must be under their charge, according as they shall assess it wisely, not with respect to the value of what is on sale at the time, but to the daily replenishment as the supplies cause a commerce and continuous exchange during the whole year. It shall be understood that the payments must be made into the proper treasuries every six months.

⟨ª Grocery stores.⟩

---

[22] See Appendix, number 17, in the original.

161

In case delay is observed in the payment of the tax mentioned, the grocery stores must be closed by the *intendant-corregidores,* or at the request of their subdelegates by the subordinate justices. But as long as they pay it punctually the intendants shall not permit the municipal councils to impose upon them or collect any municipal tax whatever, not even under color of visitations, which must be made by councilmen officially every month without salary, by the intendant in his capacity as *corregidor,* or any other royal judge. [Such inspectors] must punish any excess or defect in weights, or bad quality of foods, according to the municipal ordinance if there is one, without discrimination between [the stores] of the [required] number and those under the ordinance, for in this respect all must be equal, as also must they be in the dues according to the schedule for the sales prices of their commodities, in the expense of regulating weights and measures annually by the municipal inspectors of weights and measures (*fiel ejecutoria*), and in the cost of the signature and validation of the licenses. It is to be observed that, when these licenses are once given, they do not need revalidation, although the *intendant-corregidores* or justices may be replaced, except when the said grocery stores shall change owners.

162

ªSalable and transferable offices in my dominions of the Indies form one of the branches of my treasury. In order that the rules prescribed in the laws of those kingdoms and in the various royal *cédulas* which have since been issued for their better understanding and interpretation, may be most adequate and just for all cases of sales, renunciations, and forfeitures of those offices, I command the intendants to conform to them punctually. I also [order] that when vacancies of this kind may occur in the towns of their provinces they shall submit the bids and overbids which are made to a *junta* of auctions, and after the bids are verified along with the accompanying documents including the explanatory statement of valuation, and after observing the procedure provided for by the laws,[23] they shall send them to the [*junta*] *superior* of Mexico City, in order that, when they have been reviewed in turn by the general accountant of the royal treasury as to their purport and by my *fiscal* as an interested party, that body may decide upon the value and the award as it deems most fitting; then it shall return them to the intendant concerned so that he may put into effect what it may determine and order him to do.

When the award is made and the exact amount bid has been deposited in the treasury they shall again return the documents to the said *junta superior de hacienda,* in order that, after the auction approved by the *junta,* its president shall officially transmit to the viceroy those documents which concern the offices of the district under his special jurisdiction, so that the said viceroy may thereupon command that the proper titles be issued according to what laws 9, 24, 25, and 26, title 20, book 8 of the *Recopilación* provide. He shall place on the aforesaid documents the proper notation that they have been put into effect. When this is done, the viceroy shall return them to the superintendent of my royal treasury, who, after leaving in the general accounting-office a proper account for its guidance in the future, shall return them to the intendant concerned, in order that they may be deposited in the archives [of the intendancy].

Bearing in mind the above-cited law 24, and law 3, title 22 of the same book of the *Recopilación,* the intendant shall order that the transcripts for which litigants ask shall be granted according to said laws, so as to procure my royal confirmation for the offices which may be of the first rank, according to the quota

---

[23] *Recopilación,* leyes 1–21, tit. 20, lib. 8; leyes 1–8, 10–27, tit. 21, lib. 8.

which I have prescribed for the kingdom of New Spain by my royal *cédula* of February 21, 1776, inserted in another one of January 31, 1777.[24] What I enjoined by the said decree for the *fiscales* of *audiencias* and attorney generals of my royal treasury, in regard to seeking confirmation in positions of lower rank, shall remain under the charge of the intendants respectively.

⟨ᵃ Salable and transferable offices. By the royal *cédula* of May 2, 1797, it was ordered that accounts, information, and a memorandum should be taken as might be convenient for regulating the sale price of the offices of *regidores* of the cities and towns of these dominions, and it was declared therein that those of Mexico City were worth 4,000 *pesos*. By the royal *cédula* of December 28, 1803, the cost of the town councilorship of the province of San Luis Potosí was likewise declared.⟩

163

Since it is my royal will to preserve for the commandant-general of the frontier the powers appropriate to his office, I order that in the salable and transferable positions of the district under his command everything shall be understood to apply to him which has been explained by the preceding article with respect to my viceroy concerning the offices of his territory; but with the exception with regard to procedure that, to prevent greater delays, a memorandum of the documents shall be made in the accounting-office of the treasury of Mexico City before they are sent to the aforesaid commandant-general, in order that he may command the titles to be issued, and afterward send the documents to the intendants concerned, so that they may be deposited in the archives, and that he may put into effect all the other matters which are provided for in the aforesaid preceding article.

Therefore to avoid doubts and embarrassments in its fulfillment, I expressly annul for the territories, jurisdictions, and districts in which this ordinance must be observed, the above-cited royal *cédula* of February 21, 1776, in so far as it may be

---

24 See Appendix, number 18, in the original.

contrary to what is here ordered. In other matters the decree shall be kept in force, both in regard to [the part] which mentions my viceroy, and must be understood also in the case of the said commandant-general, just as it must in that which refers to the superintendent-subdelegate and to the intendants of my royal treasury, according to what is prescribed by this and the preceding article.

164

In order that what is commanded by the two preceding articles may have all the effect for which it is issued, the *junta* of auctions in the capital of Mexico must continue to exist, and shall perform its functions according to laws 2 and 3, title 25, book 8 of the *Recopilación*. It shall be composed of the intendant-general, of the most recently appointed judge of that *audiencia,* of the *fiscal* of my royal treasury, and of its ministers, the accountant and the treasurer. Another similar *junta* shall be established in each capital of the other intendancies. In the intendancy of Guadalajara it shall consist of the same ministers respectively as in Mexico City because there is an *audiencia* there, and in the others of the intendant, his lieutenant-assessor, the ministers of the royal treasury, and of its defender whom the intendant shall appoint, all the officials keeping the same order in regard to their seats as that with which they are named herein.

In case of the absence, illness, or incapacity of the intendant in the intendancy of Mexico or Guadalajara, his lieutenant-assessor shall attend [the *junta*], and shall take his seat after the *fiscal* and before the ministers of the royal treasury. The *juntas* and auctions mentioned must be held in precisely the same houses where the accountant's and treasurer's offices of my royal treasury are located, so that during the meeting of their superior officers the royal houses may not be left unoccupied.

165

ªThe revenue of the alms which the faithful contribute for the Bull of the Holy Crusade of the living and of the dead and for other favors connected therewith, has always received my most careful attention and that of my glorious forefathers, for the purpose of preventing all malversation and waste [of money] in regard to it, ʻand of guaranteeing the good administration, receipt, and collection of its proceeds for the commendable and pious ends to which they are assigned. With the selfsame motive, and with that of making these funds more abundant and more useful for their praiseworthy designs, my august brother, Don Fernando VI, besought and obtained from the Holy See, for himself and the kings [who were to be] his successors, by the brief of March 4, 1750, the adequate concession and control [of the Bulls of Crusade]. In the use of these faculties he dispatched his royal instruction, dated May 12, 1751, to all the viceroys of the Indies, in order that they might according to its spirit draw up the proper ordinances for a new system of collection and distribution of the aforesaid alms. Nevertheless the entire purpose at which the said royal instruction was aimed was not attained in New Spain, for these Bulls continued to be issued by treasurer-contractors at very high contract prices, to the injury of the people.

As this was not in conformity with what I piously desired, I thought well to intrust the regulation of the aforesaid revenue to José de Gálvez, visitor-general of that kingdom, and thereafter from the beginning of the year 1768 this revenue has been under an administration very advantageous to my royal treasury and to my vassals. Wherefore bearing in mind the favorable consequences produced in the branch mentioned by the method which the visitor-general established for its economic control with the advice of my viceroy, the subdelegate-commissioner of the Crusade, and with the aid and consent of the prelates of the dioceses, the efficacy of which method is shown by the lucrative proceeds obtained since then and which are continually increasing, I wish and order that the said administrative method shall continue under the same form, rules, and securities arranged for by the instruction dated December 12, 1767, which the aforesaid visitor-general issued for its establishment.

There [shall be] no other change except that the three treasurers, in the cities of Puebla de los Ángeles, Antequera de Oaxaca, and Valladolid de Michoacan must be discontinued, and their duties and functions shall be united to those of the ministers of the royal treasury, the principal accountants and treasurers of province, who must be appointed in each one of the said cities as the capitals of intendancies, in order that the summaries of the Bull may be distributed and sent by them to all the parishes within the area of their provinces, just as is done at present by the treasury officials of Guadalajara, Durango, Guanajuato, and San Luis Potosí respectively.

⟨ᵃ Crusade.⟩

166

In conformity with the pontifical brief of March 4, 1750, cited in the preceding article, the full faculty of administering, collecting, and distributing all the proceeds of the Holy Bull and of the favors connected with it belong to my supreme prerogative, with absolute independence of the commissioner-general of the Crusade and of the other apostolic officials. Consequently the two jurisdictions, the spiritual and the temporal, which intervene in this branch must be separated. And since it is proper to prevent doubts or embarrassments from arising in the free exercise of these powers under the new system of the intendancies, and to provide, besides, that in those my dominions litigants may have two instances in temporal suits concerning the Crusade, I declare that in all matters of this kind each intendant in his province must have exclusive cognizance in first instance, as is ordered for the other revenues of my royal treasury, with appeals to the *junta superior* thereof, and from its decisions to my royal person by the *vía reservada* of the Indies. For this purpose it is my sovereign will that the superintendency of this branch shall be understood to belong to the superintendent-subdelegate of my royal treasury, and in each intendancy of province respectively to the special officer at the head of each district.

⟨ᵃConcerning the jurisdiction of the Crusade see the royal *cédulas* of January 23, 1792, and July 20, 1796.⟩

167

Since it is proper that the aforesaid branch of the proceeds from the Holy Bull shall have its formal ordinance, as the other divisions of this kind have in New Spain, in order that, by this means, its administration and control in all those provinces may at once be made uniform under the rules indicated in the two preceding articles and under others besides these which may be decided upon, I command that, in the light of the instruction given by the visitor-general and cited in the first of the two articles mentioned, of what is provided in each of these latter, in the ordinances, dated March 8, 1752, which were drawn up by my viceroy of Peru for the distribution of the summaries [of the Bulls] and for the collection of the alms in that kingdom, and in fulfillment of that which was commanded by the before-cited royal instruction of May 12, 1751, and of the royal *cédula* of September 11, 1755, in which this instruction was approved, the superintendent-subdelegate, with the advice of the tribunal of accounts, shall draw up an ordinance under the terms that he may consider proper and fitting for my just and religious desires, and adapted to the local and other circumstances which must be reckoned with in order to insure success, and which shall in no wise be contrary to the economic method of administration which is defined herein. When the ordinance he makes is examined by the *junta superior de hacienda* with the special care and deliberate reflection which the subject requires in all its parts, when it has been enlarged or modified as [that body] may think fitting and convenient for the purposes stated, the [said *junta*] shall approve it and command that it be put into practice provisionally, until I may be pleased to legalize it with my royal approval after account is given to me by the *vía reservada* with [a copy] of it and an accompanying report.

168

ªUnder very appropriate titles and the papal concession of Alexander VI in his bull issued on November 16, 1501, and later confirmed by other high pontiffs, the tithes of the Indies belong to my royal crown with the full, absolute, and irrevocable right of possession, under the necessary and perpetual condition of aiding those churches with a sufficient endowment for the proper maintenance of divine worship and for the adequate sustenance of their prelates and other ministers who serve at the altar. By virtue of the foregoing grants the essential provision contained in law 1, title 16, book 1 of the *Recopilación* was promulgated, and later, by law 23 of the same title and book, the form and method were decided upon, according to which, so as to obtain that purpose, the aforesaid tithes must be divided, administered, and distributed.

In consideration of all this the crown assumed the obligation of providing from the other revenues of its patrimony for any expenditures for which the tithes might not be sufficient to cover the endowments indicated. On account of both obligations not only did it fall to the royal authority to care for the good management and administration of the proceeds of the tithes, and to see that they should be distributed with honesty and with proper exactness among the recipients interested in their total yield, in order that the holy churches, parishes, and hospitals, which are under the immediate sovereign protection, might not suffer injury in their respective incomes and that the royal treasury [might not be harmed] because of the responsibility stated, even in regard to the two-ninths (*dos novenos*) which were reserved for it by the above-cited law 23; but so likewise did it pertain to the same supreme authority to see that what was ordered in law 34, title 7, of the aforesaid book should be put into effect. Hence it was commanded by laws 27, 28, and 29 of the said title 16 that the treasury officials should attend the auctions and leasings of the tithes, and, by the following law 30, that one of them and an *oidor* wherever there may be an *audiencia,* should do this for the accounts and allotments in order that these may be made according to the act of erection of each church.

I thought best to command that the royal *cédula* or circular of April 13, 1777,[25] should be issued for the following purposes: to render uniform in all my dominions of the Indies the proper observance of the above-mentioned laws by checking the serious inconveniences experienced on account of their misunderstanding and the misinterpretation which has been given to other laws relative to the same subject; for the purpose of insuring that in the aforesaid acts the direct right of use of the tithes referred to which I possess, shall prevail and be recognized as is just and proper; and finally, for the purpose of preventing injury in any manner being caused to recipients of the total sum [of the tithes], or to my royal treasury because of its aforesaid responsibility, either in regard to the two-ninths, or the major and minor vacancies, the *mesada,* or the half-annates that belong to it.

But considering that the new establishment and system of the intendancies may cause doubts concerning the method of putting into effect the regulation inserted therein, I have decided, in order to avoid them and to facilitate the most exact execution of

---

25 See Appendix, number 19, in the original.

what is provided thereby, to make in accordance with the true spirit of the *cédula* and laws cited, the declarations which are contained in the following fifteen articles.

⟨ª Tithes.⟩

169

The *junta de diezmos* of which the before-mentioned ordinance treats, and which must be established in the cities of Mexico, Puebla, Valladolid, Antequera, Guadalajara, Durango, Mérida, Arispe, and Monterrey, as they are the capitals of the archbishopric and the bishoprics of New Spain, must, in those districts which have *audiencias*, consist of the intendant, the most recently appointed *oidor*, the *fiscal* who dispatches the business of my royal treasury, of two factor-judges, appointed, until [there may be] a new order of mine, one by the prelate and the other by the *cabildo*, and of one of the principal ministers of the royal treasury of the province. Where there is no *audiencia* the intendant, the two factor-judges, one of the ministers of the royal treasury, and the fiscal-defender thereof shall compose the said *junta*.

Because the intendants of the provinces and dioceses of Yucatan and the New Kingdom of León do not regularly have their residences in the cities of Mérida and Monterrey, those *juntas* shall consist of the respective governors, of the two factor-judges, of one of the ministers of the royal treasury of the district, and of a defender thereof whom the intendants themselves shall appoint. Also the royal accountants of the tithes and tables (*quadrantes*) must be present at this *junta*, just as they attend the other *juntas* in the remaining dioceses.

⟨ª This article and the fourteen following ones are suspended according to the reserved order of March 23, 1788, in which it was commanded that the prelates and the churches which had not put into effect the system of the *juntas de diezmos*, should continue according to the former practice until there should be another order, and without any innovation respecting the administration of the tithes and cognizance of cases concerning them. Until January, 1806, there has been no order issued.⟩

170

The members who have been assigned respectively to the *junta* mentioned must keep and observe in respect to their seats and signatures the following order and places: the intendant, who must preside over it, the *oidor*, the *fiscal*, the factor-judge (who on account of his rank or seniority shall precede the other factor in the *cabildo* of his church), the minister of the royal treasury (either the accountant or the treasurer), the other factor, and the royal accountant of the tithes; where there may not be an *audiencia*, the intendant, the factor (who must come before his companion), the minister of the royal treasury, the other factor, the fiscal-defender, and the accountant of the branch.   In the cities of Mérida and Monterrey, the governor, the aforesaid factor-judge, one of the ministers of the royal treasury, the other factor, the defender, and the royal accountant.

In case of the absence or illness of the members enumerated, his lieutenant-assessor shall substitute for the intendant, for the *oidor* the companion who antedates him in tenure of office, for the *fiscal* [the individual] who substitutes in his office, for any of the factor-judges the person whom his chief shall appoint in his place, and for the minister of the royal treasury his companion; with the proviso that, where there is an *audiencia*, when his lieutenant-assessor attends for the intendant his place shall be after that of the *fiscal*, and the *oidor* shall preside, but where there is no *audiencia* he shall take the seat of the intendant and preside over the *junta*.

171

All the members mentioned shall have in their turn a decisive vote, but the *fiscal* must not have it in those matters in which he may speak as a litigant.   The accountant of the royal tithes, or his chief.official who shall substitute for him when he cannot be present on account of some legitimate hindrance, shall have only an informative vote. He who may preside shall have a casting vote in any case of disagreement in order that he may decide it.

172

^aThe *junta de diezmos* which is established shall not be a permanent tribunal with jurisdiction extending to all the cases resulting from the branch of tithes, because the function which it is declared to have in the above-cited ordinance, although royal, must be understood to be purely directive, economic, and regulative, and consequently limited to providing the means most conducive and fitting for the best direction, administration, collection, and secruity of the tithes and of the second *casa-excusada*.[26] It [shall be limited] to determining the conditions under which leases [of tithe-collecting] must be advertised; to deciding the time, manner and circumstances under which bids must be allowed and awards authorized, encouraging their greater increase; to considering whether administration of this revenue may not be preferred within the area of some parish or parishes in which the circumstances make it appear most useful; to resolving and determining everything that may occur until the auctions or administrations are completed, and which may have direct relation to the latter or the former; to intervening in the computation of the tithes and their distribution in order that they may conform to the laws and respective acts of erection according to the later royal declarations, and that the accounts may be drawn up and published with suitable formality and exactness, and finally to putting into effect everything which may seem useful for the benefit of the aforesaid branch and its recipients.

⟨^a By the reserved order of March 23, his Majesty commands that there shall be no change in the matters of the administration of the tithes and the cognizance of cases concerning them until, the information having been obtained and the opinions which were asked for having been heard, he shall decide what is fitting.⟩

---

[26] House of a landed proprietor chosen to collect tithes of fruits and of flocks.

173

Cognizance of all contentious litigation which may occur in regard to the recipt and collection of the proceeds from the tithes and the *casa-excusada,* usurpation and employment thereof, with all their incidentals, whether they may have been leased or placed under administration (except the funds which may belong to my royal two-ninths in the total of those which may have been auctioned), shall belong exclusively to the factor-judges, who must act and proceed with only the delegated royal jurisdiction that pertains to them because of the quality and nature of the temporal income of my royal patrimony which the said tithes possess even in the part that is granted to churches. The factor-judges shall not on account of this make use of censures or other judicial compulsions than those which are permitted by royal decree for ordinary and executive judgments, with appeals to the *junta superior de hacienda* and from it to my royal person by the *vía reservada* of the Indies.

It must be understood that the aforesaid contentious jurisdiction of factor-judges is one and the same for both of them, so that they may exercise it either together or separately in all the matters of which they may take cognizance, whether by assignment or by territorial division of the jurisdiction, which the two factors shall settle among themselves, or by the decision of the prelate and *cabildo* for the easier and more prompt dispatch of the business which may occur.

They shall substitute for each other mutually in case of incapacity, absence, or illness, so that the one who remains may take cognizance of the cases which the other may have begun. Because the measures which emanate from the royal authority and jurisdiction must be intrusted to royal magistrates for execution, the aforesaid factor-judges of the tithes, in the exclusive exercise of the authority which is delegated to them must make use of the ordinary bailiffs. The intendants as *corregidores* shall appoint a bailiff or as many as may be necessary and suitable, in order that they may be ready [to do] what is commanded them by the tribunal of tithes.

174

The election and nomination of the royal notary who must perform judicial acts not only in regard to auctions and the procedure relative thereto, but also in every doubtful case within the exclusive jurisdiction of the factor-judges, shall belong exclusively to the *junta de diezmos* as one of its economic functions. Because the said notary shall receive in the aforesaid occupations as remuneration the just fees which belong to him under the schedule which the *junta* must form in conformity with what is ordered by the ordinances referred to, he shall be held adequately paid therewith and shall not receive any perquisite from the total of the tithes.

175

It shall also be the particular duty of the aforesaid *junta* to issue the orders under which the lessees must be qualified, and the authorizations which according to article 193 must be given to the ministers of my royal treasury concerning that part of the leased tithes which pertains to it as the royal two-ninths. But to simplify as much as possible the business of the *junta*, it shall be sufficient that the said orders and the authorizations to tax-collectors shall be issued in its name by only the intendant and one of the factor-judges. The clerk, who is notary, must certify them, and a memorandum must be made in each case in the accounting-office of tithes, without any fees being charged by that office.

176

Tithe collection cannot be leased to individuals who are ecclesiastics, but their administration may be conferred upon such persons if the *junta de diezmos* thinks best; they must first give legal, ample, and guaranteed bonds. Because in such a case the factor-judges may find themselves obliged to proceed against some religious administrator, who may seek means of eluding the effects of an executive judgment by alleging the exemption arising from his religious privilege so as to challenge the jurisdiction and make void or block the measures of the factor-judges, the latter must, in order to avoid and to check such inconveniences, pleas, and procrastinations at their beginning, demand beforehand from the ecclesiastical prelates, and these must grant them (as I so order) the delegation of the ecclesiastical jurisdiction, and powers sufficient for dispatching these judgments, and they shall proceed against said debtors without hindrance or embarrassment until actual collection and restoration of what may be owed to such a commendable branch [are effected.] In the manner herein stated the factor-judges of the tithes must also conduct themselves, if on account of concealment, misappropriation, or any cause relative to the tithes, it shoud be necessary to take action against any secular or regular ecclesiastic, although he may not be an administrator.

177

As the free administration of the proceeds from the tithes, which by the laws of the Indies is granted as a tenure in sufferance to the prelates and *cabildos* of the churches of America, must not be understood to obtain, nor shall it take place, except in respect to that part which remains of the total sum after what belongs to my royal two-ninths is deducted, and as this amount cannot be ascertained in the case of tithes collected by administration, until the period [of the collection] having expired, that which is chargeable to the credit of the branch is calculated, it is therefore necessary to establish fitting rules in this matter, in order that the spirit of the laws and the royal *cédulas* cited shall be fulfilled, just as is done by the rules prescribed in said laws and *cédulas* in the case of the tithe collection which is sold at auction.

In consideration of these principles, the choice and appointment of administrators must also belong to the special and exclusive jurisdiction of the *junta de diezmos*. In the name of this body and in the manner provided by article 175 for the authorizations of lessees, shall the titles of such administrators be issued for their authority; there shall also be indicated in said titles such salary or percentage as the *junta* may deem fitting.

178

All the administrators, not excepting those of the second *casa-excusada*, if it shall be in administration, shall necessarily be obliged to keep an official and accurate account and calculation of the tithes under their charge, according to the exact formula which the royal accountant of the branch must draw up for this purpose, and which, with the proof and documents that shall be provided for therein, the *junta* must approve in order that, by enumerating the proceeds which are collected, and stating the places, terms, and persons without fraud or omission, knowledge of what the respective tithes of the parish, or *casa-excusada* under its care produce in one year may be exactly known. This sworn account they must give under the penalty of the law and present it to the *junta de diezmos* when the year of administration is finished so that, after the said royal accountant shall examine it closely and revise it as may seem just to him, [that body] may approve it, if it deserves this, or decide what is necessary to do before it may be so approved.

179

The lessees, including those of the *casa-excusada*, shall also be bound by the same obligation as that imposed by the preceding article upon administrators to keep and submit to the *junta de*

diezmos a formal and sworn account in the same terms as indicated, separately by parishes, as soon as the time of the lease may
expire. For this purpose the royal accountant of tithes shall
give to each of the former and the latter the formulary prescribed in the article cited, with a book containing as many leaves
as he thinks necessary in view of the greater or less extent and
returns of the tithing district, according to the parishes, or
casas-excusadas which it must comprise. All these pages must be
numbered, and on the first one must be put a note stating how
many leaves the book contains; this note must be signed by the
intendant and the two factor-judges with their half-signatures
and with the whole name of the aforesaid accountant. The last
page must be signed with rubrics by the same officials, and all the
other pages only by the accountant. It shall also be understood
that each administrator or lessee must pay for the book that
shall be given to him.

180

In the accounts which the administrators shall thus present
to the *junta de diezmos* the net proceeds of the tithes under
administration, and consequently what belongs to my royal treasury from the two-ninths and which the ministers thereof must
receive, shall be stated. But these accounts and also those which
lessees shall present shall serve to guide the *junta* in regard to
future leases and auctions by means of the knowledge that they
shall furnish concerning what the district of each parish and its
second *casa-excusada* may yield. With this purpose, and because
of the use which the accounting-office of the branch may see fit to
make of the aforesaid books on various occasions, that office shall
be the place wherein all [the books] must be deposited and
preserved.

181

The bonds required in cases of leasing collection of the part
of tithes which do not pertain to my royal two-ninths, and those

which belong to the second *casa-excusada,* whether the function be sold at auction or administered, must be executed to the satisfaction of the intendant, or of his subdelegate where he does not reside, and to that of the factor-judges with the necessary hearing and supervision of the *fiscal* included in the *junta.* But all bonds executed for security of the tithes to be collected by administration must also have the approval of the ministers of the royal treasury, inasmuch as the amount of the two-ninths which belong to it, and which, on account of the obligation of their offices these officials must certify as collected or provided for, is included in the aforesaid revenues that are to be administered.

Inasmuch as the proceeds from these revenues, as they are gradually collected in the offices of the administration, must go to the treasury of the respective church under the official supervision of the royal accountant of the tithes, and inasmuch as there can be no good reason for depriving my treasury [of them], until such time as the administrators shall submit and liquidate their accounts concerning the part of the deposits indicated which may belong to it from the aforesaid two-ninths, the *junta* shall take very special care that at the end of each third of the year the accounting-office of the branch shall make a correct computation of this part, in order that its total may be transmitted by the said church treasury to the ministers of my royal treasury for the account of the sum which shall accrue to it because of the division of the gross sum which all the administered tithes produce as shown by the final balance of their yearly returns.

182

Not only must the legal papers, orders, and measures which are drawn up or issued by the factor-judges, in which judicial authority may not be necessary, be promulgated through the accounting-office of tithes, but also the correspondence which the aforesaid judges carry on in regard to the said branch. The royal accountant shall take the advice of these officials for everything, since he must be immediately subject to their commands in everything which concerns the administration of the revenues from the tithes in detail, their collection and receipt. Therefore the legal papers mentioned, the proceedings, correspondence, and all other documents and papers concerning this branch must be kept and deposited in the archives of the said office. The notary who draws them up shall leave in the judicial registry of his office only the writings and legal instruments which may require this on account of their nature.

183

The tithes of some one inhabitant, but not of the richest one of each parish of all those of the diocese concerned, are by the terms of their acts of erection applied to the building of metropolitan and cathedral churches. These persons are the *excusados* whom law 22, title 16, book 1 of the *Recopilación* mentions, and [constitute that group] which is described in the *cédula* of April 13, 1777, as the *segunda casa-excusada*. Since [the privilege of collecting] the tithes of all the *casas* must be sold at auction or administered under the joint cognizance and jurisdiction of the *junta de diezmos* as was indicated in article 172, the account showing what they produce by either method must be submitted to the said *junta* in order that it may examine and approve it. But the statement of the distribution of the balance shown by the aforesaid account to the credit of the building fund, and of the other income belonging to it, such as *censos,* interment fees, and others which shall enter into the fund, must be submitted annually to the vice-patron in conformity with what is ordered by the royal *cédula* circular of May 23, 1769.[26]

---

26 See Appendix 20 in the original.

In order that this may be duly observed and as is my sovereign will, I declare that, when the churchwarden to whom [this duty] belongs, shall have presented the account mentioned with its substantiating documents to the magistrate who exercises the respective vice-patronage, the latter must submit it with an accompanying letter of transmittal to the prelate and *cabildo* of the holy cathedral church in order that, after it is examined, they may express to him, in their turn and without delay, what seems to them best and fitting; with what they say and with the proper decree, the said vice-patron must transmit the account to the royal accountant or accountants of the tithes of the diocese; they, in discharge of the duty of *contador-fiscal*, which they must exercise in these cases, and keeping in mind laws 11 and 18, title 2, book 1 of the *Recopilación* and articles 188 and 191 of this ordinance, shall proceed to examine and annotate it, and to form half-margin sheets setting forth the defects and revisions which may seem to them proper.

After they have submitted their revisions to the said churchwarden, so that he may offer his justification within the time that they assign to him, they shall in the view of his representation and of all other relevant facts close the aforesaid account and return it to the vice-patron in order that, if any net balance is available, he may declare it and cause it to be recorded; and after this is done, he shall approve it if it deserves this, or determine what is yet necessary before he can do so; in this manner the [account] shall be closed. The vice-patron as well as the royal accountants respectively, must act in conformity with what is provided by the various Laws of the Indies for taking, glossing, and closing the accounts of the royal treasury.

The vice-patron shall then submit to my royal hands the original account thus closed and with it what the prelate and *cabildo* have in their turn explained, the defects which the *contador-fiscal* has brought to the attention of the churchwarden, and his representations, the certificate that the balance has been deposited if there was one, and the approval that has been obtained. A transcript of all this and the original documents of the account shall be deposited in the archives of the office of the said royal accountant or accountants.

Because, in the provision of the before-cited royal *cédula* of May 23, not only the cathedrals must be understood to be included, but also all other churches the buildings of which receive an endowment from the tithes or any other branch of my royal treasury, the same thing ordered for building cathedral churches must be observed in their accounts, with only the difference that what is enjoined respecting the prelate and *cabildo* of these churches must apply to the priests and curates of the former where they exist, and that, for greater brevity, the church-warden must require from these the account and its [accompanying] documents so that, after explaining what they in turn think fitting concerning it, they may submit it to the vice-patron; and he, if he should notice any defect in the presentation of any of the accounts mentioned, shall send an official letter to the prelate of the diocese in order that he may have it corrected in observance of what is provided by the royal *cédula* cited.

All of this I wish to be obeyed in this manner in New Spain, and in fulfillment thereof I command the intendants and the other judges of the *junta de diezmos* referred to, and encharge the very reverend archbishop, the reverend bishops, the venerable members of the *cabildos* of their churches, and each one of the factor-judges who, under the conditions explained in this and the fifteen preceding articles, in the part pertaining to each one, shall observe the laws, the ordinance, and the *cédulas* mentioned in them, and shall keep and fulfil them exactly without negligence or evasion, and without doing the contrary to this or permitting them to be contravened in any manner.

184

In order, moreover, that no doubts or embarrassments may arise concerning the manner in which the observance of what the above-cited law 29, title 16, book 1 of the *Recopilación* orders in its first part must be secured in future, namely, that wherever the tithes are not sufficient for the endowment of the churches, those which may exist shall be collected by the treasury officials in the manner prescribed, and the clergy shall be supported at the expense of the royal treasury, I declare that the leasings and auctions of the tithes which may be in suchwise conditioned shall be effected both in [those] of vacant sees of prelates and in those which have none in the *juntas* of auctions of which article 164 treats, and without the concurrence or intervention of the other judges or persons who are mentioned therein; the respective judges of the treasury, the accountant and treasurer, under whose charge [the matter] must belong, shall take action in regard to such leases and the collections according to what has been defined by general rule in this instruction for the other branches of my treasury, and the provisions of law 31, title 8, book 8 of the *Recopilación* must be observed in these auctions.

I command the intendants to see to the careful and punctual observance of what is declared herein and of that which the before-cited law 29 orders concerning the administration of the said tithes. They shall see to it that this administration is left to the prelates and *cabildos* in the part pertaining to them if they should claim this, and if they shall have obtained my *cédula* and permission therefor. They must also put into effect all the other provisions of the law mentioned for such a case, bearing in mind that the aforesaid *cédula* must be presented to them with the executive order (*cúmplase*) of the superintendent-subdelegate of my royal treasury, and after its registry in the auditor's office of Mexico City.

185

In consideration of what was provided in article 174 of the Ordinance of Intendants dispatched under the date of January 28, 1782, to the intendants of the viceroyalty of Buenos Aires, that superintendent-subdelegate of my royal treasury remitted with a letter of August 4, 1784, the tables of the tithes of the archbishopric of Charcas belonging to the preceding year 1783. With this at hand the general accountant of my Council of the Indies called to my attention in a report of July 3, 1785, the defects that he noticed in the said tables, and the doubts and exceptions which occurred to him concerning the collection, management, and distribution [of the proceeds] of the branch mentioned.

In order that the aforesaid report might be examined and an opinion of the matters concerned might be made known to me, I commanded that a *junta* composed of the judges of the supreme tribunal itself should be formed. This body in compliance with this order and in its report of last June 2, explained to me what it considered best for correcting the abuses introduced in the distribution of the tithes, and recommended for the future the general and proper observance therein of what is provided by the laws and acts of erection of the churches. Agreeing with what the said *junta* proposed to me, I resolved and ordered by royal *cédula* of last August 23, what is contained in the following seven articles, and it is my sovereign will that it shall be obeyed, fulfilled, and put into effect exactly and strictly in all the dioceses of New Spain just as is provided in them.

186

The *casa-excusada* which was discussed in article 183 must be established according to what is prescribed by law 22, title 16, book 1 of the *Recopilación*, that is, its respective tithes must be kept separate from all others. For this purpose the choice and designation of one of the tax-payers within the boundary of each parish shall be made by provision of the *junta de diezmos;* he must not be the first one in wealth, but the second. Therefore when this is done, [the revenues of] this branch shall be collected with the same distinctiveness as the others. They may be either leased at auction or administered according as the aforesaid *junta* shall judge best.

187

From the total or gross sum of all the tithes, after [the proceeds] from the *casas-excusadas* are deducted as the preceding article provides, the two fourth parts for bishops and for chapters must be separated. From the other two-fourths or half the two-ninths pertaining to my royal treasury, according to law 23, of the same title 16, book 1 of the *Recopilación,* shall be subtracted. It shall be understood that the aforesaid royal two-ninths must not undergo the deduction of the three per cent for the seminary nor the costs of collection, but these shall be levied on the proceeds of the tithes when they are not leased.

But if the ministers of the royal treasury should not then collect and separate from the total amount those funds which belong to the said royal two-ninths and these should continue with the others in the administration, in such case the royal ninths must contribute pro rata to the quota which afterwards shall be expended for the greater advantage, custody, and increase of the amount of the aforesaid tithes.

But if the ministers of the treasury mentioned should consider it fitting to lease those tithes from which the two-ninths are derived they may do so, but in this case the lessee shall receive the two-ninths at the warehouse or storehouse where they may be collected, without keeping them there longer than the brief period which the *junta de diezmos* may determine. If the lessee does not come to get them within this time he must pay what may be ordered for storage and care, and shall incur the risks therein.

188

It must be observed that the ninth and one-half destined by the above-cited law 23 and by the acts of erection of the cathedral churches to their respective building funds, must be derived only from the tithes of the district of the parish of each of them, and that what [is obtained] from the proceeds of the tithes from the other parishes of the diocese shall belong to their building funds respectively. Therefore in order that this rule may be put into effect where it is not now in observance, the amount from the aforesaid ninth and one-half shall immediately be deposited for the account of the vice-patrons and prelates of the diocese, who shall distribute it proportionally to the said parishes to which it pertains according to the need of each one. Meanwhile the tithes of every parish for its respective distribution may be leased or administered for each one separately as was ordered before and is practiced in some dioceses of those my dominions.

189

In order to decide with proper knowledge what may be best to the end that the other ninth and one-half, which is commanded by the above-mentioned law 23 to be applied to hospitals, may have the most fitting and most useful investment in such a commendable object, I wish my vice-patrons and the prelates of the dioceses jointly to inform me, with due proof and as quickly as possible, how many hospitals there are in their respective districts; how far apart they are; what the revenue of each one is, according to receipts of the last five years; which ones receive income from the said ninth and one-half and which ones do not; how this portion of the tithes is distributed and what its annual amount is in the whole diocese, computed also for five years; and what other hospitals may be established and endowed without injury to the necessary endowment of those which exist, with any other information that they may consider conducive to the proposed end.

190

The four-ninths called *beneficiales* (providing ecclesiastical livings) shall be distributed precisely according to the above-cited law 23 and the act of erection of each church. Wherever this is done its observance shall continue without alteration. But in those dioceses in which the contrary is done, either because the aforesaid four-ninths have been applied to the *cabildos* and to parish priests of the chief towns, or used in any other method, that which pertains to [the four-ninths] in the district of the parish of the cathedral shall be immediately separated in order that the use which its act of erection provided for it may be attained. The same thing shall be done respectively with what pertains to each parish of the cities and chief towns—that is, the [four-ninths] shall be given to their priests and other officials who should receive them.

All that may remain from the proceeds of the said four-ninths after the separations mentioned are made, shall be preserved and deposited in the strongbox of the three different keys which shall be located in the place which the vice-patron and the prelate of the diocese shall decide upon. The individual whom the vice-patron shall choose must keep one of the keys, he whom the bishop appoints [shall have] the second, and the [person] whom the *cabildo* designates the third. This measure must be understood as provisional until the vice-patrons and prelates of the dioceses shall inform me respectively concerning the revenues which shall be set aside for each prebendary and priest of a chief town, exclusive of the part which hitherto they may have enjoyed from the aforesaid four-ninths for ecclesiastical livings which may be deposited [in the coffer].

They shall draw up this report correctly and as quickly as possible. The vice-patrons shall accompany theirs with a complete and legalized statement of the table (*cuadrante*) of the tithes, which their accountants must form, in observance of what is ordered for them by article 200 of this ordinance and must submit it to the respective intendants, who for the purpose [mentioned] shall transmit the aforesaid copy to the vice-patrons where they [themselves] do not exercise this supreme prerogative of my crown by virtue of what is provided by article 8. Let it be understood that the vice-patron shall be held responsible for whatever negligence may be noted.

191

In order to stop the arbitrary manner with which the general and particular expenses are charged and distributed among the recipients of the tithes, I have likewise resolved : that in the class of general expenditures the gratuities of the factor-judges, in the churches where it is still the practice to make them some assignment notwithstanding what is provided in this matter by the royal *cédula* of April 13, 1777, already cited under number 19, shall be considered a legitimate expense; that the royal notary-clerk of the *junta* shall not be assigned any remuneration from the total sum of the tithes, but rather what he may have had shall be suppressed and prohibited according to article 174 of this ordinance; and that their respective salaries shall be paid to the priests and servants appointed by the act of erection of each church from the branch [of finance] for which the aforesaid act of erection may provide, and that the other servants not included in it shall be paid from the building fund of the cathedral; that the salary or perquisite of the observer of deficiencies (*apuntador de fallas*) shall be paid directly by the *cabildo* and not from the building fund or from the four-ninths for ecclesiastical livings as has been done irregularly in some cathedrals; that the special expenditures by the *cabildos* in salaries of solicitors, attorneys, and others of this class shall be under the charge and care of persons who appoint them, and in no manner may they be included in the account of the distribution of the tithes; that the three-ninths applied by halves to the building fund of cathedral churches and parish churches, and to hospitals, shall be paid pro rata from the quota due to them from the general expenses of collecting or administering the tithes; and that the same thing shall be understood in regard to the four-ninths for ecclesiastical livings, but these shall be exempt from any other levy which may have burdened them, even when it is applied for some festival agreed upon by the prelate and the *cabildo*.

192

Finally, desiring to facilitate as much as is fitting and may be possible the practice prescribed by the six immediately preceding articles, I have resolved likewise that the *juntas* of tithes shall provide in their respective dioceses (as I very specially order) that the administration or leasing [of the collection] of the tithes shall be performed in the future parish by parish exactly, and each one separately, and not by the districts, in order that with all distinction and clearness that which the area of each parish produces may be known, and the particular distribution may be made for which the already cited law 23 and the acts of erection provide. But it must not be understood on account of this that the leasing of the tithes of the districts of two, three, or more parishes shall be prohibited to one and the same individual, provided that the amount for which the offices corresponding to each one are leased shall be kept separately.

193

The royal two-ninths of the tithes of the dominions of the Indies, which, as was said in article 168, are reserved to the crown and belong to my royal patrimony, must enter into the royal treasuries. For this purpose the intendants shall watch with particular attention that, from the total amount of all the revenues from the tithes, either leased or administered, and as is provided ·by law 23, title 16, book 1 of the *Recopilación,* and as is declared in article 187 of this ordinance, the legitimate values of the said two-ninths shall be deducted and shall by virtue of the following law 24 be collected by the ministers of the royal treasury, to whom [this duty] pertains.

In order that these officials may execute the said law in the part which refers in sequence to those tithes which are leased, it is my will and I command that, because law 27 of the same title and book remains in full force and effect in regard to what relates to the aforesaid ministers of the royal treasury, as it shall remain, not only must they procure from the *junta de diezmos* the tax-collecting power which is ordained for them therein, and cause the separate statement to be made which the above-cited law and the preceding law 26 provide appertaining to the royal two-ninths mentioned; but besides this they shall require bonds to their satisfaction and approval from the said lessees against whom the said tax-collecting power is given.

They shall act, in the collection and its coincident functions, as is provided in the other branches of my treasury, with dependence upon the exclusive jurisdiction which in those matters is declared to belong to the intendants, and to the *junta superior de hacienda* in the proper case, because in this matter the beforementioned law 24 must be understood to be annulled. But with respect to the total of the royal two-ninths of the tithes which are administered, the officers of the treasury of the holy church concerned must collect it according to that which is ordered in article 181, since the collection and accounting of the total revenue which the districts of the parishes or the administrative areas paying tithes may produce, must be accepted from the administrators themselves or from their guarantors by the factor-judges until such collections shall cover whatever deficit may appear as an unpaid balance or other discrepancy in the closing of their accounts.

194

In the use of the supreme powers which belong to me in regard to the tithes of all my dominions of the Indies by virtue of the papal concession mentioned in article 168, and with the purposes shown in my royal *cédula* circular of October 19, 1774,[27] I considered it best to reserve for myself the appointments of accountants of the tithes and tables of the metropolitan churches and cathedrals; consequently by the same *cédula* I took away from the aforesaid churches the power of making them. Among other things I command at the same time that these officers appointed by the *cabildos* of these religious establishments shall immediately cease to serve, and I declared furthermore everything which I thought fitting concerning ad interim appointments, the powers, salaries, and whatever related to the beforementioned offices.

It is my royal will that everything shall continue in the area of New Spain [as heretofore], with no other innovation except that the ad interim appointments of the aforesaid accountants shall be the exclusive function of the superintendent-subdelegate of my royal treasury upon nomination by the respective intendants; and I desire that it shall so be done and that the former and the latter shall take the greatest care that the said offices may be given to individuals possessing all the ability and competence necessary for the best performance of their duties; and they shall see that, in the part pertaining to them, all other matters which I was pleased to order by my royal *cédula* referred to shall be observed with the greatest exactitude. Only the portion thereof which treats of the aforesaid ad interim appointments shall be understood to be expressly annulled.

---

[27] See Appendix, number 21, of the original.

195

With the same purposes that influenced me to dictate the measures contained in the general *cédula* which the preceding article cites, and heeding what the viceroy of New Spain proposed to me in view thereof, in order to make its success in that kingdom more sure, I made, by another special decree of October 20, 1766, some declarations concerning what was provided in the same *cédula* and applicable to only the area of the aforesaid viceroyalty. Being convinced that they must be put into due effect, I desire and command that in all the provinces affected by this ordinance they shall be understood and observed as they are contained in the four following articles.

196

The subordinate officials of the accounting-office of the tithes who, at the time the aforesaid royal *cédula* circular of October 19, 1774, was received, had been named and appointed by the *cabildos* of the metropolitan churches and cathedrals of the kingdom of New Spain, shall continue to receive the same salary which they had at that time and formerly from the total sum of the tithes, but with the condition of having to obtain the royal title which shall be sent to them by the superintendent-subdelegate of my royal treasury.

The *cabildos* shall retain the power which I grant them of proposing individuals to the respective intendants to fill these positions in future; provided that, since the officials mentioned must be directly subordinate to the royal accountants, these latter must cooperate to procure satisfactory nominations by means of confidential reports for which the intendants as their immediate superiors shall ask them concerning the said nominations, in order to give account, with everything concerned and with the opinion which they may consider best, to the superintendent-subdelegate, in order that he may command the proper titles to be issued and that they may be issued.

The *cabildos* shall receive those individuals thus elected, likewise the ad interim accountants, as such accountants and subordinate officials of the tithes, recognizing them at all times as my appointees. Their predecessors appointed by the *cabildos*, if any of them still remain, shall cause the accounting-office with all its papers and other documents in its possession, after formal inventory [is taken], to be delivered to the [newly chosen] accountants.

197

ᵃAlthough the aforesaid royal accountants are removable, they must not be removed at the will and pleasure of the *cabildos*, but in my royal name by the recommendation of the superintendent-subdelegate upon the reports of the respective intendants. But nevertheless they must be and are understood to be subject and subordinate to the said *cabildos* and also to the factor-judges, as they were heretofore, in the use and exercise of the jurisdiction that has been intrusted to them for the revenues under their charge, for the accounts, distributions, and other matters which the former officials, appointed by the said bodies, have exercised.

They shall likewise be subordinate for the correct distribution of the total amount of the tithes according to what is prescribed in the articles of this instruction which treat of the matter, and especially to everything ordered in article 182. It is to be understood that the royal accountants as well as their officials must have the same subjection and necessary subordination to the intendants and other ministers of the royal treasury who, according to what is provided, must intervene in the leasings referred to, the division and distribution of the total sum of the tithes, and the deduction of the royal ninths.

⟨ᵃ This article was protested by the royal accountants of tithes of Puebla in consequence of the superior declaration of September 17, 1775, in which it was asserted that they were of character similar to that of the accountants of the general directing offices (*direcciones*) and that the *cabildos* could not exercise or have any superior jurisdiction over them. The superior government declared afterward in the decree of October 17, 1805, that what is provided in this article for accountants must be observed until his Majesty might decide some other method, since the article itself is nothing but a restatement of what was provided in the royal *cédulas* of October 29, 1774, and October 30, 1776, against which no declaration of the superior government can stand. The decision of his Majesty is pending.>

198

The above-mentioned royal accountants and their subordinates must also exercise, without larger salaries, traveling expenses, or remuneration than those which they are to receive from the said revenues of the tithes as has been decided, all the functions which those persons appointed by the *cabildos* formerly performed respectively, including keeping account of and distributing the [funds from] anniversary masses, pious funds, and all the obventions, in case the churches desire to leave them under their care. But if they do not they may freely intrust these duties to another accountant whom they may appoint, assigning him the salary which they consider fitting from the rents and revenues of the said pious funds.

The aforesaid separation and appointment must however be understood to be without prejudice to the total amount of the tithes or to the salaries appropriated from them for the royal accountants, with the proviso that these officials (in case the churches intrust to them the functions relative to the obventions) as well as those whom their *cabildos* may appoint in their lack, must be subject to them solely in spiritual matters and nothing more.

199

ªFinally, for the important purpose that I and likewise my Council of the Indies may have individual and certain information not only concerning the total annual amount of the tithes and obventions, and of the certain and uncertain proceeds of each cathedral church, but also concerning what sum from each one of these pertains to the respective recipients, and with this necessary knowledge may proceed without delay wherever it may be fitting and convenient, to the division of the bishoprics, the restoration of suspended prebends or those awaiting the completion of the acts of erection and the inauguration of patrimonial benefices, and in order that other information and reports no less necessary and useful shall not be lacking, it was commanded by the above-mentioned royal *cédula* of October 20, 1776, that all the accounts of the tithes and other branches mentioned therein, including that [of revenues] from anniversary masses, should be submitted annually in future to the tribunal of accounts of my royal treasury for their gloss and liquidation, as must be done with all the accounts of its revenues. Afterward these accounts are to be sent to me in the manner that is ordered for the said revenues.

But considering on the one hand the embarrassments and delays which the practice of this measure would necessarily cause, and on the other that the purposes at which it is aimed and which are stated herein might be obtained more easily and completely by means of the tables of the tithes obtained in the manner and under the conditions which will be prescribed by the following article for thus there will be a general account in which not only the total amount from the revenues of the tithes and the gross amount from all the obventions of each year but also their respective distributions will be combined with due minuteness and clearness—I expressly annul the said royal *cédula* in regard to the measures referred to [wherein it ordered that] the accounts therein designated must be submitted to the tribunal of accounts.

Therefore I desire and command that everything prescribed and declared in this article and the three preceding ones shall be observed very exactly in the area of New Spain, and that the superintendent-subdelegate of my royal treasury and the intendants of its provinces shall cause it to be obeyed and executed in the part pertaining to them respectively, without doing anything to the contrary or allowing it to be violated. I also order the very reverend archbishop, the reverend bishops, and venerable members of the *cabildos* to keep, obey, and execute it in so far as it pertains to them, and cause it to be kept, obeyed, and executed as stated herein.

⟨ª As the tribunal of accounts stated on January 18, 1796, in the *expediente* marked M. P. number 94, folio 2 *verso*, concerning the gloss of the accounts of the tithes which is added to the task of the aforesaid tribunal, the royal *cédula* of October 20, 1776, is annulled by this article. By virtue thereof, all the accounts must be submitted to the accountants of the tithes in order that they may fulfil what is provided in article 200 of this ordinance.

200

ªTo the end that the important purposes which I proposed in determining to reserve for myself their appointments may be obtained as completely as is fitting by means of the royal accountants of tithes and tables, it is my will and I command them that, as soon as they have drawn up every year respectively the tables of the value and distribution of the revenues from the tithes, anniversary masses, and other fixed and incidental emoluments (even when these are not under their control) with the clearness and precision which are indicated and explained in the formulary which the general accountant of the Indies issued for the purpose under the date of October 30 of the present year [1786], they shall in conformity with the provisions of this ordinance and the special act of erection of each church, present it to the *junta de diezmos* so that, since the accounts and distribution which law 30, title 16, book 1 of the *Recopilación* mentions are included in it, the *junta* may fulfil the obligation and purposes for which the law cited was issued, and, in discharging its duties, (keeping in mind the act of erection and pertinent articles of this ordinance) shall examine the said table and compare its data with the entries and information which must be kept in [the office] of the aforesaid *junta;* and if the report does not agree with these, the *junta* shall proceed to rectify it with the help of the royal accountant himself; and when it is corrected the *junta* shall place on it its authorization and the members present shall sign [the document].

They shall do the same with three other copies of the report mentioned, the document itself being deposited in the archives of the accounting-office, and the three copies shall be delivered to the intendant, who must transmit one of them to the ministers of the royal treasury in order that it may be of use to them for guidance in making the suitable deductions in the major and minor vacancies, as will be prescribed in the articles which treat of these, since from the aforesaid report certain knowledge may be obtained of the revenues applicable to the dignities, canonships, and other prebends of the said churches from the tithes, whether from the fourth destined for the chapters or from the remainder of the four-ninths of their parishes after subtracting the allotments by which these are affected and the costs and expenditures which precede the distribution; [it will serve] also to verify the debits which must be placed in the accounts respecting the branches which have a share in the proceeds from the tithes. The intendant shall remit to me through the superintendent-subdelegate without delay the other two copies, the original and the duplicate, and the latter officer shall forward them by the *vía reservada* of the Indies. One copy shall go to the general accounting-office of the Indies for the purposes which may be best for my service.

⟨ª Since the *juntas* provided for in the preceding article have not been established, the making of the gloss of the accounts of which the royal tribunal has charge, according to the royal *cédula* of October 20, 1776, also must be understood to be suspended, as was declared by the superior decree of February 4, 1796, in the *expediente* cited in the foregoing article.⟩

201

In case that the *cabildos* of the churches do not leave the account and calculation of the obventions under the care of the royal accountants of the tithes by virtue of the free power which article 198 gave them for this, in order that the said accountants may draw up the tables as is prescribed in the preceding article, and perform all the other duties ordered for them thereby, it shall be the precise obligation of the accountants whom the *cabildos* appoint to submit to them properly and without the least delay an exact, certified, and signed copy of the account under their charge. It is to be understood that this must include and show with all accuracy and minuteness what may have been appropriated to each office of dignitary, to the canonships, and other prebends of the respective churches, and to their building fund in the year examined on account of masses, anniversary masses, allowances, money for vestments, and all the other permanent and incidental revenues which they enjoy, inasmuch as this all must be included and manifested in the same manner in the tables mentioned, and what was determined by the said preceding article must be observed.

In the exercise of the right and power which belongs to me to demand the aforesaid information, the duty of causing those accountants appointed by the *cabildos* to fulfil with due punctuality what is ordered herein, without allowing any excuse, shall be the exclusive function of the intendants. But if, as may happen, the accountants should be ecclesiastics, in any cases of negligence which they may observe the intendants shall send the proper exhortations in my royal name to the prelates and *cabildos* concerned in order that without more delay they shall cause them to obey in all its parts my royal resolution mentioned, as I now and henceforth order each one of them [to do].

202

Every defect or mistake in the tables in relation to the bestowal and distribution of the proceeds from the tithes having been guarded against as much as possible by means of the investigation and other methods ordered in article 200, thus avoiding the injuries which may from doing the contrary be caused to my royal treasury and to the other participants in the receipts from the total amount of the tithes, it shall be no less desirable to do the same thing in regard to what pertains to [the funds] from anniversary masses, obventions, and other income. Since the method which is in practice in these my dominions for accurate collection of the royal thirds, and the ecclesiastical half-annates that are collected in them, is the most judicious and best means, it is my sovereign will that it shall be adopted in New Spain.

I therefore command the intendants, when a conspicuous defect is noticed by the *junta de diezmos* of which they are presidents, in the product which the aforesaid statistics of the fees and obventions show, to proceed to obtain confidential information and ask for the documents which may be thought pertinent in order to ascertain whether it is true or not that there is a fraud, deception, or mistake. They shall also leave to the other interested individuals the right to enter a complaint before whomever it is fitting [to do this] against any abuse that they may consider injures them, with the just consideration that they shall be indemnified for it if it is legitimately proved.

203

Various special royal *cédulas* have been heretofore dispatched to the metropolitan churches and cathedrals of the Indies concerning the method that their prelates and *cabildos* should observe in the election of factor-judges of the tithes, and concerning the term during which the individuals appointed must exercise the duties of this office. Also many rules differing from each other have been given for both matters by the aforesaid *cédulas,* the injuries which have resulted from this diversity being worthy of note. Hoping to check them in their origin, as the problem is not either on account of its nature or its circumstances in any way opposed to uniformity in all the churches of New Spain, and as it is of great importance that the aforesaid office of factor-judge shall be granted to select individuals fit to perform their duties, I have decided as a general rule that, neither for the person whom the prelate of each church shall appoint in his turn, nor for him whom the *cabildo* must also choose in its turn (according as each appointment was declared in article 169 until there may be another measure of mine) shall any rotation or alternation be observed henceforth among their prebendaries, as has been done in some dioceses; but the *cabildo* shall name its factor-judge of the tithes by a plurality vote, and the prelate the judge whom he has a right to choose by his own free will, provided that both elections shall necessarily devolve upon members of the corporation of the *cabildo* and in no case outside of it. The aforesaid nominations, which must be presented to the *junta* in order that it may be informed concerning them and a transcript be placed in its record book, shall be issued to [the factor-judges].

The said elections must alternate biennially between the prelate and the *cabildo*. I command that, in order to establish this regulation without confusion or embarrassment, for the first year they both shall make these appointments, for the second the prelate shall elect or reelect his factor, and for the third the cabildo shall do it. This alternation shall be maintained successively so that each one may serve in his turn for two years, except the first one whom the prelate shall appoint if he is not reelected.

[In this way] one factor-judge will always be informed in all matters pertaining to the commission, and the serious deficiencies which have been experienced in the collection of the tithes because of the lack of this definite knowledge may be avoided. Therefore the prelates as well as the *cabildos* respectively may reelect the aforesaid judges provided they may deem this useful for [administering] the revenues. Because nothing else so well suits my royal will as this, I order both prelates and *cabildos* to observe it, cause it to be kept and fulfilled exactly in so far as it concerns each of them. I also command the intendant vice-patrons, for the same purpose if it should be necessary, to send to them in my royal name appropriate official letters and exhortations.

204

[a]By law 37, title 7, book 1 of the *Recopilación,* the collection of the proceeds from the vacant archbishoprics and bishoprics of the Indies was intrusted to the treasury officials, in order that [the amount of these revenues] might always be known to the persons who were to receive them according to law. By a decree of September 20, 1737, my glorious father, Philip V, deciding the doubt which arose and had been pending ever since the year 1617 about the possession and application [of the funds from] the major vacancies mentioned, which gave a motive for the aforesaid law, was pleased to declare among other things that just as the tithes of the Indies by the papal concession of Alexander VI belonged to the crown with full, absolute, and irrevocable dominion, so also by the same right do all revenues and tithes belong to it which were originated by vacancies in the offices of archbishops, bishops, dignitaries, canons, petty canons (*racioneros*), lesser prebendaries, and other officials who have been assigned salaries from the tithes, but which were not drawn either because of death, transfer, or resignation, in the churches in those kingdoms and in the adjacent islands. Although these incomes and revenues might consequently be applied indiscriminately to the expenses and needs of the state like those of any other branch of the royal treasury, it was his will, as a general, permanent, and unalterable rule, that they should be applied and distributed precisely in the services and pious works which

he was kind enough to order performed or assisted in these dominions [of Spain] or those [of America]; more especially [were they to be used], in so far as they would suffice, in paying the traveling expenses (*viático*), transportation, sustenance, and other expenses of the apostolic missionaries of the various religious orders who go from Spain to those kingdoms at the expense of the royal treasury and remain there for the holy purpose of civilizing and converting the heathen Indians to the pale of our Holy Mother Church, as a pious work in the highest degree acceptable and in every way commendable, and the first and principal consideration of the Catholic Kings and their successors ever since Divine Providence deigned to enlarge this monarchy with the discovery and occupation of those kingdoms.

For these purposes he likewise commanded that not only should the collection, receipt, and the separate account of the proceeds of the major vacancies be continued in charge of treasury officials, but also those of the minor vacancies under similar conditions, and both should be handled like those of other branches of the royal treasury. It was understood that the major vacancies [should be computed] from the day of the death, transfer, or resignation of the prelates [and continue] until the confirmation of their successors or the fiat of his Holiness the Pope, and the minor ones from the death, transfer, or resignation of their owners to the taking possession by those provided in their places.

In both kinds of vacancies only the income of each prebend or benefice as computed according to the distribution and allotment from the total sum or gross amount of the tithes shall be included in this measure; but those portions, which because of the obventions, anniversary masses, and other prequisites are distributed among them while alive, and those for the churches which receive an assignment for their maintenance from the royal treasuries, shall revert as they always have, upon the death of their ministers to the royal treasury.

It is my royal will that nothing be changed in what has thus been recounted and was commanded by the royal *cédula* circular of October 5, 1737,[28] and also that all [the foregoing] shall be fulfilled exactly and that the intendants shall cause the ministers of the royal treasury to observe it with due punctuality wherein in pertains to them. The latter must keep a separate account of this branch of vacancies, setting the major vacancies apart from the minor ones, this being necessary inasmuch as some of the pious funds are expressly assigned to the proceeds of one or other of these vacancies.

⟨ª Vacancies.⟩

205

By the royal *cédula* circular of October 5, 1737, cited in the preceding article under number 22,[28] among other matters it was declared that the amount of the revenues from all the vacant archbishoprics, bishoprics, dignities, canonships, petty and half-canonships, and positions of other ecclesiastics who receive assignments for their maintenance from the tithes of my dominions of the Indies belongs to the crown; and consequently it was ordered by the same *cédula* that the aforesaid amount should enter into the royal treasuries. I therefore thought best to command by another decree of July 31, 1780, that I should be informed whether the vacancies from parishes and chief sacristries which received tithes should be considered included in the aforesaid declaration.

In view of the reports which were made for me in fulfillment of the decree, and as my Council of the Indies with these reports at hand advised me, and notwithstanding that all the proceeds and dues from the tithes derived from vacancies in parishes and chief sacristries of my dominions belong to me, I resolved and commanded by royal *cédula* circular of November 16, 1785,[29]

---

28 See Appendix, number 22, in the original.
29 Found under number 23 in the Appendix of the original.

that the revenues for the parishes and *doctrinas*[30] should not enter into the royal treasuries, but be paid to the individuals who serve provisionally in those offices, not only for the four months legally prescribed as the term for which they are appointed, but also for all the time intervening between the occurrence of the vacancy and the appointment of the ad interim official, and from the time when he completes the four months until the proprietor takes possession.

But considering that the reasons and purposes that influenced me [to take] this measure relative to the parishes and *doctrinas* do not apply to the chief sacristries, I decided not to except them from the general rule. Consequently it was commanded by the same aforesaid *cédula* that the proceeds of the tithes belonging to them in the time of their vacancies should enter into my royal treasuries. These shall be computed from the natural or civil death of the proprietor until the new proprietor provided in such a case, and not an ad interim appointee, shall take possession. All of which it is my sovereign will shall be fulfilled and put into effect in the dioceses of New Spain according as is declared herein, and as I commanded by the aforesaid royal *cédula*. For this purpose I give very strict order to the intendants and other officials whose duty it is to see that it is observed, and also corresponding orders to the prelates of the dioceses and to *cabildos* of the metropolitan churches and cathedrals of that kingdom.

206

In the special royal *cédula* of May 1, 1769, issued by the advice of my Council of the Indies owing to the great decrease of revenue which had occurred in the metropolitan church of the city of La Plata and in the corresponding proceeds pertaining to the major and minor vacancies which belong to my crown

---

[30] *Doctrinas* were Christian Indian villages subordinate to a parish or mission.

as was stated in the preceding article, I was pleased to declare that, whenever the office of archbishop or magistral canonship is vacant, the royal treasury must pay and henceforth shall pay for the sermons which pertain to and are respectively assigned to either, and the salary of the capitular who defends the lawsuits and business of the church during the vacancy of the capitulary defensor.

But in no case had any quantity been rightfully deducted or must it be deducted from the minor vacancies to pay those who chant the epsitles and gospels in place of the deceased prebendaries. Next, I commanded by the same *cédula* that, since the said sermons and what is given to the lawyer who substitutes for the capitulary defensor must be paid for from my royal treasuries (into which the funds from the major and minor vacancies must be entered without any discount) the dean and the *cabildo* of the church must appoint this advocate and my vice-patron the preachers, also the latter shall determine the regular salaries suitable for all.

As the reasons which influenced me to make the decision referred to were general for all the other metropolitan churches and cathedrals of my dominions of the Indies, I command that it shall in all its provisions be observed and fulfilled punctually and exactly in the sanctuaries of New Spain, and that hereafter no deductions shall be made from the proceeds of the minor vacancies for ecclesiastics appointed in the aforesaid churches to fill the places of prebendaries who are lacking, since it is the obligation of all the members of the *cabildo* to do this themselves.

It is to be understood that [the fees] for sermons which I wish and command to be paid from my royal treasuries must be those prescribed for [those preached by] prelates and magistral canons according to the act of erection of each church, which are called *sermones de tabla;* and that the regulation of the amount which must be given to preachers for their stipends and as fees to the lawyer elected by the *cabildo* who shall perform the duties of the doctoral canon in his lawsuits and business, must be made by the magistrate who exercises the local powers of vice-patron, who must inform the intendant of this and the latter shall arrange for the preliminary proceedings which have been prescribed in order to provide for all extraordinary expense; so that in consideration of this he may order paid the amount of the [salary for preachers] and the [lawyer's fees] from the fund of the aforesaid major and minor vacancies respectively.

207

Being desirous of providing for the permanence and perpetuity of the annual endowment of 40,000 *pesos* which by decree of January 1, 1775, I was pleased to assign for the expenses and pensions of the Royal and Distinguished Spanish Order of my august name [Charles the Third] from [the proceeds of] the miters and prebends of some of the holy churches of the Indies, and considering that this could not be done unless that which accrues to me from the major and minor vacancies, as is stated, should be deducted by pro rata therefrom, I thought ·best to declare that the deduction of 40,000 *pesos* should be made by including the vacancies mentioned notwithstanding that they belong to my royal treasury, and had been freed of all discount at the time of their incorporation to the crown. For the observance and fulfillment of this idea a suitable royal *cédula* circular was issued on December 13, 1777.[31]

I therefore command the intendants of the provinces of Mexico, Puebla, Oaxaca, Michoacan, Guadalajara, and Durango to watch with special care that the aforesaid royal resolution contained in the *cédula* mentioned be exactly obeyed, observed, and executed. They shall deduct from the proceeds of the major and minor vacancies which occur in the metropolitan churches

---

31 This is found in Appendix 24 of the original.

and cathedrals of the said provinces, which are included in the assessment of the 40,000 *pesos*, what pertains to them by pro-rata according to the time of their duration, and according to the quantity which each miter and prebend receives as pension by the before-mentioned distribution.

208

[a]The tender considerations of my paternal love which recommended the important continuation of the *monte-pio militar* of Spain and the Indies, and the consequent desire of guaranteeing thereby the benefits contributed by its establishment to the widows and children of the faithful vassals who serve the state in the former and latter kingdoms in the distinguished career of arms, influenced me to pass various resolutions in the year 1777, relative to both dominions, with the purpose of attending to the urgent needs of the aforesaid *monte-pio* and of preventing [its embarrassment] if possible in the future. Among these measures was one applying to its fund one-fifth of the net amount of the major and minor vacancies of the churches of the Indies, after the legitimate expenses have been deducted from the total proceeds.

But after communicating my royal resolution to the Council of the Indies and after that body had advised me concerning it, I considered it best in view of what it explained to me, to grant as a temporary device for the benefit and aid of the *monte-pio militar* mentioned the third part of the net proceeds of the aforesaid major vacancies, after defraying the legitimate expenses of that branch, in order that that amount shall be collected as the other funds of the said *monte-pio*. For this purpose the proper royal *cédula* circular for its execution and fulfillment was issued on July 31, 1779.[32] Since it is my sovereign will that the aforesaid appropriation shall be continued for the present under the same

---

[32] See Appendix 25, of the original.

terms and with the same condition, I command the superintendent-subdelegate of my royal treasury of New Spain and the intendants of its provinces to observe it and cause it to be obeyed
punctually in the part which pertains to each one of them
respectively.

⟨ª *Monte-pio militar,* i. e., military pension fund.⟩

209

ªBy the bull of Pope Benedict XIV issued on May 10, 1754,
the favor and permanent power to collect an ecclesiastical half-
annate from each and every one of those individuals named by
royal appointment to benefices, pensions, and ecclesiastical offices
of these dominions [of Spain] and those of the Indies was
granted to King Ferdinand VI, my beloved brother, and to his
successors, provided that their certain and uncertain revenues
and proceeds should reach the annual amount of 300 ducats
of the current coin in the respective countries of their location.
Although the king my brother was nevertheless pleased to resolve that the bull mentioned should not be put into effect in
those kingdoms at that time, and ordered that the exaction of
the ecclesiastical salary-tax (*mesada*) should be continued as
was being done by virtue of the temporary concession of the
Holy See and its extensions of time; afterward, however, by my
royal decree of October 23, 1775, and with attention to the just
considerations mentioned therein, I commanded that from the
date thereof and thenceforth the aforesaid bull of Benedict XIV
should be put into execution in my dominions of the Indies. By
virtue thereof the exaction of the aforesaid ecclesiastical half-
annate shall be required under the rules of equity and with the
precautions which by the same decree I was pleased to prescribe
and declare.

I commanded the commissioner-general of the Crusade, as
executor of the said bull, to draw up and submit to me the

proper instruction for its operation, and I provided that orders conducive to the punctual fulfillment of everything decided by the royal decree mentioned should be issued. In consequence of this action and with the literal insertion of said decree, the royal *cédula* circular of January 26, 1777, was issued.[33] Therefore, since it was my sovereign will that according to the *cédula* mentioned and to what is provided by virtue thereof in another one of July 31 of the same year,[34] in which the instruction is inserted which, as was said, I ordered to be drawn up and the commissary-general of the Crusade drew it up and it received my royal approval, I commanded the intendants to fulfil and cause to be obeyed that which was decided and is contained in the two *cédulas* referred to, in so far as these concern them. In the cases and matters in which it may be necessary, they shall support the measures of the subcollectors which article 3 of the aforesaid instruction mentions, and see that ministers of the royal treasury observe and put into effect respectively and with due punctuality all that is ordered in articles 14 and 15 of the same instruction.

⟨ᵃ Ecclesiastical half-annate.⟩

210

ᵃConsidering that, notwithstanding what is provided by the two royal *cédulas* cited in the preceding article, it may perhaps be doubted whether the *mesada*, which is to continue to be collected at the appointment of those parish priests who should pay half-annates but are exempted therefrom, should be collected or not, under the same jurisdiction and rules as the aforesaid half-annate, and its proceeds be added to those of the *mesada*, I think best to declare that the *mesada* which must be exacted from the priests mentioned, being as it is, an equivalent into which the half-annate is permuted in consideration of their commendable

---

[33] Found in Appendix 26, of the original.
[34] *Ibid.*

labors as pastors, the same rules which have been given or shall be given in future relative to the half-annate must govern the regulation, exaction, collection, and application of the *mesada;* for the proceeds of them both and of the eighteen per cent which shall continue to be exacted on the amount of the aforesaid *mesada* shall form a single branch and must be included in one and the same account, although with sufficient distinction so that what each of the two taxes mentioned may have yielded can be known, and also the eighteen per cent of the *mesada,* since its yield has a different use from that of the half-annate.

⟨ᵃ Ecclesiastical *Mesada.*⟩

211

Since, in order to bring about what is provided in article 15 of the instruction cited and inserted in my royal *cédula* of July 31, 1777,³⁵ it will be necessary that all funds from the said half-annates and ecclesiastical *mesadas,* and those which in consequence of what is ordered in the two preceding articles, shall be deposited in the other treasuries, whether principal ones of province or subsidiary ones, shall be united in the general treasury of Mexico City, I command the treasury officials who administer them to dispatch respectively and punctually to the aforesaid general treasury at the beginning of each year, without delay or omission, the consignment of the funds pertaining to the branch mentioned which have been collected in the treasuries under their charge in the whole immediately preceding year.

The aforsaid officials (as also those of the general accounting-office and treasury of Mexico City) shall be governed in remitting the total net sum of those consignments and of the amount that they themselves have collected, which they must send to the General Depository of Cádiz by what is provided in the already-cited practical and provisional instruction formed by the general accounting-office of the Indies concerning [the proceeds] of this and the other branches (*ramos remisibles*)

---

³⁵ This is under number 26 of the Appendix of the original.

which must be sent to Spain. It is to be understood that, according to the said instruction, each of the treasury officials respectively must draw up an account of the branch referred to and submit it to my royal tribunal of accounts as is ordered for the other funds under their control.

212

In some places in my dominions of the Indies doubts and controversies arose as to whether the half-annates should or should not be levied and collected from individuals promoted to ecclesiastical offices of equal or greater income, as is done in the case of secular positions by virtue of my royal decree of May 12, 1774. Being informed concerning the appeals which were made to my royal person concerning the doubts indicated, and keeping in mind that I had by the *cédula* of October 23, 1775, already cited in article 209, expressly commanded that in my kingdoms [of America] the exaction of the ecclesiastical half-annates should continue under the rules, declared that those persons appointed to ecclesiastical offices of the Indies which pay the half-annates must contribute it, although they receive no advance in salary, from the entire income of the position to which they were promoted, when they have completed one year of tenure of a new position. For this same reason, and under the aforesaid conditions [I order] that those officials who receive an increase in income because of promotions are subject to the total payment of the said dues, in spite of whatever is observed in either case in the exaction of the half-annates of secular employees, the rules concerning whom have nothing to do nor must be allowed to have anything to do with ecclesiastical offices.

I command that from those individuals provided with benefices, who die before completing the year of their term, only on what is due from them during the time that they were entitled to the income from their prebend and from the proceeds thereof must [the half-annates] be collected by pro rata; and that the same thing shall be done when any holder of a benefice is promoted before finishing the year of his term. This must be done without prejudice to the half-annates which they pay upon their new positions. All this was notified by the royal circular order of June 1, 1780, to my viceroys, presidents, and governors of the Indies, also to the intendants wherever they exist, for their proper instruction, for that of the accountants, and the subcollectors of the aforesaid half-annates. It is consequently my royal will that the declarations mentioned shall be observed exactly and punctually in New Spain, and I command the intendants of its provinces to pay very special attention to the fulfillment thereof in the part pertaining to them.

213

It being proper that the subcollectors of the aforesaid half-annates and ecclesiastical *mesada*, for better performance of their duty, may have accurate and exact information of what, on account of the tithes, obventions, and other certain and uncertain revenues, pertains every year to each one of the dignities, canonships, prebends, minor canonships, livings, and half-livings, and pensions of the dioceses under their special cognizance, I command the *juntas* of tithes that, as soon as the statistical table of the tithes, which is treated of in article 200, is framed by the royal accountants and is approved every year by the *juntas*, they shall cause the royal accountants to make a comprehensive certificate of the result of the table described, and each *junta* shall transmit it to the subcollector concerned.

214

[a]In consideration of the papal concession of the supreme pontiff Urban VIII in his brief of August 12, 1625, it was commanded by law 1, title 17, book 1 of the *Recopilación* that

from any person who, by royal presentation or in the name of the vice-patrons of the churches of the Indies, might be provided with a bishopric, canonship, living, half-living, or prebend of the Indies, or any office or ecclesiastical benefice, parish or *doctrina*, a *mesada* on the annual value of his respective income should be collected, on condition that it should not be exacted until four months should have passed after his having taken possession of the position. For this purpose it was ordered by the same law that in such cases the treasury officials should proceed to the computation and collection of the aforesaid *mesada* in the manner and under the rules defined in the same law, in conformity with what is provided by the papal brief indicated.

By virtue of another brief of June 16, 1626, in which the same Urban VIII declared that the *mesada* mentioned must be paid to this court entirely and completely in silver and be free from expenses, risks, and convoy duties (*averías*), it was also commanded by the aforesaid law 1 that, beside what the *mesada* might amount to, there should be collected from the person presented with an office, and from his property and income, the costs of his transportation in freights, dues, *averías*, and other expenses [incurred] until he should arrive in these kingdoms. The total amount of each one of these shall be sent to these kingdoms, for the account and risk of the person from whom it may have been collected.

Athough that favor [of Urban VIII] was provisional for only fifteen years, it has continued until the present under the said conditions by virtue of the various prorogations of the Holy See. By force of these the collection of the *mesada* from each and every one of the persons provided by the royal presentation with the ecclesiastical offices of my dominions of the Indies, which have been enumerated, was continued without interruption, until I, using the favor and power that were granted to me and my successors permanently by the papal bull which was treated of in article 209, thought well to resolve by my royal decree cited therein that in those kingdoms of mine the exaction of the half-annates from ecclesiastical offices should be put into practice as was prescribed according to the aforesaid bull, and that in the others excepted by it and the before-mentioned decree, the *mesada* referred to should continue to be collected under the same conditions as was provided until then by various other apostolic concessions, as I commanded by the royal *cédula* circular of January 26, 1777, which also was cited in the aforesaid article 209 under number 26, and afterwards by another of October 12 of the same year.[36]

I provided in this ordinance that for the estimate of the amount of the said *mesada,* what was ordered in another decree of December 21, 1763, in so far as it did not oppose the *cédula* of January 26 should be observed punctually and exactly. But since his Holiness Pius VI afterward by a brief of June 16, 1778, was pleased to extend the favor mentioned under the same conditions as those by his predecessors and for all the time of my life, intrusting its execution to the commissary-general of the Crusade (a circumstance which should partly change the practice observed formerly in the management of this branch) I consider it best, in order that it may conform in everything to the aforesaid brief, to define by the six following articles the rules which must govern it in future.

⟨ᵃ *Mesada.*⟩

215

Because the before-mentioned commission, given by the Holy See to the commissary-general of the Crusade in article 19 of the aforesaid brief of June 16, 1778, is identical with that which he also intrusted to him for the exaction of the ecclesiastical

---

[36] Found under Appendix number 27, in the original with the other *cédula* and the brief cited afterward.

half-annates, the collection of the *mesada* shall be under his juris-diction and that of his subcollector or subdelegate for this branch in the Indies, under the same conditions and with the same powers which I have declared for them by my royal *cédula* of July 31, 1777, already cited under number 26, and by the in-struction inserted in it. But he shall be guided in estimating the amount of the *mesada* and the time of its imposition and collection, by the aforesaid brief and by the provisions of the already cited law 1 and the general royal *cédula* of December 21, 1763,[37] without falling into the errors which were therein called to the attention of the treasury officials.

He shall also as is repeatedly commanded exact that which is due at the rate of 1 per cent for freights and *averías* on the amount of each *mesada* in order that the total from both may be transferred to the respective subtreasury of my royal treasury. The ministers of the treasury shall transmit to the subcollector at the beginning of each year the detailed report in triplicate which the aforesaid law and *cédula* require, so that when the said subcollector has placed on all three copies his authorization, after comparing them with his own entries and adding also in triplicate his individual account of all that is owed and collected, with the proper steps taken for its payment, he shall send all the documents to the intendant of the province. The latter shall address a copy of them to the tribunal of accounts to serve them as a guide in examining the report which the ministers of the royal treasury must give to [that body]. He shall send the other two copies, the original and a duplicate, to my royal hands by the *vía reservada* of the Indies. Thence one shall be sub-mitted to the general accounting-office of the Indies for the uses that are best for my royal service.

---

[37] See Appendix 27 in the original for the *cédula* and the brief.

216

[a]The ministers of the royal treasury to whose care the proceeds from the aforesaid dues of the *mesada* and its 18 per cent are intrusted according to what is provided by the preceding article, must render annually to the tribunal of accounts a separate account of both, observing what is determined by general rule in this instruction for the other accounts under their care. Because the funds from the said revenue, in conformity with the purpose of their concession, have long been applied to paying for sending missionaries from Spain to those kingdoms and it is my will that they shall be thus spent, I command the said ministers of the royal treasury to send respectively and punctually at the beginning of each year without delay or omission to the general treasury of Mexico City the funds under their care pertaining to the aforesaid branch which they may have collected during the whole immediately preceding year; and I also order the general accountant and treasurer to send annually to the General Depository of Cádiz for my royal disposition, the total of those consignments and of what they themselves have collected for the same revenue, that is the net total in their possession.

Each minister of the treasury shall be guided in the aforesaid remissions by what is prescribed for every revenue that is to be sent to these kingdoms in the practical and provisional instruction of the general accounting-office cited in various articles of the present ordinance. It is to be understood that such remissions must be made in their entire transit at the account and risk respectively of the individuals from whom the aforesaid quantities have been collected, because this is in conformity with the concession of this right at its origin, and with subsequent dispositions of the said law 1, title 17, book 1 of the *Recopilación* of the Indies.

⟨[a] See article 98.⟩

217

It is generally and repeatedly commanded in conformity with the papal briefs cited in article 214 that those appointed to bishoprics or any other ecclesiastical office which pays the dues of the *mesada*[a] shall give bond to the satisfaction of the treasury officials that they will make the payment thereto corresponding, in conformity with the aforsaid law 1, title 17, book 1 of the *Recopilación,* when the four months of tenure are completed. Consequently it was determined by the royal *cédula* circular of July 5, 1690, that the archbishops and bishops should not install those persons presented with prebends of those churches, parishes, *doctrinas,* offices, or ecclesiastical benefices, without first ascertaining that the said security had been given.

But as the measures mentioned had not been sufficient to attain the just purpose for which they were issued, I thought best to resolve in the year 1765, that in all dispatches of presentations to dignities and prebends which shall be issued in future the clause shall be inserted that possession shall not be given until the interested individual shall give evidence that he has first guaranteed the payment and collection of the *mesada* which he owed because of his presentation, according to the provisions of my royal *cédula* circular of December 21, 1763, already cited under number 27.[36] Furthermore, by another general *cédula* of May 7, 1765, I was pleased to command the treasury officials, if any one of those provided with offices, did not when the four months of his possession were completed pay the *mesada* due from him according to the rules which were given for its regulation in consequence of the papal briefs mentioned, to oblige their guarantors to pay it; or, if it should seem best to them, to have recourse to the treasurer of the chapter, in order that he shall pay it to them, after deducting the necessary sum from what belonged to the chief debtor.

It is my royal will that all the foregoing up to this point in the part referring to treasury officials shall be observed by the aforesaid subcollectors, because not only does the estimate of the amount of the *mesada*, but also its collection and the authorization and acceptance of the bonds, in the same manner as they must do it for the half-annates, come under their jurisdiction and cognizance. In order to make it easy to do this with reference to each tax without incurring the risks presented by the measures taken hitherto, I command that all the orders which may be sent by the secretariats of my royal chamber of the Council of the Indies by virtue of the ecclesiastical provisions which I shall make in future for the dioceses of New Spain, except those of the archbishops and bishops, shall be submitted (when the dues that are owed are paid by the interested persons or their agents) to the superintendent-subdelegate of my royal treasury, who must give notice of the receipt of them, in order that he may send them without delay to the intendant of the province to whom they belong, and that he may transmit them to the respective subcollector from whose hand the appointees must receive them after they have guaranteed to his satisfaction the payment of the *mesada* and its 18 per cent, under the conditions pertaining to each one of these dues according to what is provided and determined. For the same purposes and under similar terms, I also command that all the orders for ecclesiastical presentations made in exercise of the powers which are granted them shall be submitted to the aforesaid subcollectors respectively by the vice-patrons as royal proprietors.

⟨ᵃ By the royal *cédula* of September 10, 1796, his Majesty declared that the ecclesiastical half-annate of the bishops is levied and must be collected from the date of the confirmation by his Holiness, that it to say, from the time when they begin to enjoy the proceeds. This is understood as an act of possession in respect to bishops although they may die before receiving it, as happened to his Excellency Señor Granados. For this purpose the royal declaration already cited was issued.⟩

218

It is fitting that the tribunal of accounts and the auditor's office may have all the information that shall be conducive to their better administration in the examination, gloss, and closing of the accounts which they must make; therefore I wish and command the superintendent-subdelegate of my royal treasury in New Spain, and the vice-patrons as royal proprietors of their dioceses, to submit to the said tribunal at the beginning of each year a detailed report in which the latter must include the ecclesiastical presentations which have been made in their districts during the whole of the immediately preceding year, and the former shall insert the orders which have been sent to the intendants, and those that have been directed to the tribunal by the secretariats of my Royal Council of the Chamber, in observance of what was provided by the preceding article.

219

In conformity with what was prescribed by the papal briefs of which specific mention was made in article 214,[38] also in consideration of what was declared by my decree of October 23, 1775, and chapters 6 and 7 of the royal instruction, this latter being inserted in the *cédula* circular of July 31, 1777, and the former in another decree of January 26 of the same year,[39] only [those persons possessing] archbishoprics, bishoprics, parishes, *doctrinas* of my kingdoms of the Indies, as also pensions, offices, and ecclesiastical benefices the income and the certain and uncertain rents of which do not exceed the annual amount of 300 ducats of the current money in those dominions of mine, or if they are not less in value in the said coins than 100 Roman ducats of the *cámara*, must pay the *mesada* here dealt with, from the date of the aforesaid decree, and they shall do it in future.

---

[38] See Appendix 27 of the original for what is written literally.
[39] Both are found under number 26 in the Appendix of the original.

Since it is necessary, for the most exact observance of this order and to avoid all doubt, to know just how much each one of the two said quantities of ducats is worth in the current coins of the Indies, according to their different kinds and values, I declare that the aforesaid 100 Roman gold ducats of the *cámara* correspond exactly to the sum of 218 *pesos* and 6 *reales* of the current coin of the Indies, and the 300 ducats of the same to 413 *pesos*, 4 *reales*, and 28 *maravedís* of the said money, each one being calculated at 11 *reales* and 1 *maravedí*.

220

In order to know whether the ecclesiastical office which may have been provided shall contribute the half-annate or pay only the *mesada*, it is necessary to find out to which of the two quantities mentioned in the preceding article its income from the tithes approximated, with its certain and uncertain revenues, in the year immediately prior to the grant and taking possession of the office. In like manner in order to regulate the *mesada* according to law 1, title 17, book 1 of the *Recopilación* and the royal *cédula* of December 21, 1763,[40] conforming with the apostolic concession, it is also necessary to know what amount has accrued during the last five years, from the same sources, to the office from which the ecclesiastical *mesada* is to be deducted.

In consequence of this, and of the fact that, among the objects which I sought in the order reserving for myself the appointment of the accountants of the tithes and fourths of the holy churches of the Indies was that of facilitating thereby the aforesaid investigation with proper exactness, by this means stopping the continual embarrassments which previously had hindered it in spite of repeated and strict measures issued concerning the matter, I order the subcollectors of both dues, that, with the certification in hand which the *juntas* of tithes must

---

40 See Appendix 27 in the original.

send annually according to article 213, they shall make investigations of the incomes and deduction of the *mesada* in the presentations of either an archbishopric or bishopric, or of any other position of dignitary, prebend, benefice, or office relating to the holy metropolitan church or cathedral of the diocese, and of the pensions which may be reserved in any of the aforesaid offices and are not expressly exempted; [I also order] that, in regard to the parishes, *doctrinas,* offices, and benefices which must be included in the tables of the tithes and consequently in the certificate mentioned, they should also make the proper investigations with an accurate report not only concerning what has accrued to them respectively in the last year of the five mentioned, and in all the five in case of need, from the share which each one of the offices ought to receive from the four-ninths of the tithes, but also concerning what the obventions and revenues have produced for them in the same time, as may be evident from the books of the collector's office (*colecturía*) which must be kept as is commanded, in all the churches of the parishes and *doctrinas,* or in their defect, from the results of the investigations and proper proceedings which the said subcollectors must take, and which, in case of necessity the vice-patrons must aid.

221

Upon appointments in favor of the religious of the mendicant orders, to *doctrinas* and curacies which have not been secularized in conformity with the general measures given for this by the *cédulas* of February 1, 1753, June 23, 1757, and of November 7, 1766,[41] the dues of the *mesada* shall be collected under the same manner and conditions as law 5, title 17, book 4 of the *Recopilación* provides. But it shall not be collected from the alms of which law 2 of the same title treats, nor from the pensions which archbishops or bishops assign from their miters

---

[41] See Appendix, number 28 in the original.

to assistants for their sustenance, from [the time of] their approval by his Holiness until the death of the chief recipient, nor from what they may receive because of the said pensions in case of vacancies from the proceeds of these, because such consignments are on account of their nature excepted from the dues referred to, according to the aforesaid law 2.

222

In New Spain there are other minor revenues that belong to my royal crown, like those from cockfights, monopolies or contracts of snow, alum, leather, and some partial dues of little consideration. Because all these, of whatever kind or nature they may be, must be subject to the exclusive control of the intendants, it shall be one of their duties to be especially informed concerning how many taxes in the aforesaid class belong to my royal treasury in their provinces, so that they may collect them by well regulated administration or justly lease them; for revenues of little importance cannot ordinarily bear the expense of administration. Therefore it is fitting that they shall be sold at public auction in the *junta* of auctions, in order that they may be awarded to the highest bidders with the formalities and under the conditions enumerated in article 162. This is to be understood to apply to the revenue from cockfighting, which at present must not be changed in so far as its tribunal is concerned, for that body is already actually established.

223

As I was informed that the *cabildos* of the cathedral churches of my dominions of the Indies and the other collectors of the tithes did not fulfil with due punctuality the strict obligation, under which they were established, of paying the parishes of their respective dioceses when the proceeds of the tithes are sufficient to warrant this, an omission which was not only an injury to the priests but also to my treasury, as the synod was collected illegally from the royal subtreasuries; and, further-more, keeping in mind the different abuses and disorders which generally, and on account of the same origin, are experienced either in regard to the exorbitant synod paid to priests, and the irregularities observed in paying them other perquisites without the prerequisite confirmation of their appointments, in defect of which their salaries should be held back from them for the benefit of the aforesaid churches, according to law 16, title 7 and law 18, title 13, book 1 of the *Recopilación*, I was pleased, upon the advice which my Council of the Indies gave me concerning everything on October 14, 1771, to take various measures for their remedy and the proper *cédulas* for their fulfillment were issued in the following year on January 21, 1772.[42]

But since in spite of the fact that the most exact and prompt fulfillment of what was commanded in them had been recom-mended, there have been no satisfactory results up to the present, and consequently this serious matter continues without receiving the proper regulation to which the aforesaid *cédulas* and my royal intentions were directed. In order that these may not longer remain without effect, I command the royal intendant vice-patrons to encourage as such with the greatest possible effort in the dioceses of their provinces the practice and the punctual observance of what is provided and enjoined by the *cédulas* referred to; and that the viceroy of Mexico, the com-mandant-general of the frontier, and the president-regent of my *audiencia* of Guadalajara shall do the same respectively in re-gard to the churches and dioceses in which they must have the absolute exercise of the royal vice-patronage according to what is provided by article 8. Each official shall give account to my Council of the Indies concerning what advance has been made in the matter.

---

[42] Found in Appendix, number 29, of the original.

224

It is likewise befitting to my sovereign authority to stop the serious abuses which some of the priests of the provinces of New Spain commit who impose upon the Indians exorbitant parochial dues (perhaps from the same cause as stated in the preceding article, which in a great part must cease immediately by virtue of what is ordered by article 190). For the remedy of these abuses I have commanded (as is done under this date) that very strict orders be directed to the very reverend archbishops, reverend bishops, and prelates in regular orders who have subordinates in parishes and *doctrinas*, commanding that they all must prohibit, under severe penalties, every irregularity in the aforesaid dues. At the same time I enjoin the first-named officials to form fair schedules concerning this matter, adjusting them to the poverty of the natives, and send such schedules to the respective *audiencia* within six months without fail, in order that their examination and approval may be completed within the precise period of one year counted from the date of receipt of the orders cited.

As I wish that watching the minute fulfillment of this just decision of mine be one of the duties of the secular magistrates, I command the viceroy, the commandant-general of the frontier, and the intendant-general of Mexico to take special heed of its punctual observance. They shall frequently order the respective *intendant-corregidores* and governors to pay close attention to the conduct of priests in this matter. Furthermore, my viceroy and commandant-general shall enjoin the *audiencias* in the areas of their respective commands to see to this matter with the attention and care which its importance and seriousness demand.

225

By the supreme prerogative of my crown and more especially because the churches of the Indies belong to my effective royal patronage and are under my sovereign protection, the vigilance and care of providing for the greater security of the tax on the property left by prelates at their death (*espolios*) pertain to me, in order that in due time such property may be delivered to the person who has a right to it. In consideration of this, and keeping in mind what was commanded in laws 37, 38, and 40, title 7, book 1 of the *Recopilación* for the same purposes, I desire and order that what is provided by these shall be observed with the amplifications and restrictions which will be defined in the four following articles.

I command the viceroy, the commandant-general of the frontier, the president-regent of the *audiencia* of Guadalajara and the intendants respectively, to obey, keep, and execute it, and cause it to be fulfilled and executed in the part relating to them as vice-patrons. [I also enjoin] the intendants as such to see that ministers of the royal treasury shall without neglect perform with promptness and energy, as is fitting, all that is ordered by the aforesaid laws and articles. None of them may do the contrary to this or permit the laws to be violated in any manner.

226

Because the personal intervention of the *fiscales* of my royal *audiencias* in the inventories of which law 39, cited in the preceding article treats, may only occur in the capital of Mexico and in Guadalajara, I command that in all the other capitals of the dioceses of New Spain the citation which the law mentioned provides shall be understood to apply to the attorney general of my royal treasury, and that according to it he shall assist in the said precedure.

227

The inventories, auctions, and leases of the *espolios* of archbishops or bishops, at which two prebendaries of the respective church and one of the ministers of my royal treasury of the district must be present, belong to the special cognizance of the *intendant-corregidores*, who consequently shall have it also in first instance in lawsuits and cases that may arise concerning the said *espolios;* they shall order according to law what is fitting for the indemnification of property of such privileged nature, and permit appeals for which there may be a cause, to the royal *audiencia* of the territory. In order that in these second instances, injury to the estates and possessions justly pertaining to the churches may be prevented by all the adequate means of my sovereign protection, I command that my *fiscales* shall come to the support and defense of them.

228

All the property inventoried in the aforesaid *espolios* of archbishops or bishops, not excepting pontifical property, shall necessarily be deposited under the control of the said ministers of the royal treasury who, by reason of such deposit, shall take charge of them under a due accounting and receipt until ordered by the proper person to deliver them according as may be provided. With all due circumspection and observing the decorum due to episcopal residences, the *intendant-corregidores* shall take very special care to prevent concealment or misplacement of any of the wealth and jewels of the aforesaid prelates, as often happens when they die or are approaching death. For the purpose stated, when occasion arises, the intendants shall place in the houses of prelates a suitable guard and custodian consisting of respectable persons of entire fidelity and proper diligence for the best performance of this duty.

229

When the claims, if there be any, made against the income from the *espolios* mentioned, are decided and settled, in either of the two cases when their proceedings are finished, they shall be sent by the *intendant-corregidor* to the *audiencia* of the territory, which shall examine them minutely and carefully. If that body finds them to be correct as is fitting for the proper fulfillment of my sovereign and just purpose, it shall approve them and return them to the intendant, commanding him to order the ministers of the royal treasury to deliver without delay to each creditor what pertains to him; and then, when all this is deducted from what is sequestered under their control, and observing what may be ordered or provided in future by my royal *cédulas* in this matter, to make a punctual and just delivery of what remains, and of the pontifical property, to the church and other destinations to which they belong. After this is done the *intendant-corregidor* shall give account to my royal and supreme Council of the Indies with a complete transcript of the proceedings in conformity with law 37 already cited in article 225.

230

ᵃAll the funds belonging to my treasury produced from administered or leased revenues, of whatever kind or nature they may be (excepting only that from tobacco which at present must continue under separate account and management as has been provided) must enter into the treasury of the territory in which they are owed and originate; either into the general treasury, or into a principal or subsidiary one. So that even the proceeds of certain revenues which are now collected separately in New Spain must be transported monthly from their administrative offices to the chief treasury of the province or to some one of its subsidiary ones which is nearer to the general treasury of Mexico City, because the surplus funds of all the subtreasuries must be collected into the latter. The traversing of distances a second time should be avoided as much as possible in their transportation and dispatch, in order to prevent the greater expenses which would be caused from doing the contrary. Under these rules I command that at present no change shall be made

in the matter of administration and management of the revenues indicated. It is the duty of the officials respectively to direct them in the manner and method which are intended and provided by their particular ordinances.

⟨ª Monthly entries. See articles 118 and 129.⟩

231

Although, according to articles 149 and 156, the factors and administrators of tobacco must also control and sell powder, playing cards, and stamped paper, notwithstanding this, at the end of the year they must render and submit entirely separate accounts of the aforesaid products or branches; that is: of that of tobacco to the general director, in order that he may give the report the course of procedure prescribed for it in the special ordinance of this revenue; those of powder and playing cards separately, and with distinction between the classes of articles and their respective directors; so that, when examined in their accounting-offices, and when the debits for goods which may have been charged to each factor or administrator (for they have to be remitted with their intervention) have been approved by said accounting-houses, they shall summarize the sales of all the factories and administrative revenue offices in the general account which the aforesaid accounting-offices must keep for their branch. These [accounts] must be transmitted with the particulars concerning them to the tribunal of accounts of my royal treasury to be balanced as is provided in the ordinance for both revenues. But the said factors and administrators must give and transmit the accounts of stamped paper to the ministers of the royal treasury of the principal or subsidiary treasuries from which the stamps were sent, so that, when a verification and summary, similar to those which have been explained for powder and playing cards, has been made for them, the [factors and administrators] shall send them with their own reports to the aforesaid tribunal of accounts.

232

Every intendant shall designate a day of the week for holding in his house a *junta* of government consisting of the principal ministers of the royal treasury of the province, the administrators, chief accountants and treasurers of any of my revenues, if there are any in the capital, each official bringing to the said *junta* a memorandum or report properly signed concerning the funds and proceeds on hand from the branches of finance under his control, and concerning the condition in which the collections or deficits of accounts in every one of them may be, so that the *junta* may find out whether all my dues are exacted uniformly and without injury to the contributors; whether the employees work with due intelligence, energy, and integrity in the fulfillment of their obligations; and whether there are subordinates who are not necessary for the good account, administration, and security of them, or whether it is fitting to add any other, with the idea that only those who are necessary and most fit for performing their duties shall be kept.

The *junta* shall discuss and confer concerning these matters and others which may arise relative to my royal treasury, means of improving and increasing its funds in every possible and just way, as much economy in its administration and collection as is possible, and the reduction to cash form as may be fitting those products found on hand by the memoranda submitted. In the *junta* of the first week of each month, with the comprehensive tables of revenues on hand which shall have been made out to the last day of the immediately preceding month according to article 235, the discussion and conference shall include whatever is shown by these with regard to the increase or diminution of receipts, and in the latter case, examination of the cause and effort to remedy it.

233

Concerning the matters indicated in the preceding article and the others which may be considered by the aforesaid *juntas* of government conducive to the better collection of my royal funds, the intendants themselves shall decide upon the measures which they may consider most effective and fitting, after having heard the opinions of the other members present which must be entirely informative, in order that their decisions may be made with greater knowledge and certainty. In the *juntas* mentioned a book shall be kept in which not only exact and specific entries shall be made concerning the particular matters which may be proposed and discussed in those bodies, and which on account of their importance and conditions deserve action, but also what the intendant may decide for each one. But if among the matters treated there should be any which need more serious investigation and decision by a higher authority the intendants shall report them to the *junta superior de hacienda* through the superintendent-subdelegate as its president, and they shall be provided for according to its decisions.

234

ªBoth in the general treasury of army and royal treasury of New Spain, and in the principal and subsidiary subtreasuries in the provinces, and in the general and special treasuries of tobacco and other branches of finance which may belong to the royal treasury under separate administration, the coffers shall, without any exception, be opened on the first day of each month. The intendants shall witness this act in the treasuries and administrative offices of the capitals of the intendancies, and in the same manner their subdelegates in the subtreasuries and administrative offices outside of the capitals.

For this purpose the officials under whose charge each treasury may be must have formed a detailed account of the funds on hand at that date, according as is ordered by sections 111 to 114 of the already cited practical and provisional instruction.[43] They shall sign this and submit it to the intendant or subdelegate before beginning the aforesaid operation, since it is his duty to ascertain the actual cash on hand in each kind of funds mentioned in the said report by means of a recount and careful examination of them according to section 115, and from a comparison only of sums pertaining to the other [revenues] in the coffers as is provided by sections 116 and 117.

Thus the intendants and their subdelegates must be responsible respectively, with the authorization of which section 118 speaks, and which they must affix as will be stated later, for any showing which may be made against the correctness and effectiveness of all that which they are required by this admonition to examine with scrupulous care; as shall they also be for neglect or omission in collection of debts and balances due, which in conformity with laws 1 and 30, title 8, book 8 of the *Recopilación*, they must watch over and expedite in accordance with what they see [recommended] in the said plan for this class of funds.

If any difference be found in the inventory and investigation, they shall try to learn the cause, without taking severe measures, until they themselves examine the entries in the corresponding books, and if there is an error in them it shall be corrected; or if when this is done, there is just reason to suspect concealment or misappropriation of funds, they shall officially command in this case that restoration of what is lacking shall be made, without prejudice to whatever the officials who are short in their accounts may prove later. But if the proper conformity is found between the cash on hand and the above-mentioned

---

[43] See Appendix, number 30, of the original for all sections cited in this article.

report, they shall keep it wherewith to verify the monthly statement which must be submitted to them afterward, and they shall order that the proceeds in the administrative offices of revenue shall be transported to the proper treasury according to what is ordered in article 230.

⟨ᵃ See article 98.⟩

235

ᵃWhen the act of checking the coffers explained in the preceding article has been performed, the officials having charge of the aforesaid treasuries and offices of revenue administration must without exception form a statement of the receipts and expenditures from the first of the year until the last of the month immediately preceding, and they shall submit it properly signed to the respective intendants and subdelegates within three days, according to what is prescribed in sections 119 to 123 and in 130 of the practical instruction mentioned[44] in which must be included what was shown by the report concerning the funds on hand, which was prescribed in the foregoing article.

The intendants and subdelegates, after making a comparison of this part of the statement with the aforesaid report, shall place their approval on the former if they find it correct. If there should be some difference in the balance of receipts and expenditure or a greater delay in its presentation than the three days prescribed, they shall investigate the cause with zealous care but also with prudent consideration in view of the inevitable mistakes to which the matter of accounts is subject, and with this advice and information they shall take action according to what is fitting and best.

⟨ᵃ See article 98.⟩

---

[44] The sections cited in this article are found in the Appendix of the original, under number 31.

236

ᵃIn order that in the future I may have promptly and with due form and clearness a comprehensive report of the receipts of each one of my revenues, of their expenditures and the balances on hand in each treasury and revenue administration office of New Spain, and that the injurious delays and embarrassments may be avoided which have been experienced before both there and here concerning this important matter, the intendants shall cause the officials of the treasuries and administrations of revenues of the capitals of their provinces, after the monthly statement is drawn up as provided by the preceding article, to submit to them without the least delay five copies of each one legalized with their signatures, on which the intendants shall place their approval.

The respective subdelegates shall collect in the proper form six copies of each statement concerning the treasuries and revenue·administration offices outside of the capitals in order that, after placing on them their approval and keeping one for their guidance, they shall send the other five without delay to the intendants. The intendants shall keep one copy of both the latter and the former statements, which must remain in their secretariat, and send the other four to the superintendent-subdelegate who, leaving also one copy of each statement in the secretariat of the superintendency and submitting another to the tribunal of accounts for the purpose ordered in law 31, title 1, book 8 of the *Recopilación,* shall transmit the two remaining ones, the original and a duplicate, to my royal hands by the *vía reservada* of the Indies, where one shall go to the general accounting-office for the proper purposes.

Inasmuch as the monthly compilation of these statements into a general one by the aforesaid tribunal, as provided in section 125 of the practical instruction referred to,[45] may cause

---

[45] Found under number 32 in the Appendix of the original.

delay in acquiring the information which they furnish, I command that the compilation mentioned shall not be made monthly, and that the tribunal of accounts shall postpone this until it receives the statements of the month of December.

It is to be understood that the transmission of these statements to me must not be suspended on account of the aforesaid compilation, nor the sending of the others because of the negligence or delay of any treasury; but that all as soon as the intendants and the superintendent-subdelegate receive them must take the above-mentioned course provided for their proper destinations, since it was for this purpose that the number of copies is increased which the aforesaid practical instruction explained. The tribunal of accounts shall submit three copies of the general statement which must result from combining those of December as is said, to the superintendent-subdelegate, who shall leave one of these in his secretariat and transmit the other two as well as the monthly statements to my royal hands by the *vía reservada,* whence one also shall pass to the general accounting-office to await the time when corresponding accounts reach it.

⟨ᵃ See article 98.⟩

237

ᵃAlthough with the act of inspecting the strongboxes and the formation of the monthly statements explained in articles 234 and 235, the purposes of the inspection and computation are fulfilled, as ordered by laws 23, 24, 28, and 29 of title 1, law 16 of title 4, and law 29, title 29 all of book 8 of the *Recopilación,* it is nevertheless fitting that the procedure of inspecting the strongboxes for the month of December, which must be made on the second day of January of each year, shall include also the taking of the regular inventory for which law 2, title 29, book 8 of the *Recopilación* provides. The senior minister of the tribunal of accounts, according to the aforesaid law 22, shall be present [during the examining of the coffers] in the general treasuries of the royal treasury and of tobacco, and in those of the revenue administration offices of the capital of Mexico, and [the annual report so made shall not preclude] the statement of the aforesaid month of December being made and submitted, as provided by general rule in the two preceding articles.

During the monthly inspection of the coffers only those valuable funds the most liable to be misplaced easily must be counted; but in the inspection of the coffers at the end of each year and in which it is proposed to close and balance the accounts of all the year and verify the proper administration by the properties on hand, not only must the said properties but also all those less valuable assets be examined and counted, weighed or measured with equal care, in the presence of the respective notary of each treasury or branch of finance. Their stamps and markings shall be inspected, and also, in the minute and detailed inventory which shall thereupon be formed of all the funds on hand in money, the proceeds and precious substances or those not valuable, the moveable goods, and other things belonging to my royal treasury or for the use of the other offices, shall all be mentioned. The officials witnessing the act referred to shall legalize it with their signatures and the notary with his certificate thereof.

A complete transcript of their respective inventory must be left in each of the treasuries and revenue administration offices, and each subdelegate shall transmit the originals of those which have been made with their assistance to the intendant of the province in order that, when he sends them, with those made by himself in the capital of the province, to the superintendent-subdelegate, the latter official may submit them, together with those made under his supervision in the metropolis, to the tribunal of accounts, so that they may serve as supporting documents for the respective accounts when they are taken and as a guidance for ascertaining whether negligence occurred in disposing of the salable commodities before they suffered deterioration. It is to be understood that the inventories of the stock on hand of the monopolized articles must be formed separately and be likewise authenticated in order that, after submitting them with the others to the superintendent-subdelegate, he shall send those of tobacco to the office of the director of this revenue because their accounts must be taken in it; and those of playing cards, powder, and stamped paper to the aforesaid tribunal because there the accounts of these branches must be taken and closed as was provided by article 231.

⟨ᵃ See article 98.⟩

238

The intendants shall require the officials of the principal treasuries and those outside of the capitals and the other administrators of their respective provinces to give them individual reports of all the employees in the offices for the collection and receiving of my royal revenues, from the first subordinate to the last customhouse guard, keeping separate the branches in which they serve and the salaries which they receive in order that, when a book is made from all the information and reports which they consider fitting concerning the capability, integrity, and habits of each one, they may watch with the greatest vigilance their conduct and the exact fulfillment of their respective duties. They shall admonish for the first and second time those who deserve punishment for some carelessness or negligence and suspend [from office] those who merit this reproof because of repeated offense. They shall give a substantiated account of this to the superintendent-subdelegate of my royal treasury so that he may determine the proper penalty according to the nature and conditions of the misdeed or crime.

239

ᵃBecause the port of Vera Cruz is the necessary passage and entrance for the circulation of maritime commerce with all the provinces of New Spain, except that of Yucatan, it is essential that the intendant of that city and its adjacent coasts shall take as many measures and precautions as he may judge fitting in order to check and suppress on all sides the frauds and contrabands which habitually occur both in the importation of fabrics, foodstuffs, and other merchandise, and in the clandestine exportation of gold, silver, and the precious products of that kingdom.

Since in the instruction made by the visitor-general on February 11, 1767, and which I have commanded to be observed, the most useful and fitting rules were determined for these important purposes, also for regulating the customhouse, royal subtreasuries, and other offices of the port mentioned, I order the intendant of Vera Cruz to observe and cause the aforesaid instruction of the visitor to be obeyed exactly in all matters which on account of this ordinance or my royal orders are not suppressed or annulled. It is to be understood that with the new establishment [of intendancies] the powers and duties which formerly were intrusted to the political and military governor of that fortress, who was judge-conservator of my revenue, are therefore annulled in this part of the said instruction of the visitation, and he must not have any cognizance of or supervision over confiscations and contrabands.

⟨a Confiscations. See the following article and 80.⟩

240

aIn view of the fact that in all the terrestrial and maritime matters and cases which occur in Vera Cruz and on its coasts, the intendant must observe the ordinances and laws concerning them,[46] I declare that, in order to avoid doubts of any kind in cases of contraband and confiscations on land and sea, he must take action, and so must all the other intendants in their respective provinces, with the advice of their regular lieutenant-

---

46 Under number 33, in the Appendix of the original, the laws and other orders mentioned are found.

assessors, and without the interference or intervention of another judge, allowing recourses and appeals in these matters from their sentences to the *junta superior de hacienda* only, and that body to my royal person by the *vía reservada* of the Indies.

[b]Let it be understood that the aforesaid *junta* as well as the intendants, even when appeal is not taken from their respective sentences, must give me account by the *vía reservada* with a complete transcript of the proceedings, including the distributions, as is commanded and is in observance, suspending its execution according to law 8, title 38, book 9 of the *Recopilación,* until I, in view of them, may condescend to determine what may be my royal approval.

⟨[a] Confiscations. See articles 80 and 239. [b] See Article 78.
The royal order of June 7, 1780, orders that the distribution shall be put into effect, there being no appeal or doubt, under the responsibility of the accounting-house which makes the comparison, in case the accounts are found to be erroneous.⟩

241

[a]It will be fitting, for the better protection of my royal revenues when parcels of cloths, foodstuffs, and products go from that customhouse to the interior of the kingdom with the proper stamp of the royal arms (*marchamo*) and the itemized certificate of landing and destination (*guía*), that the intendant of Vera Cruz shall give sufficient information concerning them to the intendants of the provinces to which they are directed. For this purpose he shall cause the administrator to give him separate reports of the shipments besides those which he himself must transmit to the other administrators at the destination [of the goods].

The governor or *castellano* of Acapulco, as a subdelegate, shall do the same respectively because that port is the only one habilitated on the coasts of the South Sea for the commerce of the Philippines, and for that which I have recently granted to the four kingdoms of both Americas. The intendants of the

Provincias Internas shall do the same thing reciprocally when produce and commodities are taken out of them and sent to Vera Cruz or to Acapulco for exportation from their ports.

⟨ᵃ By royal order of March 24, 1796, his Majesty commanded that the duplicates mentioned which article 241 prescribes shall be omitted, as was decided before respecting Vera Cruz and that the proclamation of May 14, 1776, be observed in everything, as published by this superior government, and the measures taken by the *junta superior* on August 19, 1791, which provided that the itemized certificates of lading and destination which are sent to the administrator of this capital should be dispatched with statements that the duplicates had been omitted and they were considered sufficient. This measure is to be understood for all the customhouses within the area of this dominion.⟩

242

ᵃIn regard to the exclusive functions which are granted by the various laws of the *Recopilación* to the tribunals and accounting-offices of the Indies, nothing of importance must be changed for those established in New Spain. Therefore, even though I may consider it best in future to give them new organization they shall remain as they are in observance at present while said provisions are being issued; but with the proviso that, if in the examination which the general accounting-office must make of the accounts that have been taken, closed, and approved by the aforesaid tribunal a charge shall result against any one of the individuals who drew up the accounts mentioned, in such a case the accountant who has glossed and closed the account, or the tribunal itself if the mistake has occurred on its part, shall be responsible to my royal treasury for what it may amount to, without prejudice to his or its right to proceed against whomever there may be occasion. It is to be understood that this shall be done without prejudice to the continual right of my royal treasury to bring charges anew against the officer who formed the account or his guarantors if conditions shall make this preferable.

⟨ᵃ The note of the *junta* which is cited is found in the *expediente*, marked V. I. number 3, *foja* 38, which was formed on account of the departure from Vera Cruz of two boxes of powder without a certificate of lading.⟩

243

ᵃDoubts and difficulties which may arise for the tribunal of accounting during the examination of accounts and concerning other matters handled by it but which do not reach the status of a lawsuit, must be decided by plurality vote according as laws 33 and 92 of title 1, book 8 of the *Recopilación* provide. In case of a tie vote, or the absence of any accountant, they shall be decided in the said tribunal with the attendance of the superintendent-subdelegate as its president. In this part the provision of the above-cited law 92 shall be understood to be annulled. But if the doubt or difficulty should be such as to demand further inquiry and a higher decision, and if the accountants agree to do so, they shall consult the *junta de hacienda,* to which body I also reserve power to decide in these cases and that of taking cognizance exclusively of the matters treated of by laws 36, 65, 84, 88, and 93 of the aforesaid title and book. The *junta* must observe in form and substance what these laws provide and is not contrary to that which is herein ordered.

It is to be observed that in none of the cases among all these mentioned may a minister of the royal treasury, either the accountant-general or the treasurer, vote or even attend the *junta.* But some other judge of the tribunal of accounts must be present whom the superintendent-subdelegate shall appoint, preferring whomever shall be better informed concerning the case to be judged and decided. And inasmuch as, in order to do this in the cases of which the aforesaid laws 36, 65, 84, 88, and 93 treat and in conformity with the first of these, the judges who are present must be three in number who are lawyers; among this number shall be included the president of the *junta superior* if he be a lawyer, and the *fiscal* when he does not perform the duties of his office; and my viceroy shall appoint in his absence, and in each one of the cases indicated, the *oidor* or *oidores* necessary in order that among all, excepting those which law 65 discusses, there may be only three members with a decisive vote; because among them all the judges of the tribunal of accounts shall have only a consultative vote, the decisive vote remaining for those of whom the aforesaid law 65 treats.

When the *junta superior* shall bring to trial any of the cases included under the laws cited, it shall assemble in the aforesaid tribunal of accounts, as law 63 of the same title and book provides, its own notary being present, but no other, to legalize the decisions, proceedings, and sentences. Under these directions and the general one that the duties which hitherto pertained to the viceroys in this *junta,* shall belong to the superintendent-subdelegate as president of the tribunal mentioned, the business of the tribunal of accounts of Mexico shall be controlled, with observance of the laws in everything which may not be contrary to what is prescribed in this article, because it is my sovereign will and is best adapted to the prompt exercise of its functions and the kind of business with which it is intrusted.

⟨ᵃ By the royal order of June 3, 1793, his Majesty commanded that, in spite of that which is decreed in this article, the chamber provided by ordinance should be reestablished as the laws cited provide, and that it should continue under the same method as it did before this ordinance [was issued]. As it is the only tribunal of justice erected for the cognizance and decision of matters of this kind which arise in the tribunals of accounts, everything which may be remitted by the aforesaid tribunals of accounts or appealed by litigants must belong to its cognizance and shall be dispatched in it, with absolute separation from the *junta superior* since its constitution and functions are different.⟩

244

ᵃIn consideration of that which is ordered by the first part of article 242, it shall be one of the special cares of intendants that the ministers of the royal treasury, the accountants and treasurers of the general as well as of the provincial and subsidiary ones, also the other general or special administrators of any branch of my royal treasury shall draw up, order, and prove their accounts according to what is provided in the already cited practical and provisional instruction formed by the general accounting-office of the Indies; excepting in regard to administrators those of the revenue of tobacco, who must do it in conformity with the particular rules which were given them for this; and both groups of officials shall remit these accounts by their own hand and within the exact time that has been prescribed for them, to the aforesaid tribunal of accounts or to the respective general accounting-office concerned; and in case of voluntary or culpable delay [the intendants] shall force them to obey by imprisoning them in their houses or offices.

It is ordered that the amount which the treasurer general of the revenue of tobacco must give annually concerning the funds entering into his possession and pertaining to the said revenue must be submitted also through the superintendent-subdelegate to the aforesaid tribunal for its registry, gloss, and closing, notwithstanding what was provided by articles 7 and 12 which mention the treasurer and the general accountant of the said revenue from tobacco, in the ordinance which was issued by the viceroy for its general administration under the date of March 15, 1768.

⟨ [a]See article 98.⟩

245

Experience has shown without mistake the unfavorable results for the performance of my service in the offices of the royal treasury, which develop on account of the abuse whereby aspirants for offices who are employed in them are not only admitted without the proper examination and due qualification which they should possess,[a] but in some places they are even considered by right of seniority only for regular public positions and the staff appointments in the said offices.

Since it is proper to establish concerning both matters a general rule which, with equity and justice shall hereafter prevent the continuation of abuses of such consequence, I declare that the power to decide upon the qualifications of candidates for appointment as aspirants to offices and pass upon their admission, must be the exclusive duty of the superintendent-subdelegate in those offices under the tribunal of accounts and all the others of the capital of Mexico and its province, without any exception. It shall likewise be [the duty] of each intendant in the cases of those who solicit offices in the capital and district of his intendancy. The candidates shall first present to him a memorial written by their own hand, with the documents that show them to be of honorable and genteel birth, and of regular life and habits in order that the intendant may make inquiry quietly about this and about their good or bad disposition and ability, and inform the superior or superiors of the office to which they desire to be appointed, or some other officer if he should consider it best.

The superintendent or intendants as the case may be, shall examine whether, in view of everything, the individual concerned has sufficient merit to prove him desirable in character and clerical ability. In case he has, his admission shall be decreed in the same set of documents and it shall be submitted to the office to which it belongs so that the decree may be put into effect and deposited in the archives thereof. I likewise declare that the aforesaid aspirants for office shall not necessarily have right by seniority to regular positions in the offices in which they serve; but in cases of vacancies the superiors shall be free to prefer in their nominations those who, on account of their great application and progress are found more fit and competent for the best performance of the duties of my royal service.

⟨ᵃ Aspirants for offices.⟩

246

When any aspirant for office, because of bad conduct, little application, or other cause may be considered deserving to be suspended or expelled from the office to which he has been appointed, his immediate superior shall draw up the case briefly and summarily and give account therewith to the intendant of the province or to the superintendent-subdelegate if it shall occur in the province of Mexico, in order that in view of it he may decide upon suspension if he considers it just, since this must also be the exclusive power of the aforesaid magistrates respectively.

247

ᵃAll that is provided and determined for improving the direction, administration, collection, and the account and calculation [of the funds] of its branches would be useless to the department of finance if the respective offices should continue to exist in the pernicious abandonment from which they suffered in the past because of the non-attendance of their superior and subordinate officers and the indolence with which both have looked upon their duties in my service, thereby seriously injuring in numerous ways the royal treasury and the public welfare. As under every consideration this disorder requires a suitable and effective remedy which shall check it at the roots by the punishment of those employees who, forgetting themselves and what they owe to my sovereign mercy, do not fulfil their duty, I command that the attendance of all the officials of my royal treasury, including those of the tribunal of accounts, shall be necessary and indispensable during four hours in the morning and three in the afternoon on all the days of the year, excepting only those of strict religious observance.

The superintendent-subdelegate and each intendant shall determine the hour at which they shall begin to attend in the offices of their province, taking into account the season of the year and the conditions of the climate; with the proviso that the seven hours assigned must not be diminished not even in case the matters of each department have been disposed of in the course of the day, and that if some one of the employees shall

fail to be present with due promptitude without having been excused on the condition of a just and legitimate cause, he shall
suffer the penalty provided by law 21, title 15, book 2 of the
Recopilación. In consideration thereof he shall be fined by his
immediate superior half his salary for the day, as also shall the
said superiors be fined by the intendant if, through complaisance
or indulgence they do not do this.

If a case should arise in which some subordinate should incur
the aforesaid fine for the third time,[b] the intendant shall, with
brief and summary proof thereof, suspend him from his office
and possession without delay, giving account to the superintendent-subdelegate in order that he may decide what is best for
the performance of my service; and the latter shall inform me of
everything. I order the said superintendent-subdelegate and the
intendants to apply all their attention and care so that what is
provided in this article may be strictly observed. It is to be
understood that they shall be strictly responsible to me for any
laxity which may be noticed in this matter.

⟨[a] Attendance for seven hours. [b] See article 238.⟩

248

Because it is fitting to avoid doubts or varying interpretations concerning the proper understanding of a great part of this
instruction which the distinct faculties united in some of the
officials who must observe it may cause, it is understood that the
same thing ordered in general by its various articles for the
intendants and the principal accountants and treasurers of the
province must hold good for the superintendent-subdelegate in
regard to his powers as intendant of the province of Mexico, and
for the general accountant and treasurer, who hold the same
offices in the said intendancy. Consequently all the peculiar
functions of the aforesaid offices are inseparable for each official.

249

Considering the great advantages which may result for my kingdom and vassals from making the rules in both Americas uniform concerning the collection and distribution of the royal revenues of the crown, intrusting their economic management to an authorized power that shall direct them with due knowledge, and under my immediate orders and supreme authority, I named my Secretary of State of the universal Office of the Indies as superintendent-general of my royal treasury of the Indies, as was stated in article 4, with the same amplification of right, powers, prerogatives, and privileges which I have granted to the superintendent of Spain, in order that by his measures and direction the regulation which my royal treasury needs in those vast dominions may be more completely facilitated.

DEPARTMENT OF WAR

250

It is my royal will that the intendants in their provinces shall take care of everything pertaining to war which may be connected with my royal treasury. This obligation must direct their attention and care to the most effective measures and provisions conducive to its better performance, especially in the maintenance and care of the troops and other matters pertaining to such an important object which concerns the tranquility and defense of the state, in which they must always attend to the necessary comfort of my people.

251

As it is my royal purpose to establish intendants in all the area of New Spain, I wish the intendant of army and province, as well as those who only have this last rank [the intendants of province], to see likewise to the subsistence, economy, and general administration of the troops which may be in their respective territories. Since particular affairs concerning military bodies are intrusted to their inspectors and superior officers, the entire care of the intendants in this matter is reduced to two obligations, namely, to provide their salaries in money and their subsistence in provisions when the aforesaid military bodies have not been intrusted with this duty. For these purposes, and in supplying everything extraordinary which they may need, and the important matter of their health, the intendants of province shall observe the same form and method as will be prescribed for the army, for this is the general rule which must be followed in the matter.

252

[a]In regard to the first obligation, the intendants must cause their daily wage to be paid to the troops every month and the salary for officials, not permitting any sum to be advanced on credit. I declare this in order to avoid the inconveniences and abuses which are experienced from doing the contrary. But this prohibition must not be understood to apply to the case of furnishing supplies, which generally are and must be provided for the regiments or military bodies of the army by my treasuries on the last days of each month on the credit of the payment which is to be made in the following month, and for the sustenance of the troops during the month, as they have no other way to supply what is necessary for their maintenance, the daily wage for the whole month being paid during the occurrence of the review, with the only difference that the officers who receive their respective daily salaries must not be paid until the end of each month. Therefore the aforesaid supplies cannot be considered as real advances [on credit] as are those which are prohibited by the present article. This is done for the purpose of avoiding the unfavorable balances of accounts which are charged against the military bodies in these my kingdoms because of doing the contrary.

Consequently it must be understood to be permitted, as I expressly permit it, that on the last day of each month, with the previous information and consent of the intendants, the supplies necessary shall, on the credit of what must be paid in the following month, be furnished by my treasuries of New Spain, either the general one, the principal ones of the provinces or the minor ones, to the paymasters-general of the military bodies and to those persons who exercise his functions in the distant detachments. But it is to be understood that such advances must not exceed half or more than two-thirds of that which is prudently estimated as payable to the corps or detachment according to its strength during the month concerned.

The ministers of the royal treasury shall keep account of these supplies under the title of advances on credit (*buenas-cuentas*), with the understanding that all advances in contravention of what is here ordered, found to be in excess of what has actually been earned by the troops and officers when the accounts have been balanced according to the statements offered at the review and the proper discounts have been made, are not to be accepted as debits by the aforesaid officers, but the amounts concerned are to be deposited at once in the strongbox without objection or delay, and the collection of them shall be at said minister's account and risk. In such cases the tribunal of accounts may and must take charges and set them down as liquid balances of account, carrying them with interest charges at the established rate or at four times such rate, according to the laws of the Indies, if the amount be such that it indicates malversation or voluntary neglect of the rules and the precaution with which the ministers of the royal treasury must proceed in such advances. In order that all herein prescribed may be fulfilled without the inconveniences caused by the presentation of balance sheets showing arrears at the time of the reviews, I command my viceroy of Mexico, the commandant-general of the frontier, and the general intendant of army to issue their orders with special strictness to the end that these statements may be drawn up and submitted at the proper time.

⟨ᵃ Advances on credit.⟩

253

Upon the basis of these statements at reviews of the troops their contracts must be adjusted each month promptly by the principal accountants of the provinces in which they are stationed and approved by the intendants; so that, by virtue of these documents, the receipt of the paymaster thereon, and the memorandum of the proper officers of the royal treasury set down in the book of this paymaster as prescribed by the General Ordinance of the Army in article 9, title 9, treatise 1,[47] the payment may lawfully be made to him of the balances due as shown, both for the officers' salaries and for the pay of the soldiers, and for all kinds of emoluments which the various members of the troops may respectively enjoy.

254

The intendants must examine the adjustments of salaries which are drawn up by the accounting-offices of army or province for the payment of troops, officials, and other individuals of the military bodies, as was said. It shall be one of their duties in this connection to see that none of the ordinary discounts is omitted which must be made both for disabled soldiers, the *monte-pio,* hospitals and provisions, and for special charges for advances of salaries which they have received, or the assignments thereon which some soldiers have made to their families in Spain.

It is to be noted that, by the royal circular or order of August 6, 1776,[48] it is declared for all kinds of reimbursements that the *peso* of 8 *reales* old silver (each *real* of which is worth 16 *cuartos*) or 128 *cuartos*,[49] or 15 *reales* 2 *maravedís* Spanish

---

[47] See Appendix, number 34, in the original, for the article cited.

[48] Found under number 35 in the Appendix of the original.

[49] A copper coin worth four *maravedís.*

vellon[50] which is the same thing, corresponds in the Indies to the current or common *peso* of that money, and vice versa; so that for every 15 *reales* and 2 *maravedis vellon* advanced in Spain to the troops and officers of the army, and which have not been disbursed during their journey to the Indies, a *peso* of that current money must be deducted on the first adjustments and from the salaries payable there. By the same rule a current or common *peso* of the Indies must be allowed them for each *peso* of 15 *reales* and 2 *maravedis vellon* which may have been earned on their journey from what is advanced before their arrival in Spain. Likewise for each 15 *reales* and 2 *maravedis vellon* which any officers or other employees have assigned in these kingdoms there must be discounted in America a *peso* of that current or common money, or 10 *reales*, $21\frac{1}{4}$ *maravedis* of it for each 20 *reales* Spanish *vellon*, or a *real* of the aforesaid currency of the Indies from each *real* of old silver, or of 16 *cuartos*, which have been advanced, paid, or have been assigned in these kingdoms [of Spain], which is one and the same thing.

⟨ [a] Moneys. See article 113 and the *cédula* which is referred to as I. F. also the royal order of January 17, 1791, issued concerning the adjustments of salaries of officers who go to serve in the army of New Spain, obtaining balances in their favor.⟩

255

If any troop should pass from one province to another, it must take the certificate of the respective ministers of the royal treasury showing the manner and time for which they were paid. This must be visaed by the intendant, who shall transmit the proper advise to the intendant of the territory to which the troop is assigned, and both shall respectively give proper and adequate orders so that on its march everything may be provided for it as should be in the manner and according to the rules which will be set forth. If the aforesaid troop should consist of only some company or detachment, when it is restored to its

---

[50] A copper coin of Castile worth one-fourth of a *peseta* (five cents).

corps it must bring another similar certificate from the province where it may have been, beside those concerning its reviews and hospital fund.

256

When funds from the revenues and products of some provinces are assigned for the payment of troops, the intendants thereof shall cause them to be properly deposited in the treasuries in order to prevent any delay and the difficulty of issuing warrants upon the goods assigned, because it is my royal intention, so as to free them from all embarrassment, that no orders against their wages shall be drawn on the troops, and that they shall be paid in money as all other persons are who receive remuneration from my royal treasury.

257

If the funds assigned should not be sufficient to pay all the salary of the troops, they must be applied preferably to furnishing daily supplies, and the sum which is allotted to the payment of officers shall be distributed equally and proportionally among the corps in such manner that no injustice or complaint that some suffer greater arrears than others may ensue.

258

In regard to the second point mentioned concerning the supply of provisions, since the contractors and purveyors of these are immediately subject to the intendants, the latter shall cause them to report very minutely about their condition and the measures which they take to insure completely the aforesaid supply of provisions. The intendants shall also cause the contractors to govern themselves by the measures and orders which the intendants may communicate to them about the depositories of provisions and places in which it may be fitting to keep them according to circumstances. They shall observe the form, condition, and quantity which they are required to observe so that my service may not suffer the least retardation.

259

Although the supplies are at the disposal of the contractors as their own property, they may not take any part of them out of the storehouses without the orders of the intendants, who shall first give them notice and information concerning the places of their destination. The intendants must also see that they punctually fulfil the obligations of their contracts.

260

Contractors must make the distribution of supplies according as the intendants shall command. They cannot furnish any portion except by means of receipts from the *sargentos mayores* or adjutants of the military corps, or commanders of the detachments or companies. The intendants shall especially take heed that there is no connivance or profit between officers and contractors, and they shall punish any violation of these rules with the proper penalties according to the circumstances of the cases.

261

The intendants shall absolutely prohibit contractors from purchasing for consumption the grains of the country in their respective districts, unless on account of their abundance some advantage may result for the towns; also sales of these grains to the contractors shall be made with their knowledge and permission in order that [prices] may not be exhorbitant. If during transportation the troops should consume some grain, the contractors must pay for it at the current prices of their contract under receipts which, as was said, the officers or commanders must give. They shall indemnify the village for the cost which they incurred in collecting for what they have furnished the troops. This collection shall be the duty of the contractors whom the intendants may constrain by executive measures in case of necessity.

262

When contractors or their agents distribute supplies which are not in good condition, the intendants themselves shall visit the storehouses or they may intrust this duty to officials in their confidence. They shall without fail exclude bread and all other provisions that are not of good quality, and order that these shall be replaced by those of the best quality at the cost of the aforesaid contractors. But if it should develop that the latter maliciously adulterated the supplies by mixing with them any substance injurious to the health, or if the goods are of themselves thus injurious and they have deceitfully misrepresented it without advising the intendant, or the minister of the royal treasury, or their immediate military superior concerning it, they shall be punished according to what article 87, title 10, treatise 8 of the Ordinance of the Army and the later declarations provide for such cases.[51] The same thing shall be done when contractors and purveyors falsify the weight or measure of commodities which they distribute to the troops.

263

Whenever provision of supplies is administered by my royal treasury, the intendants shall choose for its management capable and disinterested persons experienced in economy. They shall estimate the amount of grain which may be harvested within their provinces according to the scarcity or abundance of the crops, and also those amounts which at favorable times may be brought from the outside. After taking all the steps [possible] in order that maintenance may be assured, they shall make a just computation or estimate of the funds which must be furnished monthly, including purchases, costs of transportation, expenses of storehouses, and all other necessary items, so that with the proper knowledge a sufficient fund may be appropriated.

---

[51] See number 36 of the Appendix, in the original.

264

They shall establish storehouses in which the supplies that may be necessary [may be collected] according to rules of the greatest utility and economy possible for their use and distribution. The same thing [shall be done] in the manufactures of bread and biscuits which may be prescribed for necessary restocking in the military headquarters as well as in other locations. They shall set rules for the clearest account and calculation of the consumption, distribution, and expenses, so that the total amount of them, their nature and characteristics, may always be kept in mind.

265

The intendants shall likewise provide that the bread, grain, straw, and pack-animals furnished the troops by the towns when the supply of these is for the account of my royal treasury, shall be paid for punctually at current and moderate prices, so that collecting for them may not cause vexation or great expenses to the towns.

266

It shall also be the duty of intendants to see that there may be as great an abundance of supplies as possible at all drill-grounds or troop encampments. For this purpose they shall issue adequate orders and likewise take as many measures as they may deem necessary for the security of the country, and the good faith and confidence of the natives, in order that they may resort thither voluntarily with their produce.

267

When the veteran cavalry may need barley, straw, hay, or other forage on its marches or at its quarters or posts, and the towns have to furnish them, the intendants shall see that the levies are made with perfect equality. But in case these provisions are furnished under contract, they shall cause the necessary stocks to be assembled and see that rations shall be given by the contractor as assigned for each according to the memoranda of the governors or commissaries appointed for this purpose, with the statement of the present strength of the corps, detachment, or company for which they may be allotted. The contractor or his agents must take receipts for all the rations which they deliver in order to present the totals thereof at the proper time to the respective paymasters according to article 274.

268

The intendants shall take very special care that the towns do not suffer grievances when they furnish these provisions during the marches of corps, detachments, or companies, or where there are no contractor's supplies, and that they shall be given receipts which the contractor shall collect and pay for the goods at current contract figures. But if there is time they shall provide that the contractor shall transmit to the *sargento mayor* or commander of the troops sufficient money for the amount of the barley and hay which they may need on the marches, in order that the officers may buy them, paying for them in cash at the prices indicated; so that the towns may be exempted by this means from the annoyance and expense of going to the contractor for their collection, which sometimes is not worth the cost of the journey and the trouble.

269

The same thing shall be done with regard to rations of bread. For the purpose that in each case it may be done with the proper formality, in order to prevent embarrassments, the prices of the contract shall be stated in the itineraries; and when the necessary money has been delivered to the *sargentos mayores* or the commanders for buying the said commodities until reaching the place of their destination, the village need not give the troops anything except what they shall pay for at the aforesaid contract prices, but merely furnish the simple quarters in the accustomed manner. But in case the troop is large the contractor may send an agent with it to provide for quarters, and he must pay for it at the prices indicated. This circumstance shall also be expressed in the itinerary so that it may be known to the towns.

270

If it should be necessary to bring barley, hay, or other forage from distant places and the calvalry cannot do this, the intendants shall provide with the greatest fairness for the necessary number of pack-animals, in order to relieve the people as much as possible from the burden of transportation. They shall do the same thing in regard to the other lines of provision and commodities which may be transported, always seeing to the greatest economy and good order according to the needs and circumstances of the cases.

271

When firewood and other supplies must be furnished for the troops by contract or by administration for the account of my royal treasury, the intendants shall take care that the same rules are observed as are prescribed concerning the supply of provisions and that it shall be done according to the actual number of individuals whom the corps may contain.

272

The intendants shall take the greatest care that, in the requisition of vehicles or pack-animals necessary for the transportation and conveyance of supplies, no injury is caused to the people. In order to prevent it they shall assign to each town or district the number which it must furnish without harm to the cultivation of the soil and harvest of crops, unless some unavoidable necessity may occur. They shall prescribe the rules which must be observed concerning this matter by the subordi-

nate judges, and order that the pack-animals of all the inhabitants of whatever condition or rank they may be, without any
exception, shall be assigned in rotation for these requisitions and
for the transportation of the troops which may occur, under the
penalty of being fined and punished for doing the contrary and
of paying the cost of any injury.

With equal vigilance they shall see that contractors pay
punctually for transportation at the price which may be arranged, without causing delay to the conveyors; and when they
give an occasion for it, the intendants may compel them to make
reparation for the costs and expenses which they caused to the
inhabitants. Let it be understood that the supplying of beasts
of burden by requisition must only be resorted to in case the
contractors shall not have been obliged to maintain and provide
those needed for the service; because if they have done this,
then only the persons who voluntarily make a bargain with them
for these conveyances must assist.

273

Before leaving the towns the pack-animals which the troops
and officials may need for their marches must be paid for at the
established prices; and unless there is urgent need they shall
not be compelled to furnish transportation farther than their
stage, under severe penalties against the officials and justices
who cause this. But in case it cannot be avoided it shall be the
duty of the officers to pay for it in due proportion before making
another march. The intendants shall admonish the justices to
aid each other in this matter with proper cooperation and punish
those who have acted with malice or negligence.

It is to be understood that pack-animals must be given only
to detached officers who are assigned to some special business
under my royal service, either on some duty of their corps with
a passport from the viceroy or the commandant-general of the
frontier, or on some prescribed journey under safe-conduct or

permission of the intendant, and not to those who do not carry either the one or the other, because for the latter the journey shall be voluntary, and the justices shall not be obliged to furnish them with these or other aids, nor should such officers claim them.

274

In order that the officers of account and computation may punctually have the bills for bread, barley, and hay which each corps shall take from the supply, the intendants shall see very particularly that contractors or their agents shall present in the principal accounting-offices of the province every two months, or at most every four, the original receipts for the supplies they have furnished the regiments which garrison the aforesaid provinces; it being understood that the receipts mentioned must be totaled by months by the paymaster of each regiment, signed by him, and legalized by the approval of its colonel or commander. The paymaster must collect the individual receipts of the contractors under which they supplied the provisions, in order that they may serve as a guide for the regiment in the contracts of its companies.

It is to be understood that the troops must not take more rations each month than those which are due them according to the summaries of the reviews, nor the detached officers who may enjoy the privilege more than what respectively pertains to them. Likewise neither may the contractor furnish them with a quantity exceeding that which belongs to them in the same month according to the aforesaid rules. As is stated, when the said receipts are presented by the contractors or their agents, summed up in the principal accounting-offices to which they 'are referred, and their value at the contract prices is approved by these offices, they shall give to the contractors certificates of the amount due them, mentioning therein the time included and the number of rations of each kind that each corps has received, so that by virtue thereof the general accounting-office of army and royal treasury of Mexico may give the aforesaid contractors the general adjustment for everything which they have provided for the troops and detached officers, and of the debits which should be placed against these for this reason, according to the contract, in order to settle and pay the legitimate balance due to the contractors.

275

Since it is proper in drawing up adjustments for supplies furnished and terminating the computation of them, to arrange that all the offices of account and computation shall observe the same method, I wish and command that their monthly credit for provisions shall be adjusted by the offices mentioned according to the summaries of review, for all the corps of troops and detached officers who receive rations, in the same manner as they do for those of daily pay, salaries, and special perquisites. After deducting from each kind of credit what has been taken from the supply of provision in produce and the other charges properly made to them for hospitals or for any other motive, [I order] that the net balance for rations, in the case of those for bread at a fourth part less, and those for barley and hay at a third part less than their current prices of the estimate, shall be allowed and paid in money to each corps or detached officer by the respective subtreasury of my royal treasury for its account.

If it should appear from the aforesaid adjustments, that the corps received a larger number of rations than pertains to their monthly credit according to the review, I command that all the excess shall be charged, respectively, to the said corps with an increase in the prices indicated by the contract, and in the proportions thereto of one-fourth part on rations of bread and one-third on those of barley and hay, in order to prevent by this means the troops from drawing from the supply of provisions more rations than those which belong to them under the [summary of] review.

276

If, after completing the adjustments in the form provided by the preceding article, the regiments should show in the reviews of the following months some diminution of effectives which they could not show in the act of the review of the month or months already adjusted for, in such case all the charge made against them in the adjustment or adjustments of the corresponding months because proofs of the aforesaid diminution had not arrived in time to include them in the respective summaries, shall be restored in money to the said regiments by my royal treasury. So that if, because of any number of effectives not having been deducted in the review of the month to which they belonged, there should be due to the corps on its contract a corresponding number of rations, and these should be charged to it with the increases provided in the preceding article cited, then under these circumstances the same sum which was charged to it in the adjustment must be restored to it.

If on the contrary such a regiment in its adjustment of rations for the month should have been charged with too few, then the new balance of accounts rendered concerning them for that month must give it credit for them at the lower prices indicated for such balances in the article referred to; for it is my royal will that the charge of the extra prices prescribed in it, and the allowance with the rebates of prices expressed therein, shall be made respectively only in the two cases, that is, either when the rations received by the troops exceed the legitimate credit pertaining to them according to the review, or when because of it some balance for rations may be due the aforesaid troops, after considering in each case all the credits and debits for every month at whatever time the regiments and the contractors may prove them.

277

In all the business and cases which may arise concerning supply of provisions for the troops and their employees the intendants must take cognizance with exclusive jurisdiction as the special duty of their offices, allowing appeals to the *junta superior de hacienda*. They [shall see that] what is granted and stipulated in my royal name for contractors is observed exactly, without causing them any embarrassment or the least injury.

278

If, during the marches and transfers of troops, or in the places where they are stationed, it should be necessary on account of the lack of quarters to lodge them in homes of private persons, the intendants and justices of the towns, with the advice of the military commanders or quartermasters, shall try to observe whenever it is possible what was provided for these matters in article 3, title 14, treatise 6 of the Ordinances of the Army,[52] so that the inhabitants shall experience the least possible inconvenience and unusual expense, and that they may be placed near their noncommissioned officers who will restrain them, and make them observe the most strict discipline and good conduct toward their patrons and the other natives, under the penalties established in the articles of the aforesaid ordinances which were cited in article 280 of this instruction, and which their officers respectively shall impose upon them. When they do anything to the contrary the intendant of province shall give account to the viceroy, or to the commandant-general of the frontier if it should be within the area of his command, so that no misdeeds or acts of violence which my vassals suffer may go unpunished.

---

[52] Found under number 37 in the Appendix of the original.

279

For the exact observance of the aforesaid rules whenever troops must be lodged in the houses of private persons, the intendants shall provide that in the cities, towns, and villages of the provinces their *alcaldes* and judges shall make and keep beforehand a legal and official description of all the houses of which they are composed, with a statement of the owners or inhabitants who dwell in them, and concerning their capacity or limitation.

280

Whenever the towns through which the troops are transported or in which they are detached are not military posts or places in which there are quarters for their lodging, and they must be taken into houses of individuals, the *sargentos mayores*, when they leave them, and in their absence the *comandantes*, shall be obliged to obtain a certificate from the ordinary justice setting forth that during all the time [of their quartering] the troops under their command have not committed any misdeed or received in kind or in money more than what is permitted and commanded for them by article 2, title 14, treatise 6 of the Ordinances of the Army.[53]

Since the intendants, as is provided, must take particular care that their pay is given to the troops every month on time, they cannot have any excuse for such excesses nor may their irregularities therein be overlooked. Wherefore I command that, if any regiment, company, detachment, party of soldiers, officers, or detached soldiers with a passport, safe-conduct license, or without it, shall cause injury or extortion to my towns or to any of my vassals either by insulting or maltreating them, or by taking from them money, produce, commodities, or other things which are not destined for the said troops according to the afore-

---

[53] See Appendix, number 38, of the original for this article and the others which are cited afterward.

said article 2, although it may be under the title of a voluntary gift, the intendants, or justices by their order, may take action within a period of eight days to prove the outrage or grievance.

When summary information is taken concerning the circumstances or the amount concerned, according to the cases, they shall submit the report to the viceroy or to the commandant-general of the frontier if these should occur within his jurisdiction, in order that, according to their seriousness and to what is provided concerning them by articles 4 and 10, titles 13 and 14, treatise 6 of the above-mentioned Ordinances of the Army, and in the other articles of title 10, treatise 8 of the same ordinances, he may punish the delinquents and arrange for the indemnification of the injury. In conformity with what is determined by any of the aforesaid military chiefs and which must be communicated in turn to the respective intendants, who shall provide for the reparation of damages that the corps, the members of which were the aggressors, must pay, the intendants shall see that the justices distribute promptly the full amounts to the aggrieved persons in proportion to what each one has suffered, and they shall warn them that any portions which these officers may withhold, and as much again, shall be made up from their possessions.

281

When in any of the cases of which the preceding article treats it is impossible to discover who are guilty, in order that the military officers may take specific action for their punishment and the compensation [of those injured], I command that the amount shall then be paid without delay at the expense of the corps of which the company, detachment, or group was a part until, when the delinquents are discovered, the sum shall be taken from them necessary for restoring the amount according to what is prescribed in the articles of the aforesaid Military Ordinances which were cited in the preceding article.

282

In order that reviews of the corps, detachments, and of the chief staffs (*estados mayores*) which are in the provinces may be passed every month, the ministers of the royal treasury, the accountants and treasurers, either of the general ones or the principal and subsidiary ones of the province, shall require them, and fix the day for their occurrence, which must be from the 5th to the 15th [of the month], since each of said ministers must perform the functions of commissaries of war, with the uniform and prerogatives thereof, in that kingdom and within their respective districts. In the places where these proprietary ministers do not exist and which are very far distant from the capitals, the intendants shall appoint persons of their entire confidence as substitute commissaries. They shall prefer the subordinate officials of my royal treasury where these are found and must give account to the intendant-general of army for his approval. But it is to be understood that these latter officials must not wear the military uniform and that it shall be the exclusive duty of the governors of fortresses or commandants of arms to designate the hour and place in which the afore-mentioned reviews must be held.

283

As the reviews are the principal means of legalizing the payment and issue of supplies furnished to troops, officers, and to other individuals pertaining to war, the intendants must heed with the greatest care the punctuality and formality which accountants, treasurers, and substitute commissaries of their provinces must observe therein. They shall conduct the reviews by means of personal identifications according to the military registers and note clearly in their summaries those who must be considered present or absent, in order that no doubt or confusion may arise to the injury of the corps or of my royal treasury, at the time of adjustment of accounts. For this purpose they shall designate those who must be credited as present with the letter P and those absent who must be excluded with A, using the same clearness and distinction in the annotations of the summaries.

In respect to the allowances for the sick, and for detachments and officers employed in recruiting soldiers, in collections, or other indispensable operations for the benefit of the military bodies, which may be made evident by legitimate certificates, they shall also proceed with great accuracy, referring to them in the summaries in this form: "the sick, as present, the detached, as present, and the employed, as present." But the aforesaid summaries shall neither be accepted by the intendants nor in the accounting-offices of the army or the principal [ones of the provinces] unless the military officer who supervised the review shall have placed on each summary under the signature of him who has served as commissary (which must occupy the chief place, as I have declared, on account of this act being his own exclusive function) the following:

I, the undersigned, was present at this review (here his name and surname are written) and this summary is made according to the number of officers, sergeants, and soldiers present and effective, without those who are declared to be assigned [to some task] or employed [elsewhere] having been reincorporated or having attended it.

It is to be understood that the aforesaid military officer must put this same statement, legalized by his signature, on all the summaries which the commissary submits to him for this purpose, comparing them beforehand with his own list since he likewise must be as responsible as that officer for any fraud which may be committed with regard to the effective force or those employed or detached. He shall refrain from this intervention if any difficulty or difference may arise, in which case he shall report it to the intendant so that the latter with the commissary may take the proper measure in its absence.

284

In order that what is provided in the preceding article and in certain ones of the articles of title 9, treatise 3 of the Ordinances of the Army[54] may be executed and observed with due exactness, it shall be the precise duty of the intendants to examine the summaries of review and revise everything in them which does not conform to both regulations, not neglecting this trust, because of the many abuses that may result from its omission. In order that there may at no time be such negligence in regard to it, I wish the accountants, treasurers, and substitute commissaries to deliver or submit to them the aforesaid summaries in quadruplicate, and also all the documents and original proofs that may have been presented to them by the corps which they have reviewed, for the allowances of officials, soldiers, and noneffectives and those present at the review in order that, when inspected and examined by the intendants themselves with the greatest minuteness, and when the allowances which have been made by virtue thereof are found to be legitimate, they may transmit them to the principal accounting-office of the province so that they may be deposited in its archives. The officials respectively who serve in it shall give an adequate receipt to the accountants and subsidiary treasurers or to the substitute commissaries who have sent such documents, for such receipts may be of use as their vouchers in whatever matter may result.

The intendants shall leave one of the summaries referred to in their secretariat, and send the other three to the intendant-general of army, who shall submit two, the original and a duplicate, to my Secretary of State of the Office of the Indies, and he shall transmit the other to the general accounting-office of the army and royal treasury. But if from the prescribed examination it should be discovered that any of the ministers of the royal treasury in their capacity as commissaries of war, or any of the

---

54 Found under number 39 in the Appendix of the original.

aforesaid substitutes, who submitted to him the documents mentioned and their proofs, has credited more allowance than belongs to the corps which presented said documents, or that the former or the latter documents were not legalized in due form, the intendants shall cause the injury which may have resulted to my royal treasury from such credit to be reimbursed immediately from the current salary of the minister who has occasioned it or from any credit or balance which he may have against the treasury. At the same time they shall issue suitable orders that the corps may not receive more allowance than what legitimately pertains to it.

285

When any troops are encamped and the day is set for reviewing them, the intendant, with the concurrence of their commander, shall take the precautions which both judge best in order to prevent soldiers from one regiment being transferred temporarily to another for the increase of its effectives, and to watch against all other frauds whatsoever. For this purpose it shall be fitting that as many corps as possible shall be reviewed at one time, according to the number of ministers available for the purpose. They shall also arrange that besides having the troops formed in the order of battle as the aforesaid Ordinances of the Army provide, guards shall be placed between the corps, in order that soldiers may not be permitted to pass from one to the other while the review is taking place.

286

If in some month any corps is not reviewed because it is on the march or in a very far distant place with which communication may have been cut off or may be difficult, the intendants of province shall so report to the intendant-general of army, so that, with the concurrence of the viceroy, he may provide the form under which the summaries must be furnished from which the estimates for the pay and supplies of such corps must be made.

287

Whenever the intendant-general of army or other officer exercising his powers may pass with troops through any province, or when those which pertain to his care and are under the command of a single military commander go into others, he must notify the provincial intendants concerning what they shall do in whatever necessary affairs which may arise. Consequently he may give suitable orders to the subordinate justices of the said provinces if there is not time to issue them through the respective intendants. The former and the latter shall observe all that is ordered for the intendant of army concerning the maintenance of the troops during transit and all other matters relating to their commissions.

288

Since, as is provided in articles 250 and 251, the economy and general control of the troops and everything pertaining to war is under the care of the intendants, the commissaries of whatever kind, the accountants, treasurers, and the subordinate officials of hospitals and of supplies, must be immediately subordinate to them. Therefore intendants must give them the rules and measures for the storehouses of both, that is, hospitals and supplies, in the most convenient manner for my service. Let it be understood that, in case either is under administration for the account of my royal treasury, they shall propose to its superintendent-subdelegate all those persons who shall be employed in the aforesaid supplying of provisions and hospitals, in order that they may serve in these offices with the salaries which the superintendent himself with the advice of the *junta superior de hacienda* may assign [at the time] of their appointment. These offices must be only provisional, since if they should be permanent or perpetual, account would be given to me for obtaining my royal approval, or I would appoint those who might suit my sovereign pleasure.

289

When the troops are on campaign it is necessary to establish depositories of supplies and hospitals for their maintenance and care, and the intendants must provide for these when it is not done by contract. But in both cases their measures must be regulated by the order of the general or the commander. They shall pay attention to all the conditions concerning the number of troops, the season, and the nature of the military operations, and shall form separate computations of how many supplies are needed, in order to attain these important purposes opportunely and with the greatest possible economy.

They shall also give the necessary rules so that due account and calculation of everything may be kept in books of entry and discharge of the sick, and daily statements, signed by the commissary of entries and visaed by the inspector [may be made] concerning those who are in each hospital. They shall cause the latter official to visit the hospitals twice each day, once early in the morning and again in the afternoon before it grows dark, in order that he may inform the intendant concerning everything which happens in them. The same procedure that is provided for the establishment, control, and management of campaign hospitals must be observed in the cities, fortified towns, and districts. In the matter pertaining to them, both the aforesaid commissaries of entries and the inspectors must observe what is provided in article 2, title 28, treatise 2 of the general Ordinances of the Army.[55]

290

They shall likewise see that storehouses of reserve supplies are established in convenient places according to what may be needed in each. First a computation of their capacity shall be made, and then it shall be referred to the *junta superior de*

---

[55] See Appendix, number 40, of the original.

hacienda by means of the superintendent-subdelegate in order that the *junta* may give its approval and measures [concerning them]. They shall cause the depositories to be inspected by the ministers of the royal treasury or their commissaries, who shall deliver or submit to the intendants monthly reports concerning the condition and quality of the provisions, in order that before the commodities are consumed or destroyed the latter may issue at the proper time orders to renew them in equal portion, or to sell them so as to do the same thing with the proceeds, using as much economy as possible.

291

In regard to the permanent quarters which the troops occupy, it is my will to relieve the towns of every kind of burden, and in consideration of this wherever the soldiers are not supplied with beds, I command the intendants to install at the expense of my royal treasury beds conforming to the custom and practice of the country. I also order them to provide for their preservation, keeping good account of the number needed in proportion to the active soldiers by the certificates of the officers who must give them, and that the beds shall be delivered upon receipt from the *sargentos mayores* or their adjutants, in order that they may be returned in case of the corps being transferred; for, the corps being responsible for those which may be lacking, the cost of any such shall be deducted from [the funds] of the corps and they shall be so replaced.

292

Because the inspection and conservation of the magazines of war which are in the fortified places or towns of their district must also be the special duty of the intendants, they shall every month ask the inspectors or guards of magazines for a detailed statement of the supplies of artillery on hand, the gun-carriages, powder, arms, munitions, tools, instruments, and other articles which they may have, with an itemized account of their condition and quality.; so that, with the concurrence of the intendant-general of army, they may dispose of the useless articles, provide for repairing and keeping what may be of service, and replace what is lacking when it is evident that it has been consumed. In order to prevent any loss or misplacement the intendants shall frequently visit the magazines mentioned by means of the respective ministers of the royal treasury as commissaries of war, so that they may find out whether the method and arrangement under which the articles are stored are as they should be.

293

Notwithstanding that the inspectors and guards of magazines of artillery, their adjutants and other subordinates are under separate inspection, yet since it is the duty of the intendants to take care of what belongs to my royal treasury, and it is their obligation to provide directly for the expenditures which are needed, the said inspectors and guards must observe the subordination to the intendants which is fitting and give them all the information for which they may ask. If in time of war a train of artillery is assigned [to some place] the intendants shall nominate to the superintendent-subdelegate, for the time that the expedition shall last, such inspectors and other individuals as may be needed for the good account and enumeration of the articles and things which are placed under their care, and consequently they shall take cognizance of the cases which arise concerning the aforesaid employees.

294

If it should be necessary to appoint any armorers to repair or manufacture arms for the account and benefit of my royal treasury, the intendants shall see that this is executed and done as is most fitting. In the same manner they shall attend to the protection of factories or artillery and other material, if they exist, and they must give account to me by the *vía reservada*, also to the viceroy or commandant-general of the frontier respectively, and to the superintendent-subdelegate of my royal treasury concerning everything which they may order in these matters or think more useful for my service.

295

The prompt supply of all the provisions for the artillery and its service, powder, wood, instruments, and other things which are needed for any operation or work, and the measures for their transportation, shall likewise be the duty of the intendants, and they may issue the proper orders for these, first arranging with the concurrence of the military commander in regard to the quantities of any kind of article which must be provided and the places to which they shall be taken.

296

The opportune and beforehanded repair of the fortifications of strongholds or forts, and of ruined barracks and magazines is advantageous to my royal treasury in that it may thus be done with small and scarcely noticeable expense; but this does not occur when remissness in these important matters allows the fortresses to become defenseless and the ruins so extensive that they need considerable expenditure for their repair. For these reasons the intendants shall take very special care to have prompt information concerning what conditions may be in this respect. They shall order the engineers who are available to apply themselves continually to the professional visitation and inspection of fortifications and inform them punctually concerning the exact works which are needed, with a statement of their character and number, and accurate estimates of their cost, in order that the intendants may make it known to the viceroy or to the commandant-general of the frontier, if they are in his area, and to the superintendent-subdelegate of my royal treasury, so that they may decide what is best for my service in regard to that which must be repaired. In consideration of this the measures relative to the execution of such works with the promptness that the matter requires shall be determined by the *junta superior de hacienda,* and it shall inform me of everything at the same time by the *vía reservada* of the Indies.

297

For making extraordinary expenditures of whatever kind, the intendants must first observe all the formalities prescribed in article 105 of this instruction, unless they are urgent and routinary such as repairs of magazines, conveying of supplies, or other matters likewise necessary. Therefore only in these cases may the intendants take measures beforehand with the concurrence of the provincial *junta* of the royal treasury and report them afterward to the *junta superior* through the superintendent-subdelegate, in order that it may approve them provisionally while account is being given me by the *junta* and I may consider it best to grant my royal approval.

298

The intendants shall watch with especial care the extraordinary expenditures that occur in case of a war, in order to avoid the abuses which usually occur in connection with remunerating soldiers who are employed in the work of making trenches or fortifying encampments. They shall come to an agreement in such cases with the captain or commandant-general, understanding that what shall be given such soldiers must be a voluntary consideration on account of their work according as they try to deserve it, and not a precise debt, since they must perform any labor to which they may be assigned. The same thing shall be done with the corps of artillerymen. The intendants shall try to observe in all this the greatest possible economy; and when it is deemed convenient to aid and encourage the soldiers with some recompense, it must be proportioned according to the fatigue or danger which they shall experience in the work or task.

299

Although all the matters mentioned above are under the special inspection of the intendants, by the rules and conditions of which they must direct, provide for, and promote them, they must bear in mind that for their better success and their more proper dispatch it is my royal will that in everything pertaining to war the intendants of province shall have due subordination to the intendant-general of army, that he as well as they shall observe their subordination to the viceroy and to the commandant-general of the frontier as the superior authorities of the provinces under their command; and that they shall observe the proper attitude toward the other military leaders because these matters, being of such great importance directly concerning my royal service and the glory of my arms, contribute to the increase of my dominions and the general welfare of my American vassals.

In consideration of this the intendants shall communicate to the aforesaid superior officers respectively all the orders directed to them regarding general or special measures concerning the management and economy of the troops, their maintenance and health, magazines of war, repairs and works of strongholds or forts, factories, foundries, and provisions for quarters in time of peace, likewise in time of war concerning everything which pertains to it, such as official preparations for expeditions and military operations that may be planned, funds for supplies and extraordinary expenses, provisions, convoys, and trains which are provided. This communication is understood to be required in those things for the execution of which the orders of the viceroy or of the commandant-general, or of whoever should be notified and informed, must intervene.

The intendants shall make known to the said superior officers the intent and purpose of their measures in order that, in contributing to their success, they shall aid the intendants, and acknowledge their authority as they ought. And because the intendants may, in executing all other measures which belong exclusively to them in matters of justice, finance, and *policía* in the government of their provinces, perhaps need military aid, in such cases they shall come for it with their representations to the aforesaid higher military authorities or to the respective commandants, who observing the same cooperation with the intendants and my decision in this matter, shall assist them in everything they do, as I command.

300

As it is my royal intention to clothe the intendants with all the proper power for accomplishing objects so conducive to the good administration, preservation, and happiness of those dominions, I very particularly command the viceroy of Mexico, the captains-general, and military commanders of the provinces under their authority, the royal *audiencias,* and other tribunals, to respect and aid all measures taken by the intendants without any opposition. They shall observe and cause to be observed all the privileges and exemptions belonging to the great office and character of intendant, and they shall act in accord with the intendants in regard to whatever is necessary and conducive to these very important ends.

301

I also wish and command that in the *juntas* or councils of war which the viceroys, captains, or commandants-general may summon for any expedition, distribution, or movement of troops, the intendants shall be present, not only to propose what may occur to them concerning the aforesaid matters under their supervision; but also in order that they may be informed in detail about everything for the purpose of taking measures with all possible effectiveness and giving the necessary orders. In the councils or *juntas* mentioned the intendant-general of army must occupy the place next after the viceroy or commandant-general. If they are only intendants of province with a right to exercise military functions, they shall have the seat next to the brigadiers, and shall be preferred to all other officers who are present. But when it is a *junta* concerning fortifications in any stronghold, what is provided in article 4, title 6, treatise 1 of the ordinances issued on October 22, 1768, for the service of the corps of engineers shall be observed.[56]

302

To the end that the intendant of army may be looked upon by my royal troops and the towns as possessing the honors and powers which I grant him, he shall be accorded, and the viceroys, captains, or commandants-general, and other officers, commanders, and individuals, shall cause him to be accorded, the same military honors as *mariscales de campo,* and give him a guard equal to that of the latter officers, according to both articles 8 and 40, titles 4 and 1, treatise 3 of the last Ordinances of the Army.[57]

When he dies he shall have the funeral honors prescribed for the aforesaid general officers in article 48, title 5 of the treatise mentioned, since I have decided this for a general rule upon the advice of my supreme Council of War on May 6, 1779. As it is most fitting for my service to give prestige to the intendants in all the provinces of that kingdom in order that my vassals may respect their persons and the extensive powers which I intrust to them, I grant them the rank, honors, prerogatives, and uniform of quartermasters for the time being until those suitable for them may be provided, and the treatment which article 3, title 6, treatise 3 of the ordinance cited prescribes.

---

[56] See Appendix 41 of the original.

[57] See Appendix 42 of the original for these and the other articles which are cited afterward.

I command the viceroy and commandant-general of the
frontier to delegate to them respectively their military jurisdiction, and where there are troops their commanding officers shall
give them the guard which article 43, title 1 of the treatise
referred to assigns to every colonel, which shall accord them the
honors which the same article prescribes and shall serve as an
escort on their journeys whenever they may ask this. It is likewise my sovereign will that when any one of the intendants may
die in a place where there are troops, the funeral honors defined
in article 52, title 5, treatise 3, with reference to article 50 of the
same title and Ordinances of the Army, shall be granted him by
them.

303

As it is also my royal will that these officials shall receive
sufficient remuneration with which to maintain the dignity of
their rank, I assign them annual salaries. To the intendant-general of army, the superintendent-subdelegate of my royal treasury, I grant 12,000 *pesos* from the general treasury; from the
principal treasuries respectively 7,000 *pesos* to each one of the
intendants of the provinces of Puebla, Vera Cruz, Guadalajara,
and Arispe; 6,000 *pesos* to those of Oaxaca, Valladolid, Guanajuato, San Luis Potosí, Zacatecas, and Durango; and 5,000 *pesos*
to the intendant of the province of Mérida de Yucatan. The
expenses of the secretariat and countinghouse of each intendancy
shall be understood to be included in the aforesaid assignments,
with the absolute prescription that the subordinates employed
in the other offices of my royal treasury may not be occupied in
the secretariat.

In consideration of this and of the promotions which I will
allow for the aforesaid officials in those kingdoms and these [of
Spain], I declare that none of them must claim or receive (excepting the fees for signatures according to the schedule on
business papers which are not drawn up for the poor or are

from their own office) any other article or quantity of money under the title of salary, remuneration, or traveling expense for superintending, conserving, or protecting the revenues, contracts, or any other business, whether administered for the account of my royal treasury or by lessees and contractors, or either as governors, or *corregidores*, or as the subdelegates of the post-offices if there be such employment—which are separately controlled and managed.

Although the gratitude, zeal, integrity, and other qualifications of such distinguished officials, in whom I have such great confidence, assure me of the punctual observance of this invariable rule with which my royal service, likewise the welfare of my beloved vassals, are concerned, I declare also that if any intendant, forgetting what he owes to himself and to my just resolutions, shall violate this statute, he shall incur my royal displeasure and be deposed from his office, and be unable to occupy any other office in my dominions.

304

In view of the important powers which I grant to the intendants in the four departments of justice, general administration, finance, and war, and the other reasons which were considered for obliging the officials of the provinces of these kingdoms [of Spain] to give bonds, I command that the officials of the provinces of New Spain, before beginning to serve in their positions shall give bond, for the results of their extensive administration, at the rate of 10,000 *pesos* for each intendancy, to the satisfaction of the tribunal of accounts and in the form which the laws of the *Recopilación* of those dominions prescribe for the securities which the different employees of my royal treasury must give. The superintendent-subdelegate shall be exempt from this obligation on account of the high qualities and powers of his position.

⟨ See the royal order of July 4, 1799, concerning the securities of the governor of Colatlan.⟩

305

As the magistrates of the Indies are subject to the judgment of *residencia* when they conclude their terms of office, therefore I also wish and it is my will that the intendants of the kingdom referred to shall be so judged in respect to matters of justice, *policía,* and government which I intrust to them as such *corregidores.* This same thing is to be understood for their lieutenants, subdelegates, and other subordinates. These *residencias* shall be dispatched by my Council of the Indies, and what is provided in regard to them by law 69, title 15, book 2 and law 8, title 12, book 5 of the *Recopilación* shall be observed. The documents which have been closed and decreed upon therein shall be sent to the aforesaid tribunal in order that, when they are examined, it may provide what shall be just.

306

In order that everything provided in this instruction may have its punctual and proper effect, I command my Supreme Council and Council of the Indies, royal *audiencias,* the tribunals of the Board of Trade (*casa de contratación*) and that of New Spain, its viceroy, captains-general, commanders-in-chief, officials, and military superiors, magistrates, judges, and other persons to whom it refers and pertains in the whole or in part to conform exactly to this instruction and ordinance, executing and observing it with the greatest exactness in regard to what refers to each one of them. Especially the aforesaid intendants of army and province shall observe everything contained in it as fixed and permanent law and statute. They shall observe it, and cause it to be observed infallibly notwithstanding any other laws, ordinances, statutes, customs, or practices which may be to the contrary, since in so far as they may be so, I expressly revoke them and desire that none of them may have effect.

I prohibit it to be interpretéd or glossed in any manner, because my will is that it shall be observed exactly according to the letter and the meaning expressed, and that the practice of what is provided may be suspended only when there is no reason to doubt the injury which might result from it. I very especially encharge the very reverend archbishop, the reverend bishops, and venerable members of the *cabildos* of the holy metropolitan churches and cathedrals, the provisors and vicars-general, and other ecclesiastical judges, the parish priests and ecclesiastical persons of that kingdom, prelates of the religious orders, heads of colleges, and missionaries appointed in the Indian reductions all to contribute to and effectively assist the punctual fulfillment and observance of what is commanded and provided in this my royal instruction, avoiding by whatever means possible any conflicts or embarrassments, which will always incur my royal displeasure as they are injurious to the administration of justice, good government, and to the peace and happiness of the people. For these purposes I have ordered the present ordinance to be issued, signed by my royal hand, sealed with my private seal, and countersigned by my undersigned counselor and Secretary of State of the universal Office of the Indies. This ordinance is issued in Madrid on December 4, 1786, I THE KING.

JOSEF DE GÁLVEZ.

This is a copy of the original.

SONORA. [In manuscript with rubric]

APPENDIX

ORDINANCE OF INTENDANTS FOR BUENOS AIRES (1782) COMPARED WITH THAT FOR NEW SPAIN (1786)

The Ordinance of Intendants for Buenos Aires is much shorter than the Ordinance for New Spain. It consists of 276 articles while the latter contains 306. Throughout the document the "viceroyalty of Buenos Aires" is naturally substituted for "Kingdom of New Spain," "Buenos Aires" for "Mexico City," "viceroyalty" for "kingdom," and South American cities for those of Mexico. All references to the "commandant-general of the frontier" are omitted. "Political governments" are used for *"alcaldías mayores," "partidos"* for "parishes," and *alcaldes mayores* are not mentioned. In some of the articles the wording is transposed and all unimportant words and phrases are omitted; but the purport of both documents is the same. On the other hand some of the articles of the Buenos Aires Ordinance insert clauses and words for greater clearness. One hundred and eight of the articles of the two ordinances are identical.[1] One hundred and eleven are the same, except for minor differences like the omission of unimportant words and clauses, or the in-

---

[1] They are as follows: Art. 13 (Buenos Aires) = 18 (New Spain), 14 = 19, 16 = 21, 17 = 22, 18 = 23, 21 = 26, 22 = 27, 25 = 31, 29 = 35, 30 = 36, 31 = 37, 33 = 39, 34 = 40, 35 = 41, 36 = 42, 37 = 43, 39 = 45, 40 = 46, 41 = 47, 42 = 48, 43 = 49, 44 = 50, 46 = 52, 50 = 54, 51 = 55, 55 = 59, 60 = 64, 64 = 68, 65 = 69, 71 = 75, 78 = 81, 80 = 83, 81 = 84, 84 = 88, 85 = 89, 87 = 91, 88 = 92, 96 = 101, 97 = 102, 101 = 106, 102 = 107, 103 = 108, 106 = 116, 107 = 117, 108 = 118, 109 = 119, 110 = 120, 112 = 122, 113 = 123, 114 = 124, 115 = 125, 139 = 161, 150 = 168, 153 = 171, 156 = 174, 157 = 175, 158 = 176, 159 = 177, 163 = 181, 164 = 182, 172 = 198, 178 = 204, 194 = 221, 200 = 229, 204 = 232, 205 = 233, 210 = 238, 220 = 250, 223 = 253, 225 = 255, 226 = 256, 227 = 257, 228 = 258, 229 = 259, 230 = 260, 231 = 261, 232 = 262, 233 = 263, 234 = 264, 235 = 265, 237 = 267, 238 = 268, 239 = 269, 240 = 270, 241 = 271, 242 = 272, 244 = 274, 245 = 275, 246 = 276, 247 = 277, 249 = 279, 251 = 281, 252 = 282, 253 = 283, 254 = 284, 255 = 285, 256 = 286, 257 = 287, 258 = 288, 259 = 289, 260 = 290, 261 = 291, 262 = 292, 263 = 293, 265 = 295, 267 = 297, 268 = 298, 271 = 301.

sertion of clauses and words for clearness, transposition of words, or the use of synonyms.[2] Some articles of the two Ordinances differ only in certain parts. Article 1 of the Ordinance of 1782 varies from Art. 1 of the Mexican Ordinance in the wording, except in the last part, since there were to be eight intendancies in the viceroyalty of Buenos Aires instead of twelve in New Spain. The names and extent of each one of the former are given, while only the names of the latter are mentioned.

Art. 3, corresponding to 4 of the Ordinance of 1786, shows a difference in the composition of the *junta superior de hacienda*. The Buenos Aires *junta* was to be composed of the two senior judges of the tribunal of accounts, of the assessor of the superintendency, of the general accountant of the army and royal treasury, and of the *fiscal* of the royal treasury. The Mexican *junta* was to consist of the regent of the *audiencia*, of the *fiscal* of the treasury, of the senior judge of the tribunal of accounts, and of the senior treasury official, either the accountant or treasurer. When the *audiencia* should be established in Buenos Aires the superintendent, the regent, an *oidor* appointed by the king, the *fiscal*, the senior judge of the tribunal of accounts, and the general accountant of the army and treasurer were to be the members of the *junta*. This variation no doubt merely followed that of the two administrative organizations. The last sentence

---

[2] They are as follows: Art. 2 (Buenos Aires) $= 2$ (New Spain), $8 = 11$, $9 = 12$, $10 = 13$, $11 = 14$, $12 = 15$, $15 = 20$, $19 = 24$, $20 = 25$, $24 = 29$, $26 = 32$, $28 = 34$, $32 = 38$, $38 = 44$, $45 = 51$, $47 = 53$, $52 = 56$, $53 = 57$, $54 = 58$, $56 = 60$, $59 = 63$, $61 = 65$, $62 = 66$, $66 = 70$, $67 = 71$, $68 = 72$, $69 = 73$, $70 = 74$, $72 = 76$, $73 = 77$, $75 = 85$, $79 = 82$, $82 = 86$, $86 = 90$, $89 = 94$, $90 = 95$, $92 = 97$, $95 = 100$, $98 = 103$, $99 = 104$, $100 = 105$, $104 = 109$, $105 = 115$, $111 = 121$, $120 = 133$, $122 = 135$, $123 = 136$, $124 = 140$, $125 = 141$, $129 = 142$, $130 = 144$, $132 = 147$, $134 = 152$, $137 = 159$, $138 = 160$, $143 = 157$, $145 = 162$, $154 = 172$, $160 = 178$, $161 = 179$, $162 = 180$, $166 = 184$, $167 = 193$, $168 = 197$, $169 = 195$, $170 = 196$, $171 = 197$, $173 = 199$, $175 = 201$, $176 = 202$, $177 = 203$, $180 = 207$, $181 = 208$, $182 = 209$, $183 = 210$, $184 = 211$, $185 = 212$, $187 = 214$, $188 = 215$, $189 = 216$, $190 = 217$, $191 = 218$, $192 = 219$, $193 = 220$, $195 = 223$, $196 = 225$, $197 = 226$, $198 = 227$, $199 = 228$, $202 = 230$, $203 = 231$, $209 = 237$, $211 = 239$, $215 = 245$, $216 = 246$, $217 = 247$, $218 = 248$, $219 = 249$, $221 = 251$, $236 = 266$, $243 = 273$, $248 = 278$, $250 = 280$, $264 = 294$, $266 = 296$, $269 = 299$, $270 = 300$, $272 = 302$, $274 = 304$, $275 = 305$, $276 = 306$.

of the Mexican Ordinance, telling where the notary and his assistant were to sit, is omitted. Art. 4 concerning the substitution for absent members of the *junta superior* is similar to 5. It says that he who comes next to the judge in seniority, or he who precedes him if the more recently elected member should be appointed by the king, shall substitute for the *oidor,* and the treasurer general could serve for the general accountant of the army and treasury. The Mexican Ordinance merely says that his companion shall substitute for the *contador-juez* or treasurer-general of the army and treasury. For the other members of the *junta* the substitution is the same. Art. 5, which is equal to 6, states that the *junta* shall be held "once a week" instead of "once or twice a week."

Art. 6 of the Buenos Aires Ordinance corresponds to 7 and 8 of the one for New Spain. The last part, concerning the royal-patronage, is more condensed than in the latter Ordinance, which made special provision for the vice-patronage. This was to belong to all the southern intendants except those of Buenos Aires and La Plata. In Buenos Aires the viceroy was to exercise it and in La Plata the president of the *audiencia.* In Mexico all the intendants, except those of Mexico City, Guadalajara, Arispe, Mérida, and Vera Cruz, were to perform the functions of the ecclesiastical patronage.

Art. 7, concerning the suppression of *corregimientos,* differs from Art. 9 of the Ordinance of 1786. All the *corregimientos* and political governments in the viceroyalty of Buenos Aires, except those of Montevideo and the thirty towns of the Jesuit missions, were to be abolished within five years. There is no time limit in the Mexican Ordinance, and until the officials had completed their term they were to be subject to the intendant of their district. In the two excepted governments of the former viceroyalty the departments of justice and *policía* were to continue to be united to the military command. The governor was to serve as an intendant of province.

Arts. 23 and 28 are similar, except that the last sentence of the latter is omitted in the former, since it applies entirely to Mexico City. Art. 27, corresponding to 33, says "excluding their land-lease revenue (*censos*) which shall be treated of in its place" instead of "their land-lease revenue shall be included." Art. 57 of the former Ordinance differs in the first paragraph from Art. 61 of the latter, since the intendants of Buenos Aires were ordered to encourage the cultivation of hemp and flax instead of cochineal. Likewise Art. 58, similar to 62, speaks of promoting the production of the wax of wild bees and from beehives instead of wild silk. Arts. 63 and 67 are similar, except that the former does not command the intendants to aid the judges of the tribunal of *La Acordada,* as this court did not there exist.

The last sentence of Art. 74 differs from Art. 78. It states that another judge of the tribunal of accounts and the assessor of the viceroyalty may meet with the *junta superior* when a measure issued by the superintendent-subdelegate is being discussed. In Mexico the judge only met with the *junta.* The former article also adds that when the royal *audiencia* should be established then only the judge should be present. Art. 76, which corresponds to 79, prescribes that only the revenue of tobacco, powder, and playing cards shall be controlled exclusively by the superintendent-subdelegate of the treasury in Buenos Aires, while in New Spain *alcabalas* and *pulque* were included. The same omission is made in Art. 77 which is the same as 80. The former omits the part: "also in the *reglamento* or guide (*pauta*) dated July 29, 1785, formed by the general accountant, which I approved and ordered observed by my royal *cédula* of February 21 of the present year [1786]."

Arts. 83 and 87 are the same except the last sentence which mentions the composition of the *junta superior.* In Buenos Aires, until the *audiencia* should be established, the assessor of the viceroyalty was to take the place of the regent of the *audienica.* Arts 91 corresponds to 96 and it treats of the 12 royal proprietary treasuries of Buenos Aires instead of the 15 in Mexico; it also mentions where they are located. At the end of the article several lines referring to the special South American subtreasuries are added.

Art. 93 is shorter than 98. At the end of the first paragraph there is omitted: "and with the aid of the reports which the accountants commissioned by him [the superintendent-subdelegate] shall draw up for the establishment of the account and calculation ordered by the general accounting-office in its practical instruction of April 27, 1784, and which was provided for them by Article 37 of the instruction given them for the management and administration of their office under date of August 1, 1785." Art. 94 differs from 99 in regard to salaries of treasury officials. In the viceroyalty of Buenos Aires they were lower than in New Spain.

Arts. 116 and 129 are alike, except in the viceroyalty of Buenos Aires the tributes were to be entered into the treasuries by half-years, while in Mexico this was to be done by thirds. Arts. 117 and 132 are also the same, except in the former viceroyalty *alcaldes ordinarios* and subdelegates were to receive 4 per cent instead of 6 per cent of the total amount entering into the treasury from tributes. From this per cent in both viceroyalties they were to give 1 per cent to the Indian governors or *alcaldes.*

Art. 118 corresponds to 130. The wording is different and the latter article is much more condensed. The former adds in the first part: "which exclusive right [giving rules for the collection and receipt of tributes] of those domains must thereupon remain subject to the special inspection and cognizance of the intendants as chiefs of the provinces, and of all the subordinate justices, subdelegates, and administrators of them, since they must be judges of this branch with the entire jurisdiction which they have in the others of my royal treasury." It continues changing the next part: "I order the superintendent-sub-delegate of it, exactly and according to what is provided in this ordinance for the exaction and entrance of the said dues, and keeping in due consideration that which is in practice in the provinces of the new viceroyalty for these purposes, and what is observed in New Spain, and what the various documents affirm which my Secretary of State of the universal Office of the Indies will send to him by my order, especially the regulation which he considered well to issue on July 8, 1770, for the government and administration of the said branch in that kingdom, and with the advice of the chief accounting-office of Buenos Aires, he shall form the instruction which he may judge fit, adopting as far as possible, and as this and the local circumstances may permit, the rules which the said documents prescribe." When the instruction was finished and approved by the *junta superior* that body was to send it to the tribunal of accounts and also to the intendant of province. The *junta* was also to transmit a copy to the king and give account to him by the *vía reservada*. Arts. 119 and 131 are similar, but the former is more condensed.

There are some slight differences between Arts. 121 and 134. The former says that the visitor-general, instead of the superintendent-subdelegate of the treasury, shall draw up the ordinance which he thinks best to prevent frauds in tribute collection. The visitor was to take the regulation when it was drawn up to the superintendent of Buenos Aires instead of to the *junta superior de hacienda*, and he was also to send a copy to the king, while in Mexico the *junta* was to do this. Art. 126 corresponds to 137, but there is much variation in it. The former begins by showing that both in Peru and in the viceroyalty of Buenos Aires the contribution of the royal tributes was not equitable and that the quota should be fixed according to the classes of people, the quality of their arable lands, the profits from their trade, and incomes. There is no mention made of reducing the tribute to the amount of 16 *reales* as in New Spain. It only says that the contribution must be regulated according to what is just without injury to the treasury or to the contributors. The *junta superior* with the advice of the *fiscal* was to determine a just quota. There were the same exemptions as in Mexico, but there is no reference to fixing the tribute for Negroes, free mulattoes, and other castes.

Art. 127 adds at the end a sentence which bids the intendants to regulate the prices of the products of industry and agriculture which Art. 138 of the Mexican Ordinance does not have. Art. 131, corresponding to 145 of the Ordinance of 1786, omits the last paragraph entirely, since it treats of the superintendent-administrator of the customhouse of Mexico City. There is some variation between Arts. 133 and 150. The chief difference is that the former adds: "the intendants themselves and their inferior justices shall see that grievance, extortion, or violence are not caused to those who are employed in the discovering and working of mines, and that the operators of these shall not commit robbery or abuses against their owners, nor the latter tyrannize over or injure the former by increasing their labor or decreasing their day's wages or salaries according to their occupations, or the contracts which they have made."

Art. 136 differs somewhat from Art. 154 of the Mexican Ordinance. The last part of the first paragraph which treats of the *junta superior* acting in regard to the officials of the branch of quicksilver and their salaries is omitted by the former. Art. 140 is similar to 148, but the wording is different. In the former the monopoly of powder was united to those of playing cards and tobacco, and the king commanded that its revenue should be as uniform as possible, according to the rules which governed that of New Spain. The superintendent-subdelegate of the royal treasury with the advice of the tribunal of accounts was to draw up the rules he thought best for it, and when approved and corrected by the *junta superior* they were to be put into effect and account given to the king. Art. 141 varies little from 149; the former states that at the same time (1778) that the king ordered the monopoly of tobacco to be formed in Buenos Aires he decided also to establish that of playing cards in all the provinces. Their direction and administration were to be united, and the superintendent-subdelegate, with the advice of the director of the monopoly of playing cards, was to make the proper ordinance for its management.

Art. 142, corresponding to 156, omits the first part concerning the sale of stamped paper in Mexico City, but otherwise it is practically the same. Arts. 144 and 158 are similar in regard to subject matter only. The former article is longer than the latter and is worded entirely different. The accounting-house for *lanzas* and half-annates of Buenos Aires was to be subject to the rules observed in New Spain. It was to be under the control of the most recently appointed accountant of results of the chief accounting-office. Art. 144 adds to the end that the revenues from *lanzas* and half-annates must be included in the general statement of the treasury and the judges of the accounting-office should submit at the beginning of each year a report of their amounts separately to the superintendent-subdelegate.

Art. 146, corresponding to 164, shows a difference in the composition of the *junta* of auctions of Buenos Aires. It was to consist of the intendant-general, of his lieutenant-assessor, of the judges of the treasury, and of its fiscal defender; while in Mexico City the members were to be: the intendant-general, the most recently appointed judge of the *audiencia*, the *fiscal* of the treasury, and its judges, the accountant and treasurer. When Buenos Aires should have an *audiencia* the composition was to be the same as for Mexico City. The membership of the *juntas* in the other intendancies of the viceroyalty of Buenos Aires and Mexico where there was no *audiencia* was the same. Arts. 147 and 165 are alike until Peru is mentioned, then they vary and the wording is entirely different. Since the revenues from the Bulls of the Crusade were so well administered in New Spain under José de Gálvez and were so advantageous to the treasury, the king decided to apply the rules to the whole viceroyalty of Buenos Aires. The said branch of revenue was to be united to the subdelegation of the royal treasury in each of the intendancies of province, and the superintendent-subdelegate, with the advice of the tribunal of accounts, was to draw up a new ordinance to be applied to the South American viceroyalty. The last paragraph of the latter article is omitted, as it treats of discontinuing the treasuries for the funds from the sale of the Bulls of the Crusade in certain cities of Mexico.

Arts. 148 and 166 are the same, except that the former omits the last sentence, which says that the superintendency of the branch of revenues from the Bulls of the Crusade shall belong to the superintendent-subdelegate of the royal treasury, and in each intendancy of province to the special officer at the head of each district. Arts. 151 and 169 are similar, except there is some variation in the last paragraph concerning the members of the *junta de diezmos* in Tucuman and Córdova from that in Mérida and Monterrey of New Spain. In the former cities the *junta* was to consist of the subdelegate, of two factor judges, of one of the judges of the royal treasury, and of a lawyer-defender of it whom the intendant should appoint. In the latter cities the composition was to be the same, except the governor was to be present instead of the subdelegate. Art. 152 gives the membership for the *junta* of Córdova and Art. 170 does it for Mérida and Monterrey, otherwise the articles are the same.

The chief difference between Arts. 155 and 173 is that the former omits the second paragraph and the first sentence of the third paragraph of the latter. The part omitted relates to factor judges of the *junta de diezmos* substituting for each other in contentious jurisdiction, or exercising it together or separately. Art. 165 omits the second, third, fourth, and fifth paragraphs of Art. 183, which concern the giving account of the building fund of each church: the churchwarden first to the vice-patron, the

latter to the *cabildo* of the church, next the vice-patron sent the
report to the royal accountant of tithes of the diocese, then the
revised account was returned to the churchwarden who again
delivered it to the vice-patron, and the latter sent it to the king.

There are some differences betwen Arts. 174 and 200. The
former says that the royal accountants should submit annually
three copies of the statistics of the fourth of ecclesiastical revenues to the intendants who would send one to the judges of the
royal treasury of the province, so that they might make comparison between the report and the income from church tithes.
If the accounts did not agree they were to be corrected in the
presence of the royal accountant who made them. The latter
article declares that the accountants shall send the statement to
the *junta de diezmos*, and the *junta* was to make the corrections
and place on it its approval. Then the original document was to
be placed in the archives of the accounting-office, but three copies
were to be sent to the intendant who transmitted one of them to
the judges of the royal treasury. Arts. 179 and 206 are almost
identical, except in paragraph three the former omits the
statement that no deductions should be made from the proceeds
of minor vacancies for ecclesiastics who were appointed in
churces to fill the place of prebendaries who died.

The last parts of Arts. 186 and 213 vary. In the former the
king commands the intendants to send the reports of the fourths,
submitted to them by the accountants of tithes, to the subcollectors; while in the latter he orders the *juntas* of tithes to do this.
Arts. 206 and 234 are similar, but with some variations. The
first omits all reference to the intendants and their subdelegates
being responsible for the approval which had to be affixed also
to statements of the funds on hand in the treasuries after the
treasury officials had signed them. Art. 207 is longer that Art.
235. It adds that each intendant should send the statements of
receipts and expenditures, with those from their treasury and
other administrative offices of the capital, to the principal ac-

counting-office of the province where they could all be united into one general and comprehensive statement of all the branches of the treasury in each province. The originals of these documents were to remain in the accounting-office.

Art. 208 says that intendants should cause the treasury officials to submit to them three copies of the general financial statement, while Art. 236 declares that they shall send them five copies of the monthly statement, and besides the intendants were to collect six copies of each statement concerning the treasuries and revenue administration offices outside of the capitals. Art. 212 omits the last paragraph of Art. 240, which concerns the *junta superior* giving the king account by the *vía reservada*. Arts. 213 and 241 have a similar meaning, but they are worded differently and do not refer to the same places. Art. 214 is much longer than Art. 242, since, besides treating of the tribunal of accounts, it also deals with the annual accounts of all the treasuries and administration offices.

Art. 222 omits all but the first two sentences of Art. 252. The part omitted refers to manner of daily payment to the troops, supplies furnished, and treasury officials account of advances given to them. Art. 224 omits all but the first sentence and a half of Art. 254. The part omitted concerns the deductions that are to be made or added to soldiers' pay due to differences of coins in Spain and America. Art. 273 varies from Art. 303 in regard to the salaries of intendants, those in the viceroyalty of Buenos Aires being lower than in New Spain; and there is no mention made of the expenses of the secretariat and counting-houses in the former article.

The thirty-three articles of the Ordinance of 1786 which are omitted by the Ordinance of 1782, for the most part, apply only to Mexico or make more definite special cases which were not thought of when the Buenos Aires Ordinance was formed. Art. 3 treats of the viceroy of New Spain putting his countersign on the titles of intendants, and Art. 10 of the political and military governments of Mexico which were still to remain in existence after the intendancies were established. Art. 16 states who must substitute for intendants when their assessors are also absent. Art. 17 tells how a judge of the treasury may appoint a subordinate to perform his financial obligations when he may be substituting for an intendant or his assessor. Art. 30 refers to the general accountant of municipal finance performing the duties of secretary of the *junta superior de hacienda.* Art. 93 mentions the precautions which must be taken when an individual intrusted with the collection of the funds of any branch of the royal treasury is imprisoned.

Art. 110 tells what divisions of finance the general memorandum book of the royal treasury must include in the class of entries. Art. 111 shows how and with what minute enumeration the same book must give an exact and detailed report of each one of the branches of entry. Art. 112 states what information the same book must contain in respect to the landed property of the royal patrimony. Art. 113 asserts how the same book shall divide into classes the permanent expenses and make a statement concerning the number and kind of employees connected with each class and their annual salaries. Art. 114 makes known when the same book must contain notations. Art. 139 takes up the exemption from tribute granted to free castes who serve in the militia. Art. 143 treats of ecclesiastical estates which fall into mortmain and their proceeds; Art. 146 of the administration of the revenue from *pulque;* and Art. 151 of the presidency of the tribunals of appeals of mining. Art. 153 deals with the control, administration, and collection of the funds of the branches of quicksilver, stamped paper, half-annates, and fees for titles of nobility. Art. 155 sets forth the regulation which must be made for the control and administration of the branch of quicksilver.

Art. 163 applies only to Mexico, since it concerns salable and transferable offices of the district of the *comandancia general* of the frontier.   Art. 167 gives instructions for forming an ordinance to administer and control the branch of the Bulls of the Crusade.   Art. 185 mentions the measures taken for correcting abuses in the distribution of the tithes, and Art. 186 the selection of members for the *casa-excusada* and the collection of its funds.   Art. 187 treats of the tables relating to bishops and chapters and royal ninths; Art. 188 of the ninth and one-half for church buildings; Art. 189 of the ninth and one-half for hospitals; Art. 190 of the four-ninths for ecclesiastical livings; Art. 191 of general expenses in the collection and administration of the tithes; and Art. 192 of administration or lease of the tithes.   Art. 205 refers to vacant parishes, *doctrinas,* and chief sacristies which receive dues from the tithes; Art. 222 to minor revenues and partial dues belonging to the crown; and Art. 224 to parochial dues.   Art. 243 shows how the tribunal of accounts must decide doubts that arise during the examination of any account or other matter with which it may deal.   Art. 244 discusses the annual account of all the treasuries and administrative offices.   The functions of the four *causas* or departments in the viceroyalty of Buenos Aires were not noticeably decreassed by the omission of the foregoing articles.

The Ordinance of 1782 adds several articles which are not found in the later one. Arts. 48 and 49 relate to the administration of Indian *censos.* Art. 128 treats of the stipends (*sínodos*) of parish priests; Art. 135 of the rules which must be observed in the *Reales de Minas* while the new ordinance was being approved and published; and Art. 149 of offices withdrawn from the tribunal of the Crusade and how this must be done.   Art. 201 concerns the exclusive supervision of the intendants in the lesser branches of the royal treasury, and in the municipal treasuries.

BIBLIOGRAPHY

I. Manuscripts Cited

All MSS cited are originals or copies in the Bancroft Library, University of California. Those marked AGI are from the Seville Archives. Those marked Archivo General are from Mexico City.

Aguilar sobre expulsión de los Franceses de Nueva España, 1795–1796. AGI, Est. Mex. leg. 5.

Angulo, Lopez. To the king, New Orleans, July 13, 1801, AGI, 86–5–23. Audiencia de Santo Domingo.

Branciforte to Varela, Orizaba, March 30, 1795, num. 982 reservada.
To Alcudia, September 28, 1795, num. 169 reservada.
To the Prince of Peace, August 27, 1796, num. 325 reservada.
To the king, November 26, 1796, AGI, num. 376. Est. Mex. leg. 6.
To the Prince of Peace, August 30, 1797, AGI, num. 498. Est Mex. leg. 7.

Bucareli to the king, Havana, October 16, 1769, AGI, 80–1–7, num. 1220. Audiencia de Santo Domingo.

Cedulario, MS, 3 vols. [Royal decrees of the eighteenth century.] BL Mex. MSS 60–62.

[Circular concerning the distribution of the diezmos of the churches of the Indies.] August 23, 1786, AGI, 141–6–6.

Consejo de Estado. Cádiz, February 3, 1813, papeleta 106, AGI, 88–19. Audiencia de Mexico.

Consejo de Indias. April 7, 1790, AGI, 86–5–22. Audiencia de Santo Domingo.
April 2, 1799, AGI, 141–3–17. Indiferente General.

Croix, Cavallero de. To the king, Lima, May 16, 1789, AGI, 146–6–14. Indiferente General.

Documentos historicos sobre Durango. BL. Mexican MS, 93.

Expedientes sobre la aprehensión de 2000 pesos. New Orleans, 1795–1799, AGI, 86–5–22. Audiencia de Santo Domingo.

Gálvez, José de. Informe y plan de intendencias que conviene establecer en las provincias de este reyno de Nueva España. Mexico, January 15, 1768. Ayer Collection, Newberry Library.
To the king, Havana, June 11, 1778, AGI, 81–4–36, num. 3.
[Proposals concerning the intendancies.] Madrid, October 4, 1778, AGI, 146–6–14. Indiferente General.

To the king, Havana, October 4, 1780, AGI, 146–2–7, num. 690. Infi-
ferente General.

To the king, Mexico, November 24, 1781, AGI, 90–2–13. Audiencia
de Mexico.

GARDOQUI, DIEGO. To the captain-general of Cuba, New Orleans, January
21, 1797, AGI, 87–1–24, num. 85. Audiencia de Santo Domingo.

To the captain-general of Cuba, New Orleans, March 3, 1797, AGI,
87–1–24, num. 94. Audiencia de Santo Domingo.

GOVERNOR of Cuba to the king, Havana, September 28, 1783, AGI, 80–1–24,
num. 168. Audiencia de Santo Domingo.

GOVERNOR [Estevan Miró] of Louisiana to the king, New Orleans, January
15, 1784, AGI, 87–3–10, num. 51. Audiencia de Santo Domingo.

HORMAZAS, MARQUÉS DE. Philadelphia, December 16, 1797, AGI, 146–2–9,
num. 11. Indiferente General.

INTENDANT of Louisiana [Martín Navarro] to the viceroy, New Orleans,
July 24, 1781, AGI, 87–3–10, num. 54. Audiencia de Santo
Domingo.

To the viceroy, New Orleans, April 30, 1782, AGI, 87–3–10, num. 112.
Audiencia de Santo Domingo.

INTENDANT of Louisiana [Juan Ventura Morales] to the king, New Orleans,
1802, AGI, 87–1–29, num. 75. Audiencia de Santo Domingo.

To the king, New Orleans, February 28, 1802, AGI, 87–1–29, num.
66. Audiencia de Santo Domingo.

To the king, New Orleans, June 12, 1802, AGI, 87–1–29, num. 109.
Audiencia de Santo Domingo.

To the king, New Orleans, October 21, 1802, AGI, 87–1–28. Audiencia
de Santo Domingo.

KING to the contador and tesorero of Louisiana, July 21, 1776, AGI, 86–
5–24. Audiencia de Santo Domingo.

To the viceroy, Aranjuez, February 27, 1793, AGI. Est. Mex. leg. 2.

Lizana to Saavedra, Sept. 26, 1809, AGI, 90–1–10.

New Orleans, August 10, 1796, AGI, 86–7–9. Audiencia de Santo Domingo.

Ordenes de la corona. 7 vols. Mex. MSS, 170–176. BL.

OTERO, BERNARDO DE. To Arriaga, New Orleans, June 15, 1775, AGI,
86–5–21.

Provincias Internas. San Luis Potosí, August 12, 1788, tom. 111, 743 num.
4, expediente 4, fojas 16. Archivo General.

Revillagigedo to the governor of Texas [Pacheco], February 10, 1790,
tom. 99, num. 6, expediente 2, fojas 344.

Commandant general [Conde] to the viceroy, Monterrey, May 16, 1819,
tom. 252, num. 934. Archivo General.

Conde to the viceroy, Durango, February 7, 1820, tom. 252, num. 505. Archivo General.

Conde to the viceroy, Durango, February 28, 1820, tom. 252, num. 519. Archivo General.

Conde to the viceroy, Durango, July 31, 1820, tom. 252, num. 663. Archivo General.

REALES CEDULAS 1750–1789, num. 161, lib. 103. Archivo General.

1752–1789, num. 150, lib. 102. Archivo General.

1752–1789, Porlier to the viceroy of Mexico, El Pardo, February 21, 1788, num. 108, lib. 134 p. 172. Archivo General.

1755–1790, Valdez to the viceroy of Mexico, San Lorenzo, November 1, 1789, P. Y. 78, lib. 142, p. 241. Archivo General.

1790–1795, king to the viceroy, Aranjuez, March 23, 1792, V, num. 65, lib. 145. Archivo General.

REVILLAGIGEDO to Floridablanca, Mexico, January 15, 1790, AGI, leg. 1, num. 55. Papeles de Estado, Audiencia de Mexico.

To Pedro de Lerena, Mexico, August 29, 1790, num. 55 reservada. Archivo General.

To Floridablanca, Mexico, October 30, 1790, num. 97 reservada. Archivo General.

To Floridablanca, Mexico, October 30, 1790, AGI, leg. 1, num. 55.

November 26, 1790, num. 162 reservada. Archivo General.

To Lerena, Mexico, March 27, 1791, num. 7 reservada. Archivo General.

Dictamen que en cumplimiento de reales ordenes de S. M. produce el virey de Nueva España Conde de Revillagigedo, sobre la precision de adicionar la Ordenanza de Yntendentes expedida en 4 de Dizre de 1786, Mexico, May 5, 1791. Mexico, Archivo General y Público, 54, num. 402.

To Lerena, Mexico, May 27, 1791, num. 400. Archivo General.

To Floridablanca, Mexico, June 1, 1791, AGI, 1–69, num. 35. Papeles de Estado. Audiencia de Mexico.

Mexico, September 1, 1791, AGI, num. 128.

To Gardoqui, March 31, 1792, num. 17. Archivo General.

To the king, November 5, 1792, papeleta 206, AGI, 103–7–22. Audiencia de Guadalajara.

To Gardoqui, June 30, 1793, num. 21. Archivo General.

Royal decreto, May 31, 1785, AGI, 141–5–11.

SALCEDO, BRUNO DÍAZ DE. To Revillagigedo, San Luis Potosí, December 4, 1792, papeleta 77, AGI, 89–6–19, num. 512. Audiencia de Mexico.

SOLER, MIGUEL CAYETANO. To the captain-general of Cuba, New Orleans, March 31, 1799, AGI, 87–1–25, num. 286. Audiencia de Santo Domingo.

SORIA, JUAN JOSEPH MARTÍNEZ. To the king, Mexico, October 30, 1770, AGI, 146–6–14, num. 1. Indiferente General.
To the king, Mexico. October 9, 1777, AGI, 146–6–14, num. 2. Indiferente General.

Testimonio [concerning measures of confiscation] . . . . New Orleans, December 9, 1783, December 29, 1783, AGI, 86–7–20. Audiencia de Santo Domingo.

VALIENTE, JOSÉ PABLO. [Account concerning the system of government in America], Seville, September 16, 1809, AGI, 141–5–11.

VILLARROEL, HIPÓLITO. Enfermedades políticas que padece la capital de esta Nueva España en casi todos los cuerpos de que se compone; y remedios, que se la deben aplicar para su curación si se quiere qué sea util al rey y al público. Tomo. 4. MS contemporary copy in BL.

II. PRINTED DOCUMENTS

BELEÑA, EUSEBIO BENTURA. Recopilación sumaria de todos los autos acordados de la real audiencia y sala del crimen de esta Nueva España y providencias de su superior govierno. 2 vols. Mexico, 1787.

Colección de documentos inéditos, relativos al descubrimiento, conquista y organización de las antiguas posesiones españolas de América y Oceanía. 42 vols. Madrid, 1864–1884.

Colección de reales cédulas. 12 vols. Madrid, 1749–1799.

Documentos historicos del Peru en las epocas del coloniaje despues de la conquista y de la independencia hasta la presente. 10 vols. in 6. Lima, 1863–1877.

Documentos inéditos o muy raros para la historia de Mexico 35 vols. Mexico, 1853–1857.

Documentos para la historia del virreinato del Rio de la Plata. 3 vols. Buenos Aires, 1912–1913.

FERNÁNDEZ, LEÓN. Colección de documentos para la historia de Costa Rica 10 vols. Barcelona, 1881–1907.

GÁLVEZ, JOSÉ DE. Informe general que en virtud de real órden instruyó y entregó el Exmo. Sr. Marqués de Sonora, siendo visitador general de este reino, al Exmo. Sr. Virrey Frey D. Antonio Bucarely y Ursua con fecha de 31 de Diciembre de 1771. Mexico 1867.

Instrucciones que los vireyes de Nueva España dejaron a sus sucesores. Mexico, 1867.

Memorias de los vireyes que han gobernado el Peru. 6 vols. Lima, 1859.

PÉREZ Y LÓPEZ, ANTONIO XAVIER. Teatro de la legislación universal de España é Indias, por orden chronólogico de sus cuerpos, y decisiones no recopiladas. 28 vols. Madrid, 1791–1798.

Real ordenanza para el establecimiento é instrucción de intendentes de exército y provincia en el reino de la Nueva España, Madrid, 1786.

Real ordenanza para el establecimiento é introducción de intendentes de exército y provincia en el virreinato de Buenos-Aires. Madrid, 1782.

REVILLAGIGEDO, JUAN VICENTE GÜÉMES PACHECO DE PADILLA HORCASITAS Y AGUAYO, CONDE DE. Instrucción reservada que el conde de Revilla Gigedo, dió a su sucesor en el mando, marqués de Branciforte sobre el gobierno de este continente en el tiempo que fue su virey. Mexico, 1831.

Revista del Archivo General de Buenos Aires. 4 vols. Buenos Aires, 1869–1872.

ZAMORA Y CORONADO, JOSÉ MARÍA. Biblioteca de legislación ultramarina. 6 vols. Madrid, 1844–1846.

III. OTHER MATERIALS

ANTEQUERA, JOSÉ MARÍA. Historia de la legislación española. Ed. 2; Madrid, 1884.

AUSTIN, SISTER MARY. The Reforms of Charles the Third in New Spain in the light of the Pacte de Famille. MS (Ph.D. Thesis, Dept. of History, University of California). Berkeley, 1927.

BECKER, JERÓNIMO. La política española en las Indias. Madrid, 1920.

BIEDMA, JOSÉ JUAN AND BEYER, CARLOS. Atlas histórico de la república Argentina. Buenos Aires, 1909.

DANVILA Y COLLADO, MANUEL. Significación que tuvieron en el gobierno de América la Casa de Contratación de Sevilla y el Consejo Supremo de Indias. Madrid, 1892. In Anteneo científico, literario y arístico de Madrid, el continente Americano; conferencias dadas con motivo del cuarto centenario del descubrimiento de America. Tomo. III. 3 vols. Madrid, 1894.

Diccionario universal de historia y de geografía. 10 vols. Madrid, 1853-1856.

ESCRICHE, JOAQUÍN. Diccionario razonado de legislación y jurisprudencia. Nueva ed; Paris, 1896.

ESCUDERO, J. A. Noticias estadisticas del estado de Chihuahua. Mexico, 1834.

FABIÉ, ANTONIO MARÍA. Ensayo historico de la legislación española en sus estados de ultramar. Madrid, 1896.

FISHER, LILLIAN ESTELLE. Viceregal Administration in the Spanish American Colonies. Berkeley, 1926.

FONSECA, FABIÁN AND CARLOS DE URRUTIA. Historia general de real haci- enda escrita por . . . orden del virey, ʌonde de Revillagigedo. 6 vols. Mexico, 1845–1853.

Gazetas de Mexico, 1796–1797, VIII.

GROOT, JOSÉ MANUEL. Historia eclesiástica y civil de Nueva Granada. 5 vols. Ed. 2; Bogota, 1889–1893.

HALL, FREDERIC. The Laws of Mexico: A Compilation and Treatise Relat- ing to Real Property, Mines, Water Rights, Personal Rights, Contracts, and Inheritances. San Francisco, 1885.

HUMBOLDT, ALEXANDER VON. Ensayo político sobre Nueva España. 5 vols. Paris, 1836.
  Versuch über den politischen zustand des königreichs Neu-Spanien. 5 vols. in 2. Tübigen, 1809–1812.

JUARROS, DOMINGO. Statistical and Commercial History of the Kingdom of Guatemala. London, 1823.

LEVENE, RICARDO. Historia Argentina. 2 vols. Buenos Aires, 1913.

MARTÍNEZ ALCUBILLA, MARCELO. Diccionario de la administración española, peninsular, y ultramarina. 12 vols. Ed. 2; Madrid, 1868–1870.

MORA, JOSÉ MARÍA LUIS. Obras sueltas. 2 vols. Paris, 1837.

MOSES, BERNARD. Spain's Declining Power in South America, 1730–1806. Berkeley, 1919.

OROZCO, WISTANO LUIS. Legislación y jurisprudencia sobre terrenos baldíos. 2 vols. Mexico, 1895.

PELLIZA, MARIANO A. Historia Argentina. 3 vols. Buenos Aires, 1888–1889.

PINKERTON, JOHN. Modern Geography. A Description of the Empires, Kingdoms, States and Colonies, with the Oceans, Seas and Isles, in All Parts of the World. 3 vols. London, 1807.

PRIESTLEY, HERBERT INGRAM. José de Gálvez. Berkeley, 1916.

QUESADA, VICENTE G. Historia colonial Argentina. Buenos Aires, 1915.

RIVERA, AGUSTÍN. Principios críticos sobre el vireinato de la Nueva España i sobre la revolución de independencia. 3 vols. San Juan de los Lagos, 1884–1888.

RIVERA CAMBAS, MANUEL. Los gobernantes de México. 2 vols. Mexico, 1782–1787.

ROBERTSON, WILLIAM S. History of the Latin-American Nations. New York, 1922.

SMITH, DONALD EUGENE. The Viceroy of New Spain. Berkeley, 1913.

SWEET, WILLIAM W. A History of Latin America. Ed. 3; New York, 1929.

VALDÉS, ANTONIO JOSÉ. Historia de la isla de Cuba. 3 vols. Havana, 1876–1877.

ZINNY, ANTONIO. Historia de los gobernadores de las provincias Argentinas. 3 vols. Buenos Aires, 1879–1882.

INDEX

Abascal, José Fernando de, viceroy of Peru, opinion concerning intendancies, 92.

Abastos, 124. *See* Supplies.

Acapulco, frontier province of, 29; administration of, 105; subtreasury of, 165, 169; *castellano* of, 289; 290.

Accountant-general, not voting in or attending *junta superior*, 291.

Accountants, general, extortions of, 13, 36; of treasury, 37; general of Mexico City, 47; 52, 53, 54; of army, 63; general, of tributes and assessments, 79; senior, 100; 101, 112; appointment of, 118; general, of municipal finance, 119, 123; attendance at *junta superior*, 120; having key of coffer, 128; of province, 129, 131; aiding intendants, 132; salaries of, 133; 148, 150, 152; as commissary of war, 157; privileges of, 163, 164; of treasury, 166; reports of, 167; general of Mexico City, 168; of subtreasuries, 169; 170; prohibition for, 171; of treasury, 173, 180; of the *contaduría general*, 185; bonds of, 186; 187; general, of assessments, 187, 188; of tributes, 188; 206, 208, 214; attending *junta* of auctions, 216; 218; of tithes and tables, 222, 223, 228, 229, 230, 231; royal, 232, 233; of treasury, 234; general, of Council of the Indies, 235; of tithes and tables, 239, 242; royal, 243, 244, 245; general of the Indies, 247; of tithes, 248, 249; 263; of half-annates, 263; general, of treasury, 267; appointment of, 271; attending *junta* of government, 280; held

responsible, 290; absence of, 291; drawing up accounts, 292; general, òf tobacco, 293; of province and general, 296; adjusting contracts of troops, 300; fixing day for military reviews, 315; 317; subject to intendants, 319.

Account book, of royal treasury, 48, 175, 176, 178.

Accounting-house, of royal treasury, 165; 289.

Accounting-office, of municipal finance, 37; of tribute, 49; of Mexico City, 51; of tithes, 52–53; 57, 58, 118, 123; general, 126; general, of municipal finance, 130, 133, 134; of army, 157; administration of, 167; general of the Indies, 168, 170, 175; 179; of assessments, 185; 186; information for, 188; of *Provincias Internas*, 189; of assessments, 191; documents submitted to, 192, 193; 203; of treasury, 206; 207; of *lanzas* and half-annates, 210; general, 214; of treasury, 215; of tithes, 226, 229, 230, 243, 244; general of the Indies, 248, 261, 266; of powder and playing cards, 279; general in Spain, 284, 285; 290, 293; making adjustments for military salaries, 300; of the province, 309; general, of Mexico, 310; of the army, 316; general in Spain, 317.

Accounts, local and certified, 37; of towns, 120; of municipal finance, 126, 127, 128; of revenue and expenditures, 129; closing of provincial, 130; depositing of, 131; revision of 132; examining and comparing of, 133; 135; of products, 145;

into effect, 15, 16; 18; changes suggested in Ordinance, 19; 32, 55, 66, 75, 217, 331.

García, Alejo, intendant of Sonora, 93.

General administration, department of, 21, 33, 41, 97, 103; united to military, 105; 157, 329. *See* also *Policía.*

Gifts, to king, 91; voluntary, 314.

Gobierno, defined, 64.

Gold, dues from, 203; concealment of, 204; payment for, 205; extraction of, 206; exportation of, 288.

Gospels, payment for chanting of, 256.

Government, change in, 27–28; uniformity of, 72; superior, 83, 84; decentralization of, 90; centralization of, 92; political, 97 n. 1; 102, 103; of provinces, 105; 106; excepted, 108; 115, 149, 174; of Lima, 191; superior, 245, 290; 326, 330, 331.

Governors, corruption of, 4; 13; of Louisiana and Vera Cruz, 15; Indian, 19; military, 21; of the frontier, 23; 25, 26, 27; of Yucatan, 29; of Costa Rica and the Philippines, 30, 31; of Cuba, 41; confirming landgrants, 42; 62; *residencia* of, 63; 64; power of, 65, 66; 70, 72, 73, 77, 89; replaced by intendants, 97 n. 1; viceroy as, 99; 103; exercising vice-patronage, 104; of fortress of Acapulco, 105; 106; confirming elections of *ayuntamientos,* 107; 108; of natives, 110, 111, 128; 129, 149; subordination of, 150; 155, 185, 187, 188, 189, 192, 194; membership in *junta de diezmos,* 222; 223, 263, 275; powers suppressed, 288; 289, 306, 315, 329; of Colatlan, 329.

Grain, sale of, 303; of provinces, 304.

Grana fina, 138. *See* Cochineal.

Granados, Señor, 269.

Granaries, 43, 69, 146; investigation of, 147.

Grand Pragmatic of Free Commerce, 8.

Gratuities, assigned, 122; of factor-judges, 239.

Great Britain, 40. *See* England.

Grocery stores, tax on, 51; 211, 212; closing of, 213.

Guadalajara, capital of intendancy of, 26; intendant of, 27, 29, 60; *audiencia* of, 77; 78, 80, 82; city of, 98; 103, 104; subtreasury of, 165; 184, 204, 208, 216; treasury official of, 218; *junta de diezmos* of, 222; 257, 274, 276; salary of intendant of, 328.

Guamanga, intendancy of, 22; bishop of, 68, 85.

Guanajuato, capital of intendancy of, 26; intendant of, 27, 80; *alcaldías* of, 103; subtreasury of, 165; treasury officials of, 218; salary of intendant of, 328.

Guancavelica, 84.

Guarantors, 163; of tax-gatherers, 183; of tithe administrators, 241; of ecclesiastical officials, 268; 290.

Guards, coast-guard boats, 80; of the *Santa Hermandad,* 143; of warehouses, 167; revenue, 202; in prelates' houses, 277; military, 318, 321, 322; of intendants 327, 328.

Guatemala, captaincy-general of, 31.

Guayana, in intendancy of Venezuela, 17.

Guía, 289. *See* Certificate of landing and destination.

Guide, for confiscations, 152.

Hacendados, 142.

Half-annates, 5; revenue from, 51, 53; 82, 178, 205, 206; dues from, 210; 221, 250; collection of, 259; 260; rules concerning, 261; of individuals promoted, 262; 263; exaction of, 265; 266, 269, 271.

Half-canonships, 254.

Half-livings, revenue from, 263; 264.

information, 121; transmission of funds by, 127; 133, 135, 136, 137; dealing with vagabonds, 138; distributing lands, 139; road and bridge repair by, 141; supervising buildings, 143; dealing with smugglers, 152; as judges, 153, 154, 157, 158; care of subtreasuries, 169; not to draw upon treasury, 170–171; 173; suspending payments, 174; 175, 177; giving orders, 179; 180, 181; supervision of tax assessments, 182, 183, 184, 187, 188; aiding officials, 189; 190; computing tribute rates, 192; 193, 195, 196; prevention of revenue fraud, 197; proclamations of, 198; 199; visiting *pulque* shops, 200; exercise of contentious jurisdiction, 202; relations to mining, 203, 204, 205; 206; enforcing laws, 209; 211; as *corregidores* and chief justices, 212; protection of grocery stores, 213; 214; confirming positions, 215; judicial cognizance of, 218–219; attendance at *juntas*, 216, 222, 223; 226, 229, 230, 233, 234; of Buenos Aires, 235; duties regarding tithes, 239, 240, 241, 242; 243; subordination to, 244; 246, 247, 248, 249; presidente of *junta de diezmos*, 250; 254, 255; paying extraordinary expenses, 257; 260, 263, 266, 269, 270, 273, 274; keeping the laws, 276; guarding wealth of dying prelates, 277; 278; naming day for *junta* of government, 280; financial duties of, 281, 282, 283, 284, 285, 286, 287, 292; dealing with contraband, 288, 289; 293; relation to treasury officials, 294, 295, 296; control over military finances, 297; providing military salaries, 298; 299; military duties, 300, 301, 302, 303, 304, 305, 306, 307, 308, 309; cognizance of military cases, 312; furnishing lodgings for troops, 313; 314, 315, 316; examining summaries of review, 317; 318,

319; establishment of military depositories, 320; 321; providing munitions, 322, 323; 324, 326; attending *juntas* of war, 327; funeral honors of, 328; deposition of, 329; *residencia* of, 330.

Intendants of province, 27, 28, 47, 50, 53, 61, 70; power of, 95; subordination of, 99; 110; assistants of, 111; 125, 131, 150, 191; supervision of *lanzas* and half-annates, 210; 259, 297, 318, 325; salary of, 328.

Intendant system, introduction into Spain, 7; extended to America, 9; opposition to, 12; of Buenos Aires, 17; of Chile, 22; of the Philippines, 30–31; success of, 65; criticism of, 71–73; change in, 74; criticism of Revillagigedo, 75–82.

Inventories, making of, 162; of *espolios*, 276–277; differences in, 282; of revenues, 285; of funds in treasury, 286; of monopolies, 287.

Irrigation, development of, 43; 136, 140.

Itineraries, military, 306, 307.

Jamaica, 38, 40, 56.

Jesuit missions, 20.

Joint responsibility, 170.

Jones, Evan, American trader, 39.

Juan Fernández, island of, 23.

Judge-conservator, of revenue, 288.

Judges, of *audiencia*, 4; of commission, 35; of first instance, 44; of the treasury, 47; visiting *pulque* shops, 50; 59; of *residencia*, 63; corruption of, 72; 74, 79; viceroy as, 80; 84, 85; idleness of, 87; 89, 93; of tribunal of accounts, 100, 101; ordinary, of appeal, 102; 108; in Indian towns, 110; 111, 112, 113; appeal from, 114; 115; inferior, 116; 117, 119, 120, 128, 129; subordinate, 137; 141, 142; of *La Acordada*, 143; 147, 148,

royalty of, 95; 98, 103, 104, 257.

Mexico City, capital of intendancy, 26; 29, 43, 47, 51, 78; customhouse of, 79; 104, 157; subtreasury of, 165; 199, 204, 206, 208, 210, 214, 215; *junta* of auctions of, 216; *junta de diezmos* of, 222; 234, 261, 267, 278.

Michoacán, 83, 257.

Middlemen, 146. *See* Retailers.

Military affairs, 7, 26, 95, 177.

Military bodies, 58; supplies for, 298; 299, 300, 316; discipline of, 312; campaign of, 320.

Military chiefs, 78, 79; intendants as, 157.

Military Department, 29. *See* Department of War.

Military *fuero*, 46.

Military government of, Costa Rica, 30.

Military pensions, 46. See *Monte-pio militar.*

Military privileges, of intendants, 46, 156; 157, 159, 160.

Militia, 8, 18; provincial, 60, 195.

Miners, 203, 204, 205, 211.

Mines, 41; protection of, 43; 138, 177, 194, 203, 204.

Mining, 18, 35; encouragement of, 51; 72; backwardness of, 86; 118, 141; corporation of, 203; prevention of abuses in, 204; camps, 206; 207.

Minister of the Indies, 18, 32; appeals to, 45; 66, 78, 84.

Minister of the Interior, 97 n. 1.

Ministers, in Philadelphia, 63; 69; of the treasury, 159; of Charles III, 96; of the treasury, 164, 166, 168, 169, 170, 171, 172, 173, 174, 178; of accounting-offices, 179; treasury, 180, 181, 187, 188, 192, 193, 199, 205, 206, 208, 209, 212, 216, 218; ecclesiastical, 220; members of *junta de diezmos,* 222; 223, 226, 229, 230, 236, 241, 244, 248; of the church, 253; 254, 260, 266, 267, 276, 277, 278, 279, 280; of tribunal of accounts, 285; 291, 292, 299, 301, 304, 315, 317, 318, 321, 322.

Minor vacancies, 253; keeping separate, 254; 255, 256, 257, 258.

Miró, Estevan, intendant of New Orleans, 63.

Misiones, governor of, 21.

Missionaries, 85, 253, 267, 331.

Missions, 14, 255 n. 30.

Misteca, 140.

Miters, 257, 258, 272.

Mobile, 40, 61.

Mojos, military government of, 21.

Money, defrauding of, 147; 162; value of, 177; 185, 194, 204, 205, 217, 270, 286; comparison of Spanish with Mexican, 300–301; 302, 306, 310, 311, 313, 329.

Monopolgy, 2; cases of, 45; 53; avoidance of, 124; of *pulque,* 200; of powder, 201; of playing cards, 202; of quicksilver, 203; of tobacco, 209; of salt mines, 211; 212; of snow, alum, leather, 273; 287.

Monte-pio, 57, 163, 176, 300.

Monte-pio de ministerio, 164.

Monte-pio militar, 46; intendants included in, 163; 258, 259.

Monterrey, *junta de diezmos* of, 222; city of, 223.

Montevideo, 20, 21, 30.

Morales, Juan, intendant of New Orleans, 63.

Morales, Venturo, intendant ad interim of Louisiana, 39.

Mortmain, 198.

Mulattoes, paying tribute, 190, 194.

Municipal councils, 35; appointing *alcaldes ordinarios,* 106; 107, 114, 122, 212, 213.

Municipal finance, 19, 74; intrusted to viceroys, 94; 97 n. 1, 101; under *junta superior,* 102; under intendants, 105; 113, 119, 120,

ERRATA